D1405818

JUL 1 8 2~~ DATE DUE

Revolution & Political Change in the Third World

REVOLUTION & POLITICAL CHANGE IN THE THIRD WORLD

EDITED BY

BARRY M. SCHUTZ
ROBERT O. SLATER

LYNNE RIENNER PUBLISHERS, BOULDER

ADAMANTINE PRESS LIMITED, LONDON

Published in the United States of America in 1990 by
Lynne Rienner Publishers, Inc.
1800 30th Street, Boulder, Colorado 80301

and in the United Kingdom by Adamantine Press Limited
3 Henrietta Street, Covent Garden, London WC2E 8LU

Library of Congress Cataloging-in-Publication Data
Revolution and political change in the Third World / edited by Barry
M. Schutz and Robert O. Slater.
    p. cm.
  Includes bibliographical references
  ISBN 1-55587-153-4 (alk. paper)
  ISBN 1-55587-216-6 (pbk. : alk. paper)
  1. Revolutions—Developing countries. 2. Decolonization—
Developing countries. 3. Legitimacy of governments—Developing
countries. 4. Developing countries—Politics and government.
I. Schutz, Barry M. (Barry Mayer) II. Slater, Robert O. (Robert
Owen), 1950-
  JF60.R46 1990   90-8035
  321.09'4'091724—dc20   CIP

British Library Cataloguing in Publication Data
Revolution and political change in the Third World. —
(Adamantine studies in international political economy and
development, ISSN 0954-6065; V. 5).
1. Developing countries. Revolutionary movements
I. Schutz, Barry M. II. Slater, Robert O., 1950–
322.42091724
ISBN 0-7449-0025-5
ISBN 0-7449-0026-3 pbk

Printed and bound in the United States of America

To our parents

Contents

3
CONCLUDING PERSPECTIVES

Preface

This project represents the confluence of long-term reflection by the editors and the opportunities presented for bringing together an international group of renowned scholars of Third World revolution and political change. The groundwork began in late 1987 with a concept for a conference encompassing theories and case studies of Third World revolutions. Papers were commissioned according to a preliminary conceptual framework developed by the editors. During the more than eighteen months that ensued between the presentation of conference papers in June 1988 and the completion of the manuscript for this book, extensive substantive revisions were made both in the essays of the contributing authors and the development of the editors' theories.

Contemporaneous with our revisions, events have unfolded transforming the shape of the international system. Conditions in Central and Eastern Europe, and in the People's Republic of China, reflect the impact of revolutionary challenges to existing Marxist political systems. While these changes reveal the importance of legitimacy (or lack thereof) to regime survival, the anti-Marxist orientation of these events has not yet affected the ideological nature of revolutionary movements in the Third World.

We are intellectually indebted to a number of individuals who provided inspiration and help for this endeavor. For both of us, General Eugene Tighe (former director of the Defense Intelligence Agency) has been invaluable as a major proponent for open dialogue between U.S. government defense analysts and academic specialists on critical Third World issues. Bob DeGross, provost of the Defense Intelligence College, supported and defended the program that allowed us to produce the book.

We would also like to acknowledge the influence of Robert C. Tucker, David C. Rapoport, and the late James S. Coleman, who provided conceptual and personal motivation for our focus, and Nick Onuf, whose attentive concern and intellectual guidance led to an acute appreciation for the role of theory in knowledge building.

We owe a debt to the authors for their willingness to undertake major and timely revisions of their essays based both on comments of the editors and on the extensive discussion that took place during and after the conference. We would also like to acknowledge the endless energies of the staff at the Defense Intelligence College, particularly Ed Collier, Steve Dorr, and Pat Lanzara, and to thank Max Gross and Mark Kauppi, teachers at the Defense Intelligence College, for their stimulating contributions to the development of the conference agenda.

Finally, we owe a personal debt to Lynne Rienner for accepting our proposal, encouraging our effort, and providing sage advice at important points along the way.

Barry M. Schutz
Robert O. Slater

PART ONE

APPROACHES TO UNDERSTANDING
THIRD WORLD REVOLUTIONS

CHAPTER ONE

A Framework for Analysis

BARRY M. SCHUTZ
ROBERT O. SLATER

> The revolutions and ideologies likely to be most important in the second half of the twentieth century are those of the underdeveloped countries. This proposition does not denigrate the obviously great continuing importance of the Communist revolutions of the first half of the century or of the Marxist ideology. They will go on working themselves out. But the new revolutions, having altered the terms on which the senior revolutionary ideologies can continue to be influential, may be regarded as the critical new factor in the problems of revolution and ideology of the next several decades.
>
> —C. B. MacPherson

More than any other political phenomenon of the twentieth century, revolution has aroused the awe and curiosity of scholar and layman alike. And with the proliferation of new states reshaping the international system after World War II, the number of revolutionary events has increased exponentially. Revolutionary phenomena have been most characteristic in the Third World; and these revolutions have been richly varied in their social contexts, ideology, type of leadership, and organizational composition.

Despite the diversity of Third World social and political contexts, revolutionary movements in the developing countries all tend to be motivated by a common perception of regime illegitimacy. This perceived illegitimacy—causing deprivation of economic equality, opportunity, and civil rights to the mass of the population—combines with a burgeoning sense of national identity to promote one or more groups bent on seizing power. More often than not, the movement for change is imbued with an ideological message of economic equality—either prescriptive Marxism-Leninism or some form of eclectic socialism.

The critical element in all revolutionary movements is legitimacy: a concept fundamental to the existence of the state, to all political systems (traditional or modern), and to other social and cultural organizations subordinate to and beyond the state. The traditional political science literature defines *legitimacy* to make it coincide with the rule of constitution and law.

3

The heightened awareness of diverse traditional political systems and the concomitant burgeoning of new states in the international system after World War II generated a broadening of the study of politics and created the need for a more inclusive definition of *legitimacy* that would encompass a people's sense of the good, rightness, or acceptability of the authority over them. While this sense of legitimate authority had its roots in the social constructs of Max Weber, it did not really pervade the formal study of politics until the late 1950s. Some political scientists from the old legalist school distinguished legalist legitimacy from normative legitimacy (Oppenheimer, 1975). In this view a type of de facto legitimacy was defined as distinct from the more rigid de jure notion that characterized traditional Western-oriented political concepts. Oppenheimer cites Hanna Pitkin's apt reference to this more normative connotation: "Legitimate authority is precisely that which *ought* to be obeyed" (Oppenheimer, 1975: 321–322). M. G. Smith, in his conceptualization of plural societies, further elaborates this distinction between political legality and political legitimacy.

> Legality connotes conformity to the law, the quality of lawfulness; while legitimacy refers to a wider order of norms and principles, and ultimately to the traditional moral system, not all the elements of which are adequately represented in the law. That which is legal is normally legitimate also, but all that is regarded as legitimate may not have legal sanction. *Whereas law circumscribes legality, legitimacy is often invoked to sanction and justify actions contrary to existing law.* Such processes suggest that where these two sets of norms conflict, certain principles or values are on occasion held by different groups to possess a moral authority superior to that of the law; and it is in terms of this superior moral authority that legal codes and procedures are evaluated and judged to be more or less satisfactory according to their correspondence with the system of values and rules which together form the basis of legitimacy within the society. (Smith, 1960: 20; emphasis ours)

The legalist perspective tended to eschew the dynamic impulse of legitimacy within revolutionary regimes and movements to the conceptual trash bin of totalitarianism and authoritarianism. Indeed, such revolutionary movements would not emerge if the existing government were perceived as legitimate, that is, as possessing consensus among the body politic. In fact, revolutionary movements spring from a publicly emerging or intruding lack of government legitimacy. The movement lays claim to that legitimacy, but at first only among its followers. If successful, a revolutionary regime must ultimately institutionalize both its program and, even more significantly, the means of transmitting its policies to a successor government in an orderly, predictable way.

Although the development of "surrogate" measures of legitimacy has been a major focus in the study of comparative political behavior, we prefer to view the concept in broader structural terms because of the difficulty in adapting the legal-institutional concept of legitimacy to Third World contexts. Indeed, most of the attempts to measure legitimacy as an aspect of political behavior have been focused on developed, Western polities. Much of the comparative politics literature reviews the concept within the context of Western democratic values and investigates its operational impact inside these systems with ongoing democratic myths, values, and institutions. Our effort focuses more on Third World political contexts, where legitimacy has never been ensconced in a modern form and traditional elements of legitimacy did not comprehend the modern nation-state.[1]

In those more recently established states, legitimacy inheres in the expectation of political and economic development. To the extent that these regimes fail to "deliver the goods," that is, allocate expected political and economic resources, legitimacy dissipates or, more likely, never achieves institutionalized form. Thus, if no public consensus believes in or accepts the government's right to rule (possesses authority), the probability increases for the formation of a revolutionary movement. Other causes must also exist for such a movement to form, but the perceived illegitimacy of the sitting regime remains necessary.

Following the moral-normative suasion in the interpretation and delineation of political legitimacy, we utilize an analytic framework identifying specific political contexts that revolutionary movements react to and interact with. This framework is implied in a theoretical overview of the dynamics, perspectives, and factors characterizing revolutionary change in the Third World—from inside the unit itself to regional and global levels.[2] Further, such an overview also suggests the impact of time, seeing such developments in changing historical perspective. Secondly we organize various contemporary case studies according to a typology defined by the context of regime legitimacy in the country (or countries) under analysis.

THIRD WORLD REVOLUTION AND POLITICAL CHANGE

Major works have tended to focus on revolutions as history-transforming events. Great revolutions have been the focus on Crane Brinton's *Anatomy of a Revolution* (1965), Barrington Moore's *The Social Origins of Dictatorship and Democracy* (1966), and Theda Skocpol's *States and Social Revolutions* (1979). However, great revolutions take place in established states with traditional, consensual forms of legitimacy. Samuel Huntington's oft-cited definition of *revolution* as "a rapid, fundamental, and violent domestic change in the dominant values and myths of a society, in its political institutions, social structure, leadership, and government activity and policies" (1968: 264) underscores the point that revolutions, that is, great revolutions, occur in states that are *also* societies where a legitimate form of government has existed. Skocpol adds to the definition of *revolution* the Leninist dimension that revolutions are "festivals of the oppressed and the exploited. At no other time are the masses of the people in a position to come forward so actively as creators of a new social order" (1986: 69). These two dimensions of structural transformation and class breakthrough from below effectively define and circumscribe revolution as "great revolution." For Theda Skocpol—and probably for Huntington as well—France in 1789, Russia in 1917, and China in 1911–1949 (in two stages) stand out as salient examples of successful social revolutions. Other theoretical inquiries into the causes of revolution are either social-systemic, like Chalmers Johnson's *Revolutionary Change* (1982), or social psychological, like Ted Gurr's *Why Men Rebel* (1970), or fall under the rubric of interest group theory, like Charles Tilly's *From Mobilization to Revolution* (1978). None of these theoretical inquiries, however, makes any conceptual distinction between revolutionary change in societies with established forms of legitimacy and those where such "values, myths, and political institutions" have not yet taken root.

Social scientists have not altogether ignored Third World revolutions. Even Huntington, in his classic *Political Order in Changing Societies* (1968), offers a protomodel with his distinction between "Western-type" and "Eastern-type" revolutions. "Western-type" revolutions incline more to the classic great revolution with its initial regime collapse occurring from above, that is, at the center; whereas "Eastern-type" revolutions resonate more clearly with the emerging Third World pattern, in which contesting groups push up from below to challenge the sovereignty and legitimacy of the existing regime.[3] In the early 1970s some scholarly focus on unfolding Third World revolutions began to appear, John Dunn's *Modern Revolutions* (1972) being the most theoretical and comprehensive. Gerard Chaliand's 1977 landmark *Revolution in the The Third World: Myths and Prospects* (rev. ed. 1988) demonstrated a comparative, in-depth understanding of the phenomenon resulting from the author's extensive field inquiry into such Third World movements as the South Vietnamese National Liberation Front and the Guinea-Bissau African Independence Party of Guinea and Cape Verde (PAIGC) under the leadership of Amilcar Cabral. Chaliand discerns the ideological dominance of nationalism, borrowed from the Western experience, as well as the unique staying qualities of the sinicized Asian movements. But scholarly discomfort with the appellation *revolution* applied to the Third World was manifest in Claude Welch's *Anatomy of Rebellion* (1980) and John Walton's *Reluctant Rebels* (1984). Walton's exegesis of revolution in its Third World context leads him to prefer *national revolt* as a more accurate description of the variegated group movements toward, and achievement of, regime control.

The term *revolt* suggests, however, a resistance to a regime without any necessary political change or completion. *Rebellion* is even less applicable to the phenomenon of Third World revolutionary movements. The *Concise Oxford Dictionary* defines *revolution* as "complete change, turning upside down, great reversal of conditions, fundamental reconstruction, especially forcible substitution by subjects of new ruler or polity for the old." Since movements with revolutionary intent either engender revolution or some other significant political change, directly or indirectly, we are content to stay with the term and concept of revolution in its "pure," dictionary definition with the full proviso that revolutionary impact, especially in its Third World context, can vary depending on the context of the specific body politic on which it is impinging.

REVOLUTION AND LEGITIMACY

Every revolution or revolutionary movement emerges out of a crisis of legitimacy for the regime in question. In the established states of Europe these crises arose when traditional principles of legitimacy collapsed or were challenged by new revolutionary ideas. The late Italian historian Guglielmo Ferrero poignantly describes this crisis in its Western historical context:

> Principles of legitimacy are born, grow up, age, and die; sometimes they come into collision and clash. Their life cycles and their clashes are the invisible foundations of history. Invisible because it is extremely difficult for mankind, though perforce submitted to them, to understand these cycles and clashes, which take place in the obscure depths of society. . . . They seem inexplicable because they originate in the struggle between the hereditary, aristocratic, and monarchic principle of legitimacy and the elective and democratic principle of legitimacy—a dark and mysterious struggle, with its roots in the dim past, that for two centuries has caused men to fight each other without knowing exactly why. (1942: 49)

However, Ferrero's astute retrospective on legitimacy and revolutions does not comprehend the peculiar problem that the newly independent Third World state has in establishing a principle of legitimacy, nor does it appear to accord a decisive role to the unique revolutionary principle of legitimacy.[4]

In order to locate this decisive role for the process of revolutionary legitimization, particularly as it might apply in Third World settings, we turn to Max Weber. Weber's ideal types of legitimate authority insert the *charismatic* basis of legitimacy between the *traditional* type (Ferrero's monarchical-aristocratic-hereditary principle) and the *legal-rational* type (Ferrero's elective-democratic principle). Historically, this charismatic basis derives from the supramundane; but in the contemporary Third World context it takes a more secular, ideological form.[5]

While the Weberian typology might apply to a state that is undergoing a revolutionary crisis and transition, it is difficult to apply the model to a newly independent Third World state. David Apter's attempt to apply the Weberian schema to Ghana was at best a partial theoretical explanation of Ghana's movement to independence. The application of the charismatic type to the Ghanaian independence movement did not fit, because (1) power was handed down from the colonial metropole, Great Britain, to Ghana without revolutionary conflict and (2) Ghana did not possess the rudiments of nation statehood that would allow it to have a traditional type of legitimate authority (Apter, 1963).

In the Third World, therefore, the problem of legitimacy is fundamentally bound up with the manifestation of nationalism and more clearly represents an attempt to establish a new national order internally and a greater sovereignty internationally. Revolutionary mass movements in the Third World are fixed on either establishing a new nation-state,[6] expressing the national will more purely or asserting national identity over perceived alien or minority rule. Shaping this emergent nationalism are a variety of unique forces and perspectives deriving from the mass of the population: perceptions of economic dependency on, and exploitation by, the landlords or national bourgeoisie; colonial status; perceived settler, foreign, or minority domination; and weakness of the state within the international system.

This need to establish the fundamental elements of nationalism and to construct an operational state with internal legitimacy from these elements precludes the capacity to generate a revolutionary challenge to existing political legitimacy. In many new Third World states the term *state* refers to legitimacy within the international community, not domestic legitimacy (Jackson and Rosberg, 1986: 51–55). Laidi (see Chapter 3), Zolberg (1966), and others have pointed to the legitimizing function of the single-party system in these new states. Ferrero's notion of "conditional" prelegitimacy in the new, nineteenth-century states of Germany and Italy provides a useful paradigm for the conditions existing in newly independent Third World states. During this prelegitimate period the new regime has an opportunity to forge the nation-state and to convince the population that the regime is indeed the manifestation of that new nation-state: "Every government began by being a government that had not yet won, but was attempting to win, universal acceptance and had a good chance of succeeding; it became legitimate the day it succeeded in conciliating the opposition aroused by its advent" (Ferrero, 1942: 139).

However, the tendency for most prelegitimate Third World regimes has been to succumb to military intrusion into government, leading to the consequent illegitimization of that government. But some military coups have attempted to acquire legitimacy through revolution from above (Trimberger, 1978; and see Chapter 5). But this dynamic is driven by specific groups or individuals within government with no preexisting links to a popular revolutionary movement. Revolutions from above can also be "second-stage," that is, they can be the second stage of prior revolutions from below. Stalin's collectivization campaign in the Soviet Union was a revolution from above piggybacked on the initial Bolshevik Revolution led by Lenin. In Cuba, Castro's Marxist-Leninist revolution from above derived from his prior populist, nationalist, not-obviously-Marxist revolution from below.

Regimes with revolutionary legitimacy must inevitably confront the waning of the charismatic foundation of that legitimacy. Either that base of legitimacy must be routinized, that is, converted to a legal-rational, elective-democratic base, or the regime will have to rely on pure coercion. Illegitimacy will then ensue, as the regime can no longer rule with a revolutionary rationale. Indeed, some revolutionary regimes never develop any sense of obligation to win universal acceptance from the population. Achieving power through the application of force, revolutionary regimes often try to sustain themselves and the revolutionary belief in their rule by that same force and by propaganda. Never trusting the conciliatory process of legitimizing their newly acquired rule, revolutionary regimes proclaim their commitment to democracy as sufficient through being revolutionary and nationalist. While Mexico might serve as an example of a revolutionary regime that faced up to a process of legitimization (if only a partial one), Ethiopia stands as an example of a revolutionary regime that has not yet made the slightest pretense toward such a process.

THEORETICAL PERSPECTIVES
ON REVOLUTIONARY LEGITIMACY

Huntington's distinction between "Western" and "Eastern" types is a neat conceptual point of departure for a legitimacy-based typology of Third World revolutions. Huntington's "Western" type of revolutionary movement and process, derived from the French Revolution prototype, is especially vulnerable to the problems of first establishing revolutionary legitimacy and later routinizing the charismatic legitimacy of the revolution toward an elective-democratic basis. In these highly bureaucratized ancien régimes, the collapse of legitimacy is at the center, thus creating a massive political void that needs to be filled as quickly and as fully as possible. In these circumstances, revolutionary movements rush in to replace the discredited despotisms without feeling the need or having the time to establish the conditions for prelegitimacy. Having stood for values opposed to the prior aristomonarchical principles of legitimacy, the new revolutionary regime resists the imperative of respecting or inculcating a new, elective set of rules for institutional government. Edmond Keller's case study of Ethiopia and John Voll and Fred von der Mehden's jointly authored analysis of resurgent Islam emanating from Iran provide some perspective on this process and condition.

The Huntington "Eastern" type, identified with the Maoist phase of the

Chinese Revolution, in which the authority of existing regimes is challenged by revolutionary movements usually based in the countryside, presents a process more likely to lead to a transition toward prelegitimacy once the movement gains power. Having been confronted with the necessity of winning the allegiance, or at least acceptance, of the inhabitants in its areas of operation, the "Eastern-type" movement already has a leg up in the process of proving itself legitimate. Prelegitimacy is not a guaranteed development once such a movement achieves power; but the examples of Cuba, Vietnam, and Nicaragua suggest that those regimes, whatever their missteps and excesses, are viewed by their populations as attempting to prove themselves legitimate by their own institutions, policies, and, most importantly, mechanisms of succession. William LeoGrande's analysis of revolutionary change in Central America, Henry Dietz's assessment of Sendero Luminoso in Peru, and David Rosenberg's essay on movements and change in the Philippines contribute to our understanding of this type of process while such movements are in train.

Huntington's "Eastern" type also includes revolutionary movements where national identity is denied by a foreign, minority, settler-colonial regime (Rhodesia); an immigrant society imposing its own national ideology (Israel); or an ethnically defined communal minority (South Africa). In each of these cases, the ethnically distinct indigenous population defines its own national rights and identity and proceeds to challenge the dominant regime. Here we see an ongoing struggle between competing legitimacies where the regime-dominating group attaches *only* its own ethnopolitical authority and legitimacy to the state. Variations on this type are covered in the essays by Stephen Davis on the African National Congress in South Africa and As'ad AbuKhalil on the Palestine Liberation Organization and Israel.

Huntington's dichotomy suffers, however, from vague labels and the fact that the occurrence of Third World revolutions since the publication of his essay (1965) has introduced new cases not easily comprehended by the original Huntington framework. For example, Iran's revolution contains elements of each type: the Mujahadeen a priori challenged the shah's claim to legitimate authority, thus resembling Huntington's "Eastern" type; while the final collapse of the shah's rule mirrored his "Western" type. Consequently, we have been informed by another conceptual indicator, which focuses on the context of *legitimacy*. In the first two cases, Ethiopia and Iran, legitimacy collapsed at the center, bringing forth an urgent need to fill the void of legitimate authority. In the remaining cases—Peru, the Central American states, the Philippines, South Africa, the Palestine Liberation Organization (PLO), and the anti-Marxist regime operations in Angola and Mozambique—the question centers around groups outside the locus of formal government power that challenge the government's claims of legitimacy.

Chapters 2 and 3 of our volume focus on historical, theoretical, and international factors in Third World revolutionary change. Four different authors offer four distinct approaches to the analysis of revolution in the Third World. Gerard Chaliand takes a distinctly historical approach; T. David Mason develops a structural perspective culminating in the state's internal revolutionary dynamics; William J. Foltz also employs a structural approach, but his focus is on external impact; finally, Zaki Laidi comprehends the revolutionary orientation through the transformation of external ideology into internal functional utility.

First, noted specialist on Third World revolutions Gerard Chaliand overviews the historical precedents with his "tool box" concept, referring to Third World acquisitions of the "tools" of the Western political experience. While Chaliand stresses the elements of nationalism, ideology, and the state, he is really arguing that the entire notion of legitimacy, as it has been understood in the West, has been embraced by Third World revolutionary movements. But Chaliand also suggests that the concept suffers when these movements become revolutionary Third World regimes.

T. David Mason's internal-structural perspective on Third World revolutionary legitimacy focuses on the process of group formation and conflict, wherein the painful effects of the unequal distribution of economic resources gradually alienates popular support for government and leads ultimately to a cycle of revolutionary mobilization–economic claims–regime repression–regime illegitimacy–enhanced revolutionary mobilization. Mason's entire sequence of revolutionary mobilization is a narrative on revolutionary claims for legitimacy against existing regime illegitimacy. But perhaps Mason's most significant contribution to the study of Third World revolutionary processes is his seamless reconciliation of the diverse strands of theory deriving from the schools of political conflict and structural dependency. Mason tempers rational choice theory, relative deprivation theory, and resource mobilization theory with the dependency perspective presented by André Gunder-Frank, Immanuel Wallerstein, James Cockroft, and others. This multilevel, multiple-theory approach is woven into an engrossing narrative that illuminates the drive for legitimacy in Third World revolutionary movements at a level of abstraction easy to comprehend but not easy to exposit.

While Mason's analysis elaborates the internal aspect of revolutionary mobilization, William Foltz's external-structural view identifies and assesses four external sources of revolutionary legitimacy: instigation, contagion, imitation, and impact engendered by world structural transformation. Thus, legitimacy is not some totally contained internal phenomenon. It grows within the soil of one distinct culture (or emerging culture), but it is the product of processes that are historically and geographically global. In this sense Foltz's analysis conceptually frames some of the processes and elements of revolutionary legitimization suggested in Chaliand's essay.

In spite of this importation of Western principles of legitimacy into Third World revolutionary movements, the most salient legitimizing principle has been (and still is) Marxism-Leninism. Zaki Laidi's essay shows how the Marxist-Leninist idea—and even more specifically, Marxist-Leninist institutions—have been borrowed and employed (*instrumentalized* is Laidi's term) by Third World movements and regimes trying to establish regime legitimacy after coming to power. And despite the "zero-sum" perception that characterized past U.S. policy orientations toward Soviet-derived ideas and institutions in Third World countries, these ideas and institutions have ultimately not had the revolutionary impact originally attributed to them by the United States. Indeed, the chronicle of U.S.-Soviet battles over Third World "hearts and minds" in places like Angola and Ethiopia is rapidly being overtaken by events, and revolutionary legitimacy within the Third World may stand or fall on the ability to develop internal consensus within the countries in question.

MOVEMENT TYPES IN THE CONTEXT OF REGIME LEGITIMACY

Our use of the case study approach is essentially driven by a typological framework that orders Third World revolutionary transformations and movements in the context of conditions and factors shaping legitimacy-illegitimacy in the existing (or prior) regime.

Legitimacy is a concept that benefits most from case comparison. Consequently, we chose to use case studies as a way of ordering and exploring the subject of Third World revolutions.[7] But a question persists regarding the organization of the case studies. This question is answered by the establishment of a set of types based on the social, cultural, and geographic context of the regimes under study.

Our selection of the relevant Third World cases involves identifying major "classical" revolutions based on salient societal-geographic variables. Huntington's classical "Western" type—the Russian Revolution of 1917—inspired our choice of Ethiopia as an example of the first type. Huntington's classical "Eastern" type—the latter phase of the Chinese Revolution (1932–1949)—stimulated our choice of the Sendero Luminoso (Shining Path) movement in Peru. The anticolonial revolutionary nationalism of the Algerian Revolution (1954–1959), points to the more contemporary examples of the African National Congress (ANC) in South Africa and the Palestine Liberation Organization (PLO) involving Israel.

A group of more recent revolutionary phenomena in the Third World appear sui generis and thus pose even knottier conceptual dilemmas. The first example, the revolutionary transformation of Iran in 1979, ushered in a distinct type of revolutionary religious resurgence defined by a radical, comprehensive commitment to political and social Islam combined with a collapsing centralized monarchy. A second example for case selection refers to the increasing number of movements directed *against established* Marxist-Leninist revolutionary regimes. The case of the National Union for the Total Independence of Angola (UNITA) selected here (and with even more certainty the case of the Mozambique National Resistance [RENAMO] do not qualify as "revolutionary movements" per se, but they might represent phenomena similar to nationalist, populist, anti-Marxist and even prodemocratic movements in countries like Burma and the Peoples' Republic of China.

Finally, we include in this typology (but not among the case studies) ethnonationalist movements oriented toward secession, boundary alteration, or a rearrangement of state power.[8] The Eritrean People's Liberation Front (EPLF); the Sudanese People's Liberation Army (SPLA) from the Southern (non-Muslim) Sudan; and the Kurds of Iran, Iraq, and Turkey are three relevant cases of this type. However, it should be noted that outside of Pakistan and Bangladesh there have been no successful state-achieving movements of this type.

Following the theoretical expositions, Chapters 4–9 include eight case studies representing each of the movement types in this study. The movement types are briefly and conceptually described below.

Type 1. Collapse of Monarchical Legitimacy and Revolutionary Change

Type 1 illuminates the collapse of traditional monarchy and its replacement by a new state organization, Huntington's classical "Western" type, based on the revolutionary principles of economic equality articulated in Marxism-Leninism but deeply affected by militarism and ethnic nationalism. Our contemporary case is Ethiopia; Edmond Keller analyzes the collapse of the regime of Emperor Haile Selassie and the aristomonarchical principle of legitimacy on which it was based. With the gradual eclipse of monarchical regimes in the Third World, Saudi Arabia, Morocco, and the Gulf emirates remain vulnerable to such revolutionary challenges in the future.

Type 2. Islamic Resurgence and the Revolutionary Legitimacy of Religion

While Type 2, in its Iranian format, resembles Huntington's "Western" type, there is also an aspect of the "Eastern" type within it. The shah's regime was losing its legitimacy, that is, its consensual acceptance when Khomeini's movement began to challenge it. The movement's reliance on distilled Shi'ite Islam as the basis of its revolutionary appeal furnished a religious foundation for its potential legitimacy. This religious base, however, confused its attempt to establish political principles of legitimacy, so that it became elective in appearance but aristomonarchical in substance. John Voll and Fred von der Mehden analyze this phenomenon as a pattern in the Middle East,

North Africa, and Southeast Asia. The Mujahadeen movement in Afghanistan and the revolutionary claims of Qaddafi in Libya reveal aspects of this type. Egypt stands out as a potential stage for this type of revolutionary movement in the future.

Type 3. Revolutionary Legitimization in the Countryside

Type 3 is Huntington's classic "Eastern" type, in which the peasants play a major role in the character and legitimization of the movement. Mao's Communist movement in the Chinese countryside furnishes the seminal example. The movement has to organize outside of the urban core of the existing regime and win the legitimate support of the peasants in its organizing environment. Finally, success occurs when the movement marches from the countryside back to the city to achieve revolutionary power. The extension of its countryside legitimacy to the city remains a difficult problem. Henry Dietz's study of Peru's Sendero Luminoso (Shining Path) portrays a developing revolutionary movement in the Western Hemisphere that consciously and effectively imitates the classical Maoist example. Next-door neighbor Colombia's revolutionary movements increasingly reflect similar characteristics.

Type 4. Regime Illegitimacy and Revolutionary Mobilization

"Soft" illegitimate regimes such as Batista's in Cuba, Somoza's in Nicaragua, and Marcos's in the Philippines are rejected by their own populations because they are exploitative *and* perceived to be inextricably linked to a dominant external power (in the cases mentioned, the United States). In these cases revolutionary groups mobilize to challenge the exploitation, corruption, and externally backed heavy-handedness of these remarkably inept and unpopular regimes. Without external support these illegitimate regimes would be even more vulnerable to internal revolutionary mobilization. The studies of Central America and the Philippines by William LeoGrande and David Rosenberg, respectively, reflect two distinct but related examples of the processes in this type of regime. Nicaragua displays a new revolutionary regime attempting to achieve legitimacy. The Philippines represents a case currently "on hold." Guatemala is an increasing prospect for such a revolutionary challenge in the very near future.

Type 5. Anticolonial Revolutionary Nationalism

In certain racially or ethnically dominated states, the ethnic outgroup challenges the partial (and often narrow) legitimacy of the ruling group. These states, often referred to as international "pariahs," have governments that are considered legitimate only to those ethnic affines who benefit from their rule. The classic colonial cases in which such revolutionary movements challenged settler-colonial rule were Algeria, Kenya,and Rhodesia. We have included two such case studies, though important differences exist between them. The African National Congress's challenge to white minority rule in South Africa is examined by Stephen Davis, while the Palestine Liberation Organization's claims for legitimate representation of the Palestinian people is analyzed by As'ad AbuKhalil. While the South African case represents one of clear minority rule over the majority, the Israeli-PLO case manifests a more problematic conflict. The Israeli population within the legally established borders is still composed of a Jewish majority with a significant minority of Arabs. But the inclusion of the West Bank and Gaza Strip alters this balance to near equality with a rapidly declining Jewish majority. These two internally divided states appear the last of their kind.

Type 6. Anti-Marxist Insurgencies?

Not wishing to avert controversial inquiries in this volume, we decided to open up the question of anti-Marxist movements. Events in Burma in 1988 and China in 1989 stimulated the notion that revolutionary movements could conceivably emerge to challenge the authority and expose the illegitimacy of certain Marxist-Leninist regimes. Changes in Eastern Europe reveal the delayed impact of seemingly unsuccessful anti-Marxist-Leninist (or at least anti-communist-regime) movements of an earlier era. A salient contemporary example of an anti-Marxist-Leninist movement that has more than held its own might be the Mujahadeen of Afghanistan. However, we chose the UNITA insurgency in Angola. The international legitimacy of movements of this type is nil, and serious questions have persisted regarding their internal legitimacy as well. Hence, the essay on UNITA by Marina Ottaway is really a critical query on the legitimacy of such movements. Third World anti-Marxist movements could appear in the future in Cuba, Cambodia, or Ethiopia.

Type 7. Ethnonationalist Movements

Our last type of revolutionary movement has been excluded from this volume because of its subnational character. Ethnonationalist movements such as the Kurds in Iran, Iraq, and Turkey; the Sikhs in India; the Southern Sudanese in Sudan; the Tamils in Sri Lanka; and the Eritreans and Tigreyans in Ethiopia often have revolutionary nationalist objectives but operate in terms of the legitimacy of the region and people on whose behalf they are in combat. Ironically, perhaps the most successful ethnonationalist movement in modern history was that of the Afrikaners (Boers) in South Africa. They not only succeeded in establishing their own ethnic national legitimacy, but they have actually become the rulers of a state targeted by a majoritarian revolutionary movement (see Type 5 above and Chapter 8).

The following chapters provide an overview and a framework for comprehending the diversity of revolutionary challenges in the Third World. Moreover, the chapters provide new insights into the different contexts and processes that produce legitimacy, either within a particular regime or in a revolutionary movement. Focusing on the context of existing regime legitimacy, the movements analyzed in this volume reflect that diversity. We have attempted to provide as broad a conceptual vista as possible and have included essays from authors who evince that range of perspective.

NOTES

The epigraph is quoted from MacPherson's "Revolutions of the Late Twentieth Century" (1966: 139).

1. For more behavioral approaches and models to legitimacy, see the works of Rogowski (1974), Eckstein (1975), Almond and Verba (1965), Eckstein and Gurr (1975), the review by Lichbach (1989), and the extensive references cited in the essay by T. David Mason (see Chapter 3).

2. A necessary distinction exists between internal and international legitimacy, and Skocpol (1979) and others clearly and justifiably stress the relationship between internal and international legitimacy in the revolutionary dynamic. The primary emphasis throughout this book, however, is on the internal dimension, or on the relationship between external factors and internal regime legitimacy.

3. See Huntington (1968: 266–274). His discussion of "Eastern-type" and "Western-type" revolutions comprehends our Types 1, 3, 4, and 5. This distinction is made even clearer:

In the "Western" pattern, the political institutions of the old regime collapse; this is followed by the mobilization of new groups into politics and then by the creation of new political institutions. The "Eastern" revolution in contrast, begins with the mobilization of new groups into politics and the creation of new political institutions and ends with the violent overthrow of the political institutions of the old order. (266)

4. It should be noted that Ferrero does acknowledge the unique salience of revolutionary legitimacy and that it does possess some endurance. However, Ferrero wrote in the earlier half of this century, and as a historian he focused on the reverberating political changes within Europe itself.

5. See especially Eckstein and Gurr's excellent critical discussion of Weber's conceptualization of legitimate authority (1975: 201–204).

6. Although the term *nation-state* can be conceptually distinguished, we see no theoretically advantageous purpose in this exercise. We prefer rather to fall back on Rupert Emerson's commonsense definition, which was designed for the Third World process:

The nation is today the largest community which, when the chips are down, effectively commands men's loyalty, overriding the claims both of the lesser communities within it and those which cut across it or potentially enfold it within a still greater society. . . .

As in earlier times the state achieved legitimacy through, say, its monarch or religion, it is now legitimate if it is the embodiment and expression of a nation. . . .

Once the people of such a state have come to a consciousness of national identity, the presumption is that the state will shortly be swept away, to be replaced by another cleaving as closely as possible to the national foundations. Where the peoples of several nations are seriously intermingled, as they are at so many points on the face of the globe, discord and trouble are the inevitable result. (Emerson, 1960: 95–96)

7. Our own approach conforms to Harry Eckstein's "ideographic-configurative" type of case study. This approach is extensively inferential, deductive, and visceral. It is a starting point for more precise and potentially even empirical study further down the road of comparative research on the subject. See Eckstein (1975).

8. Excellent research is being organized and written on ethnonationalism and ethnonationalist movements. The notion of "marginalizing" ethnic minority populations is, for example, the subject of a series of case studies edited by Ted Robert Gurr and Barbara Harff. The imminent publication of Gurr's volume as well as the existing publication of Joseph V. Montville's edited *Conflict and Peacemaking in Multi-Ethnic Societies* (1989) and Donald Horowitz' *Ethnic Groups in Conflict* (1985) precludes the necessity of including ethnonationalist movements as case studies in our volume.

REFERENCES

Almond, Gabriel A., and Sidney Verba (1965). *The Civic Culture*. Boston: Little, Brown.

Apter, David (1963). *Ghana in Transition*. New York: Athenaeum.

Brinton, Crane (1965). *Anatomy of a Revolution*. rev. ed. New York: Random House.

Chaliand, Gerard (1988). *Revolution in the Third World: Myths and Prospects*. Rev. ed. New York: Penguin Viking.

Dunn, John (1972). *Modern Revolutions*. Cambridge: Cambridge University Press.

Eckstein, Harry (1975). "Case Studies." In Fred I. Greenstein and Nelson W. Polsby, eds. *The Handbook of Political Science*, vol. 7. Reading, MA: Addison-Wesley.

Eckstein, Harry, and Ted Robert Gurr (1975). *Patterns of Authority: A Structural Basis for Political Inquiry*. New York: John Wiley and Sons.

Emerson, Rupert (1960). *From Empire to Nation: The Rise to Self-Assertion of Asian and African Peoples*. Boston: Beacon.

Ferrero, Guglielmo (1942). *The Principles of Power*. Salem, NH: Ayer.

Gurr, Ted Robert (1970). *Why Men Rebel*. Princeton: Princeton University Press.

Horowitz, Donald L. (1985). *Ethnic Groups in Conflict.* Berkeley: University of California Press.

Huntington, Samuel P. (1968). *Political Order in Changing Societies.* New Haven: Yale University Press.

Jackson, Robert H., and Carl G. Rosberg (1986). "The Marginality of the African State." In Gwendolen M. Carter and Patrick O'Meara, eds. *African Independence.* Bloomington: Indiana University Press.

Johnson, Chalmers (1982). *Revolutionary Change.* 2d ed. Stanford: Stanford University Press.

Lichbach, Mark I. (1989). "An Evaluation of 'Does Economic Inequality Breed Political Conflict?' Studies." *World Politics,* June.

MacPherson, C. B. (1966). "Revolutions of the Late Twentieth Century." In Carl J. Friedrich, ed., *Revolution: Nomos VIII.* New York: Atherton.

Montville, Joseph V., ed. (1989). *Conflict and Peacemaking in Multi-Ethnic Societies.* Lexington, MA: Lexington.

Moore, Barrington (1966). *The Social Origins of Dictatorship and Democracy.* Boston: Beacon.

Oppenheimer, Felix (1975). "The Language of Normative Political Inquiry." In Fred I. Greenstein and Nelson W. Polsby, eds. *The Handbook of Political Science,* vol. 1. Reading, MA: Addison-Wesley.

Rogowski, Ronald (1974). *Rational Legitimacy: A Theory of Political Support.,* Princeton: Princeton University Press.

Russell, D. E. H. (1974). *Rebellion, Revolution, and Armed Force: A Comparative Study of Fifteen Countries with Special Emphasis on Cuba and South Africa.* New York: Academic.

Skocpol, Theda (1979). *States and Social Revolutions.* Cambridge: Cambridge University Press.

———— (1986). "France, Russia, China: A Structural Analysis of Social Revolutions." In Jack A. Goldstone, ed. *Revolutions.* New York: Harcourt, Brace, Jovanovich.

Smith, M. G. (1960). *Government in Zazzau.* London: Oxford University Press.

Tilly, Charles (1978). *From Mobilization to Revolution.* Reading, MA: Addison-Wesley.

Trimberger, Ellen Kay (1978). *Revolution from Above: Military Bureaucrats and Development in Japan, Turkey, Egypt, and Peru.* New Brunswick: Transaction Books.

Walton, John (1984). *Reluctant Rebels: Comparative Studies of Revolution and Underdevelopment.* New York: Columbia University Press.

Welch, Claude E., Jr. (1980). *Anatomy of Rebellion.* Albany: State University of New York Press.

Zolberg, Aristide (1966). *Creating Political Order: The Party-States of West Africa.* Chicago: Rand McNally.

CHAPTER TWO

Historical Precedents

GERARD CHALIAND

The roots of revolutionary movements in the Third World, as illuminated by Gerard Chaliand, are found primarily in the era of pre–World War II European colonial domination. Chaliand argues that a thorough understanding of Third World revolutionary nationalism is attainable only if we recall the development and evolution of European nationalism in the nineteenth and early twentieth centuries. Ironically, this European experience was transplanted through colonial policies and provided the seeds of revolutionary consciousness. The pre–World War II demonstration of self-confidence by European colonial powers furnished indigenous peoples with an example of successful nationalism and effective legitimacy. Chaliand's chapter focuses on the continuity between European and Third World revolutionary nationalisms.

—THE EDITORS

There may be nothing more complex to understand than the concept of change, especially for those who have come to enjoy, and benefit from, the status quo. Few, if any, Western decisionmakers immediately following World War II seemed capable of grasping the new trends in world politics, whether they pertained to the nature of the bureaucratic and totalitarian regime of the Soviet Union or the feeling of humiliation and frustration of the Third World. It was not simply that the new problems faced by Western powers after World War II were so strange that they took a long time to understand, but that conventional thinking tended to dominate in the West, as elsewhere. Little attention has historically been paid (except by a few scholars) to the historical and political background that nurtured revolutionary movements.

One must only recall that the French from 1946 to 1962 fought two colonial wars, in Indochina and Algeria, both being *combats retardateurs*. Or recall the United States' assumption during its initial involvement in Vietnam that it was ultimately fighting against Chinese expansionism. Was it sophisticated to believe that Nasser's nationalism was so anti-Western that it had to be wholly procommunist? Why did it take a decade for the United States to recognize the Republic of China after it had openly started manifesting its antagonism toward the USSR?

It is essential, then, to understand the historical background to Western domination of the Third World if we are to grasp the changes that have taken place in the Third World since World War II. These changes and the history of Western domination hold a key to comprehending the causes and outcomes of revolutionary movements in the Third World.

DOMINATION BY THE WEST: PRE–WORLD WAR II

Particularly through direct colonialism, domination by the West has left a legacy of resentment in the Third World. This resentment is the result of the major elements that characterized European colonization at its height: the will to impose European civilization on the colonized, a subordination of the economic activities of the colonized, and a racial discrimination justified by an attitude of European-white superiority, both cultural and religious.[1]

Little can be understood about Third World revolutionary movements without recalling that at the turn of the century Europe dominated, either directly or indirectly, all of Asia (except Japan) and Africa. While the United States was already the first industrial power, it was geographically marginal vis-à-vis the center of imperial and military might of the European powers: the United Kingdom, Germany, and France. Japan was still a minor power, ranking just after Italy in terms of industrial power. Russia was still generally considered semi-Asiatic.

The superiority of the European powers remained a fact. The industrial revolution was a Western and European phenomenon. Japan was the only exception, eager to catch up in order to avoid subjugation. Demographically, by 1900, "whites" constituted 33 percent of the world population, and Germany was the fifth most populated country of the world. If we exclude China and India, the most populated Third World country was Indonesia, ranking only ninth with 38 million. The whole of Latin America was only 90 million, Africa 110 million, the Arab world a little over 30 million, and the Ottoman Empire 25 million. Never had the Europeans been so powerful: even the countries of empires still not colonized, such as China and Persia, were economically and financially semicolonized.

While many have attributed Western domination to technological superiority, cultural factors seem the more logical explanation for European domination during the nineteenth century. The subjugation of the colonized peoples was due, in no small degree, to a sense of white conceptual superiority. In fact, with the exception of Japan, it took the colonized and semicolonized two to three generations to make up much of this gap, that is, to turn the Europeans' own weapons and concepts against them.

The European domination of Asia and Africa during the latter half of the nineteenth century confronted those countries with a superiority that was conceptually incomprehensible. The countries' initial reaction was an outright xenophobic rejection and a withdrawal into traditional values. Though forced to open its doors after 1840, China initially retained its confidence in the superiority of its own culture. However, as one humiliation followed another in the face of European arms, the mandarins became concerned about their country's obvious weakness. Young Chinese were sent to study science in Europe and the United States in the belief that the superiority of the West lay in its advances in science and technology. The Ottoman Empire also tried to assimilate Western military and technical concepts while continuing to think within a traditional framework. Such efforts eventually proved fruitless.

After World War I there were only marginal increases in the area under European colonial domination: the British and French mandates in the Middle East and Italy's colonization of Libya. It was at this time that the dismemberment of the Hapsburg Empire led to the creation of states such as Czechoslovakia, Yugoslavia, and Poland. Yet at the Paris Peace Conference colonial problems played only an insignificant role. The Japanese delegation's request that the League of Nations add to its covenant an article condemning racial discrimination was rebuffed by U.S. representatives. Moreover, in spite of the great names who raised their lonely voices against servitude (such as Ho Chi Minh) and who today are recognized as the founding fathers of modern nationalism, the colonized peoples themselves were neither conscious nor mobilized. The immediate postwar period saw only the very first manifestations of what a quarter of a century later, after a new world war, was to become a clamorous freedom movement.

The principle of nations being able freely to determine their fate was proclaimed simultaneously by U.S. president Wilson and Lenin. But the application of the principle of self-determination depended not entirely on the good will of the imperial powers but also on the will of the colonized elites and their ability to get popular support. Nationalism, the main ideology of Europe in the nineteenth century, was really a new idea in the modern sense of the nation-state. The idea that a people or nation has "natural rights" and that the nation legitimizes the state was first formulated as a proposition of universal validity at the end of the eighteenth century. This revolutionary idea implied that if the citizens—not subjects—of a state no longer approve of the political organization of their society, they have the right to replace it with a better system. It was the assimilation of this concept that made it possible to achieve national liberation, recover a sense of identity, and begin nation building. Europe thus diffused, willy-nilly, its main ideas: the nation-state and the notion that anything less than self-government is servitude. Societies with a glorious state tradition and a great civilization such as China could no longer afford to ignore or despise the new barbarians with long noses. Their most complex problem remained how to assimilate the conceptual core elaborated by Europe. Here were totally new, revolutionary ideas that were difficult to put into practice without the necessary preconditions. It took the local elites in the colonial and semicolonial societies half a century to discover the tool box containing the instruments providing access to Western superiority and power.

Virtually all the insurgent movements until World War II were crushed for at least three reasons: (1) their popular support was very limited; (2) Europe had a strong imperial will and wide public support; and (3) there was no outside help for insurgents. Japan's victory in the Russo-Japanese war in 1905 had been an important landmark in East Asia. It was the first victory in the modern era of nonwhites over whites. The victory had brought Japan many students from other Asian countries fascinated by the Nippon example and eager to learn how an Asian country had been able to defeat a European power.

Yet no country was able to follow the Japanese example. The power of the West and the political-military preeminence of Europe remained intact until World War II. But World War II shook the foundation of imperial Europe overseas just as World War I had shaken European empires in Europe. In 1941–1942 the sweeping Japanese victories over U.S. forces in the Philippines, the Dutch in Indonesia, the French in Indochina, and the British in Malaya had a considerable impact. They showed that it was possible to overthrow colonial order and that the whites could be defeated. Resistance to the harsh rule of the Japanese was also an opportunity for both communists and nationalists. In Indochina and Indonesia the interval between Japan's surrender and the arrival of the French or Dutch enabled the national liberation movements to consolidate their forces before the colonial powers returned.

The disruption of the old order by war and the weakening of the European powers immensely aided the anticolonialist movements, which were simultaneously becoming more and more mass-based. In India, for example, there was a very active anticolonialist, massively backed movement culminating in the Quit India Campaign of 1942. Though Gandhi was imprisoned and the Congress party outlawed, the break with the colonial past was so definitive that the British left India soon after.

Barely ten years separate a war that had left Europe exhausted and at the end of its hegemony from the Bandung Conference of 1955, a highly symbolic moment in the emancipation and political independence of Asia and, before long, Africa. The appearance of modern nationalism marked, at least for the West, not only the break with an order based on "divine right" and its replacement by the "natural rights" of individuals or nations but also the shift from a world where the referent was essentially religious to one that was first *national*. In Muslim countries, however, religion remained of fundamental importance because it represented both religion and state (*dar wa dawla*).

POST–WORLD WAR II

After 1945 the international community's recognition of self-determination as a basic human right spurred the decolonization process in Asia and Africa. The spirit of the times had changed. After the defeat of Nazi Germany, social Darwinism was no longer a fashionable ideology. Racial equality was becoming the new norm, and racial discrimination was gradually banned or condemned in Western democracies. The allies had fought World War II in the name of freedom. Colonized elites now wanted freedom as well: white domination had to be eradicated. As for the nation-state, it was the only model that could replace colonial domination, whether it was well suited to a country's ethnic and religious composition or not.

Two serious problems existed with the concept of the nation-state. First, the state frontiers marked out by the colonizer, especially in Africa, had marginal historical bases and coincided only accidentally with more or less homogeneous ethnic groups. In the Afro-Asiatic world, the creation of nation-states has almost universally led to minorities being discriminated against or oppressed. Second, the Western concept of democracy—the rule of law and human rights—has not been assimilated. Very few states in Asia and Africa have established anything approaching democracy as defined by the West.

Theories of imperialism—stemming from Lenin—suggested that the simplest explanation for the poverty of the Third World was the existence of an industrial and imperial world. Leninism, rather than Marxism, gave a coherent and straightforward conception of the world with its division between imperial countries and dominated countries and between exploiting classes and exploited classes. A rather partial and simplistic explanation (as revolutionaries would later discover), it was not without some degree of credibility. But obstacles were not just created by foreign interference and domination. Why didn't China at the end of the nineteenth century succeed in producing a revolution like that of Japan's Meiji? Is it because of the Westerners or the Chinese elite? The corruption of the Manchus, their passivity, and the inability and unwillingness of an overwhelming majority of the mandarins to adapt tradition in order to face Western challenge cannot be discounted. To explain underdevelopment only by economic dependency seems shortsighted.

Nevertheless, to those who were in China with Mao, Indochina with Ho Chi Minh, the Philippines with the Huks, or Malaya with the (mainly) Chinese communists, Leninism made sense: it explained the contemporary world and their own backwardness, subjugation, and frustration. The fact is that the West did not fight only against communism and its spread. To a large extent, in the years following World War II the West was fighting to restore the status quo ante. Wasn't this the aim of the French in Indochina. unwilling to grant independence to anyone and fighting to keep their empire?

Wasn't this also the fate of the Dutch between 1946 and 1949, trying by force to keep rule over the Dutch Indies? Only the British withdrew shrewdly, often leaving behind political problems for the new states to solve. The British withdrew from India after having agreed to implement, but without implementing, partition. In Malaya between 1948 and 1957, the British fought successfully against an essentially Chinese-based communist insurgency while getting the support of Malayan traditional elites through promises of independence as soon as order had been restored. They successfully fought the Mau Mau in Kenya and by jailing Jomo Kenyatta gave him the stature of a revolutionary and fiercely nationalist leader, which he was obviously not. All in all, the British decolonization was so well managed, with campaigns of pacification reduced to low-profile professional troops, that the overall perception in world public opinion has been one of smoothness and success even though many of these counterinsurgency campaigns were bitter and protracted.

It is a fact that between the mid-1950s and the mid-1970s—from Dien Bien Phu to the collapse of Portuguese colonialism—the West has almost always been politically defeated in the end while trying to keep the status quo. This has been due, above all, to a very important change: the domination of the West was no longer either legitimate or unavoidable. Nationalism, in the modern sense, became gradually stronger. Opposition to independence was sometimes nurtured by the fact that the movements of national liberation, as in Vietnam, were Marxist-Leninist. But even when this was not the case, as in Algeria, conservative forces argued that they were fighting for Western interests against a movement helped by the East.

Since World War II, revolutionary guerrilla warfare and terrorism have been the predominant techniques of violence. These are decades during which the industrialized nations, sheltered from the danger of war because of the existence of nuclear power, have not had to fight a war on their own territories.

Between 1945 and the end of the Algerian War (1962) the values that underpinned or seemed to underpin the legitimacy of colonial domination were rejected, often by force. By 1973, the year that saw both the completion of the U.S. withdrawal from Vietnam and the beginning of the oil crisis, the spirit of the age had been widely altered. Throughout this period, however, the Western industrialized countries enjoyed exceptional growth. The period was marked by the military hegemony of the U.S.; the rise, at least militarily, of the USSR as a superpower; and the resulting development of a bipolar world with sharp ideological antagonism expressed during the Cold War by a series of indirect strategies: Berlin, Korea, Cuba, Vietnam. In the meantime, with the political decline of Europe and its rise as an economic power, the period is marked by the emergence of Asian and African states. Gradually, some of them will show their will as regional powers. Political autonomy has become active in spite of the military bipolarization that dominates the world.

The period of decolonization ended somewhat late with the 1974 coup that swept away the fascistic regime of Portugal and the subsequent independence of Angola, Mozambique, Guinea-Bissau, and Cape Verde. With the accession of Zimbabwe to independence in 1979, the era of armed struggle whose success was guaranteed by Western colonialism's obsolescence had come to an end. In the colonial context of the aftermath of World War II, revolutionary guerrilla warfare played a fundamental role as an indirect strategy intended to seize independence politically.

The success of anticolonial struggles was due to the fact that none of these wars was seen as of crucial importance to the metropolis. Metropolis public opinion (or a significant part of it) was more and more in favor of a withdrawal of the colonial army. There was a growing desire for independence not only among elites but among the masses in the colonies. The era of nationalism had arrived. The strength of nationalism, whether mixed with a dose of Leninism or not, proved to be decisive.

The great wave of decolonization drew to an end in the mid-1970s and was marked by the physical withdrawal of Westerners from Asia and Africa. It was a period characterized by a Europe trapped in flagrant contradiction with the very principles it claimed to incarnate: the right of peoples to self-determination and, in general, the ideal of freedom. This false position undermined the very foundations of a previously unshakable imperial consensus. From an ideological and psychological point of view, it partly explains the political weakness of a Europe already economically drained by World War II. During the period 1968–1973, the United States, though the world's leading military and economic power, suffered a similar malaise in Vietnam.

The Cold War, fought on an ideological and psychological level, brought the center of the East-West crisis to the Far East and Southeast Asia from 1950 to 1973. It was only in 1955 that the USSR started to pay attention to the Third World (with the exception of its direct periphery: Turkey, Iran, Afghanistan, and Mongolia). The USSR took note of the change in international relations as symbolized by the Bandung Conference in 1955. After the Suez crisis of 1956, a new Soviet strategy began to take shape. This wholly new strategy, based on support to liberation movements struggling against Western colonialism and imperialism even when the movement was not led by Marxists, was finally endorsed at the Congress of eighty-one Communist parties held in Moscow in 1960. The Congress was, moreover, the last to be held by what had been called, up to then, the "socialist camp." The Sino-Soviet conflict, already visible in Albania's positions, became an official breach two years later.

From the second half of the 1950s, the USSR moved from discreetly providing aid to the Algerian Front for National Liberation (FLN) to a 1960s systematic policy of aid to a number of movements: the Popular Movement for the Liberation of Angola (MPLA), the Front for the Liberation of Mozambique (Frelimo), the African Party for the Liberation of Guinea and Cabo-Verde (PAIGC), all struggling against Portuguese colonialism backed by NATO; the Southwest Africa People's Organization (SWAPO) of Namibia; and the African National Congress (ANC) of South Africa. In the middle 1960s China sought to lead a new kind of "Third World International" while trying to become the Mecca of the revolutionaries of Africa and Asia. China systematically but often clumsily set off to support all movements opposed to those backed by the USSR.

The Cold War period provided the Soviet Union with a major opportunity in the Third World. Although a totalitarian state that oppressed its own people as well as those of Central Europe, the Soviet Union was also helping liberation movements gain independence; while Western democracies respected human rights at home but were helping repressive regimes or colonial status quo dictatorships like Somoza's or Trujillo's in Latin America. It is ironic that for many movements in the Third World the West has appeared as the oppressor because it dominated the colonial world just as it dominated the world economy. Opposition to, and resentment against, it has been the price the West paid for hegemony. No wonder that radical movements in Latin America have developed anti-U.S. attitudes—just as history and geopolitics dictate the attitude of Turkey (and ultimately Iran) vis-à-vis the Soviet Union.

What kinds of changes have we seen in the philosophy of insurgency and revolutionary movements in the last decades? The Leninist-Marxist organizational structure of insurgency has been challenged unsuccessfully by the Cuban theory of rural *foco*. First described in 1960 as a novelty of the Cuban Revolution by Ernesto "Che" Guevara (1963) in his book *Guerrilla Warfare*, this theory holds that it is not necessary to wait for objective conditions to be ripe but that the armed struggle itself can create them. It was later elaborated as a contribution to the conditions of Latin America by Regis Debray in *Revolution in the Revolution* (1967). In the meantime about ten *foco* had collapsed or were engaged in a hopeless fight in various countries of Latin America: Argentina, Peru, Ecuador, Venezuela, Guatemala, Colombia, not to speak of the final failure of Guevara himself in Bolivia (1967) after eleven months of guerrilla fighting during which not a peasant joined the movement.

This failure brought about new lines of thought. One reverted to the classical Leninist-Maoist line of building political backing among the peasantry and the population in general. This has been the way of the Sandinistas of Nicaragua, the Fronte Farabundo Marti in El Salvador and the Guatemala contemporary movements. On the same organizational structure, with a harsher Maoist line influenced by what they thought the Cultural Revolution was, we can also add the Peruvian Communist movement.

The second line was an important shift from the classical line of Leninism-Maoism and rural guerrillas: the urban guerrilla. Introduced both by the Tupamaros of Uruguay and by Carlos Marighella of Brazil, urban guerrilla warfare involved the use of sabotage and selective terrorism within cities. This shift to terrorism just a few months after the death of Guevara brought about a totally new type of revolutionary movement. The novelty was that for the first time in decades, small groups became self-proclaimed vanguards without the support of the population and used terrorist actions as their only tools.

This does not suggest that at their inception, movements such as the Tupamaros did not wish to win popular support. However, popular support did not come. The basic tenet of the Tupamaros was that the bourgeois democratic state was not democratic and that this could be made apparent to the masses through the use of violence, which would, in turn, bring about a repressive state that would exhibit the very nature of the regime. Unfortunately, this succeeded in bringing to power for twelve years a harsh, ultraright regime. The Tupamaros faced the dilemma of all small, clandestine, armed organizations: how to build a political infrastructure when all the militants were mobilized in underground military tasks. Carlos Marighella's movement also collapsed before winning support because, like the Tupamaros, it finally became an urban *foco* more than a political mass movement.

These movements inspired others, which collapsed either quickly, like the Front de Liberation de Québec, or slowly, like the Rote Armée Fraktion, better known as the Baader-Meinhof group. The Marighella and Tupamaro concept that inducing the authorities to repression would ultimately bring about their downfall was simply wrong. In practice, the repression had the effect of dismantling the revolutionary organization without leading to anything more than passive sympathy from public opinion, eventually yielding to a growing hostility toward violence.

What is the revolutionary status of the Third World, and what are its prospects? What we call the Third World has been strongly divided between countries or areas that have developed economically, such as parts of Southeast Asia and the Far East, and those that have not, like tropical Africa. The demographic dimension must be kept in mind; and it is worth remembering that the nonindustrialized countries of Africa, Asia, and Latin America, which represented 67 percent of the world's population in 1900 will represent 83 percent by the end of the century. Urbanization on a large scale is the major phenomenon of the Third World. In ten years, seventeen of the twenty most populated cities will be in the Third World, with New York, Tokyo, and Los Angeles making up the balance.

The conditions that bring about insurgencies, racial oppression, ethnic discrimination, injustice, crisis, and so on will not be lacking in the future.

It is then highly probable that the cities will become more and more the focal points for social and political unrest. Clearly, this may be one of the lessons of the Khomeinist revolution in Iran.

We are reaching a time of developing unrest, of rapid deployment operations, urban fighting, terrorism, and the whole range of indirect strategies. The experiences of the past have not been adequately assimilated, nor has sufficient knowledge been adapted to today's world.

NOTES

1. For a more in-depth discussion of the historical forces that have shaped and produced a Third World revolutionary milieu, see Chaliand (1989); Fanon (1965); Magdoff (1969); and Worsley (1965).

REFERENCES

Chaliand, Gerard (1989). *Revolution in the Third World: Currents and Conflicts in Asia, Africa, and Latin America*. Rev. ed. New York: Penguin.
Debray, Regis (1967). *Revolution in the Revolution?* New York: Grove.
Fanon, Frantz (1965). *The Wretched of the Earth*. New York: Grove.
Guevara, Ernesto (1963). *Guerrilla Warfare*. New York: Monthly Review.
Magdoff, Harry (1969). *The Age of Imperialism*. New York: Monthly Review.
Worsley, Peter (1965). *The Third World*. Chicago: University of Chicago Press.

CHAPTER THREE

Dynamics of Revolutionary Change

The intention of this chapter is to inquire theoretically into the internal and external conditions that create and sustain revolutionary legitimacy. The essays synthesize established explanatory frameworks of revolutionary change and provide innovative expositions of the internal and external factors that shape the revolutionary environment.

T. David Mason articulates a comprehensive theoretical framework for revolutionary choicemaking at the level of the individual and the state. Deriving his theory from the major works of Tilly, Gurr, and Skocpol (among others), Mason identifies the indigenous factors essential to revolutionary mobilization. The essay provides an essential analysis of popular rejection of existing governmental authority and the development of active support for an alternative legitimacy claimed by the revolutionary movement.

Third World revolutions do not, however, occur in a vacuum. They occur in, and are influenced by, the context of an international milieu that reflects to a considerable extent the conduct of relations between major external actors.

William J. Foltz focuses on the external structural variables that characterize the international revolutionary "culture." His essay, formerly subtitled "Who First Seduced Them to That Foul Revolt?", provides a fourfold typology and examines how the dynamics of internal legitimization exploit the international marketplace of revolutionary experiences and ideas.

Zaki Laidi examines how Third World regimes selectively assimilate and apply revolutionary ideologies in the interest of their own consolidation or survival. His primary focus is on how Third World regimes, revolutionary or otherwise, use elements of Marxist-Leninist ideology for the purpose of building up regime legitimacy. Furthermore, Laidi suggests that a regime's or movement's ideological choices are frequently misperceived by external actors as delegitimizing despite the fact that these same choices are often functional or necessary for survival.

—THE EDITORS

Indigenous Factors

T. DAVID MASON

Although revolution has become an increasingly pervasive feature of the political landscape in the Third World, it remains perhaps the least understood and most intractable form of conflict with which governments and scholars alike must concern themselves. No doubt our puzzlement over the etiology of Third World revolutions derives in part from the many forms these conflicts assume, the wide variety of forces that appear to be at work in them, and the equally diverse array of theories that have been brought to bear in our efforts to understand, foresee, and perhaps even control them. What, then, do we know about Third World revolutions? Have we been able to identify the causes, describe the dynamics, and predict the outcomes of these all-too-frequent convolutions in the politics of contemporary Third World societies? Even if we could, would that enable us to formulate and implement any remedial measures that might preserve nations and their people against the pain and destruction of revolutionary violence without in the process condemning them to a more tragic and lamentable fate?

The answer to the first question is that there is much that we think we may know about them but much more about which we can only be certain of our ignorance. As for the second question, the very abundance of competing explanations, conflicting evidence, and contradictory policy recommendations attests to the apparent lack of any strong consensus—scholarly, political, or other—on what the causes and consequences for the Third World revolutions might be. The answer to the third question, about possible remedies, is even more disturbingly ambiguous in that many of the explanations that have been offered point to causes that are structurally embedded and thus perhaps beyond the reach of conventional, policy-manipulable variables.

What we do know and can agree on is that there is a great deal of revolutionary violence going on in the world and that virtually all of it has been for some time concentrated in the Third World. Kidron and Smith (1983) tell us that since World War II there has not been a single day in which there was not a war of some sort going on somewhere in the world. Sampson (1978: 60) has estimated that on any given day there are on average twelve wars underway in various parts of the world. The overwhelming preponderance of these clashes have occurred in the Third World, either as internal violence or as interstate violence involving one or more Third World nations (Starr and Most, 1985: 33). Indeed, what is especially remarkable about the patterns of conflict in the Third World is that a such a substantial portion of these wars have *not* been classic interstate battles but some form of civil conflict, such as a civil war, separatist revolt, or anticolonial insurgency. Thus, in contrast to earlier eras, internal war—not interstate violence—has become by far the most pervasive and destructive form of armed conflict in the years since World War II (Starr and Most, 1985: 39).

While our ability to document the occurrence and describe the dimensions of Third World revolutions has grown substantially in the last two decades, one could reasonably question whether our understanding of the nature of revolutionary conflict and the conditions that affect its inception and outcome has advanced in proportion with our accumulating experience of dealing with such incidents. Certainly, our persistent perplexity over Third World revolutions cannot be attributed to a lack of effort at understanding their origins, dynamics, and outcomes. The vast proliferation of case studies, theoretical and empirical inquiries, and strategic analyses on the subject attests to its salience as an object of inquiry for strategic analysts and social scientists alike. In the post–World War II era, scholarship has presented us with explanations of revolutionary violence based on "relative deprivation" theories depicting the emergence of the "revolutionary state of mind" (Gurr, 1970s; Davies, 1962) and structural theories pointing to the disruptive effects of rapid modernization in agrarian societies (Moore, 1966; Huntington, 1968; Skocpol, 1979; Jonson, 1982), especially its corrosive effects on traditional patron-client networks (Migdal, 1974; Scott, 1976; Popkin, 1979; Kerkvliet, 1977; Race, 1972; Wolf, 1969; Paige, 1975). A variety of empirical studies have explored the links between civil violence and extreme inequality of income (Muller, 1985), land tenure (Midlarsky, 1982; Midlarsky and Roberts, 1985; Russett, 1964; Mitchell, 1968; Paige, 1970; Paranzino, 1972) or both (Muller and Seligson, 1987; see also Linehan, 1980), as well as the links between instability and various aspects of a nation's dependency relationship in the international arena (Jackson et al., 1978) or the systemic dimensions of indigenous social change (Hibbs, 1973; Feierabend and Feierabend, 1972; Bwy, 1968). An element of formal rigor has been brought to the analysis of civil conflict in the body of works that apply the logic of rational choice theory to the analysis of individual behavior under conditions of civil violence marked by extremes of government repression and rebel coercion (Tullock, 1971; Silver, 1976; DeNardo, 1984; Lichbach, 1984, 1987; Heggen and Cuzan, 1981; Cuzan, 1980; Lichbach and Gurr, 1981; Leites and Wolf, 1970).[1]

Indeed, when confronted with the profusion of recent studies on the subject, one might be tempted to conclude that the failure of governments to translate rigorous analysis into effective policy for dealing with Third World revolutions may be less a matter of the misapprehension of the phenomena by government analysts than of the confusion on the part of policymakers confronted with a cacophony of such widely disparate studies, findings, and recommendations. Instead of presuming to resolve this confusion, I shall attempt to integrate several diverse perspectives into a reasonably coherent analytical essay on the social, economic, and demographic roots of Third

World revolutions. As such, my focus will be almost exclusively on indigenous factors contributing to the outbreak of civil war. International forces and foreign intervention will not be examined, except insofar as they may catalyze the indigenous forces of change that fuel revolutionary violence. However, even if we confine ourselves to indigenous causes, our task is not measurably simplified, as we must still choose from an extensive menu of macroeconomic, social-structural, social-psychological, and rational choice theories. How, then, does one synthesize the contributions of such widely divergent paradigmatic traditions?

At the risk of falling into a reductionist trap, I will approach this task by arguing that the fundamental question we must ask in assessing the causes of Third World revolutions is what syndrome of social, economic, and political dynamics would induce an otherwise politically inert peasant or urban dweller to risk violent death by taking up arms and joining a movement intent on the overthrow of the incumbent regime. The individual participant in revolutionary violence provides us with a useful common denominator by which to integrate theories as diverse as structural dependency, relative deprivation, resource mobilization, and rational choice. One cannot deny that there is a vast and complex array of forces at work in the eruption of revolutionary violence in the Third World. However, revolutions are fought by collections of individuals who joined the movement for their own reasons. Therefore, if we are to make any sense out of the otherwise baffling array of explanations that have been offered for the inception of revolutionary violence, it would seem reasonable and prudent to ask how the dynamics depicted by each of these theories actually effects the life conditions of individual citizens in Third World society.

The analysis that follows begins with an assessment of how a Third World nation's entry into the modern world economy alters the local economy in such a way as to displace large numbers of peasants from the land, while in the process disrupting the traditional patron-client networks that had formerly afforded peasants some measure of security against economic disaster. Their resulting economic vulnerability is further exacerbated by the rapid population growth that typically accompanies the early stages of modernization. Population growth intensifies land pressures and competition for a limited supply of occupational alternatives to agriculture. Unless the regime takes measures to relieve their economic distress, this displaced population becomes susceptible to the appeals of opposition political elites who promise the restoration of economic security through redistributive reforms of various sorts.

Faced with a growing opposition challenge, the government can respond with one of two broad strategies: it can institute a program of economic reforms that restores the economic security of marginalized sectors of the mass public to minimum levels, or it can attempt through repression to eliminate opposition organizations and intimidate their actual or potential supporters into withholding support from the opposition. However, the very conditions of dependent development that gave rise to opposition activity in the first place also constrain the ability of the state to respond with anything other than repression. It lacks the redistributable resources, institutional machinery, and political will to undertake reform. Repression thus becomes the expected policy response by default, if not by choice. However, though it may deter active opposition support in the short term, repression does not relieve the grievances that gave rise to opposition activity in the first place. As the dynamics of population growth and economic dislocations continue unabated, the size of the population that the regime must control through repression continues to expand, eventually crowding the regime's coercive capacity. If in response to unabated mass support for political opposition the regime escalates its repressive activity, this violence will eventually become more indiscriminate with respect to both the selection of targets and the level of violence applied. As repressive violence becomes indiscriminate, it eventually begins to stimulate, rather than deter, support for the opposition: nonelites come to realize that they may become victims of repressive violence whether they support the opposition or not and thus be motivated to join it if only to seek protection from regime-sponsored repressive violence. By approaching the question in this manner, we can perhaps bring some coherence to what would otherwise appear to be a confusing and often contradictory set of explanations, descriptions, and prescriptions.

DEPENDENT DEVELOPMENT AND THE CRISIS OF RURAL POVERTY

Most studies of Third World revolutions point to transformations in the local economy, social structure, and political system catalyzed by the nation's integration into the world economy as having eventually produced the set of conditions that rendered the nation susceptible to revolution. The integration of Third World nations into the modern world political economy brings many nations to a state of dependent development. The economy of the dependent nation is centered around the production of agricultural products or other primary goods for export to the industrialized North. This leaves the Third World nation dependent upon the North for capital, technology, transportation, and manufactured goods. Since that nation's ability to pay for those imports and service the national debt is dependent on the market price of the primary goods it exports, the nation's economy is highly vulnerable to fluctuations in the world market price of its primary goods exports. Over time, the unfavorable terms of trade that accrue to nations in the periphery of the world economy serve to retard and distort the growth and diversification of the economy, polarize the distribution of wealth and income, and disrupt the traditional mechanisms by which rural and urban masses assured themselves of some margin of subsistence.

The local effects of dependent development are especially severe for the Third World nations that were integrated into the global economy as exporters of agricultural products. Prior to their penetration by the global economy, these nations typically existed as agrarian societies, with land tenure and land use structured along traditional clientelist liens. Patterns of land ownership varied widely, but in most cases there was a small landed elite that controlled large amounts of land in the form of large estates and a vast peasant majority that lived perilously close to the margins of subsistence. While most of the population did exist in poverty, they were usually afforded some measure of security from subsistence crisis through traditional clientelist mechanisms. Peasants existed as smallholders producing food crops for their own consumption and for sale in local markets; as tenants or sharecroppers renting land on a large estate to produce cash crops for the landlord and food crops sufficient to meet the family's subsistence needs; as permanent workers on large estates; or as seasonal agricultural laborers. Even the permanent workers on large estates were usually afforded access to some land as a matter of usufruct. On this they could grow food and some livestock for their own consumption. Moreover, the local landed elite were typically expected to provide local peasants (especially their own tenants) with various services (e.g., crop loans, rent delays, emergency grain, and a host of other services) that amounted to a subsistence floor. In return, peasants were expected to provide the landlord with such things as free labor, a share of their crop, political support, and other acts of deference. Thus, tradition defined a set of diffuse, face-to-face relations between the local landed patrons and their peasant clients that provided peasants with some degree of security against frequent subsistence crises.[2]

For such nations, the entry into world markets for export crops stimulated a profound change in traditional patterns of land use, land tenure, and the accompanying structures of social stability and economy security. As the demand among the metropolitan nations for the commodities of the Third World nation increases, the opportunity structure facing traditional landed elites is altered, making it more profitable for them to shift their land from the production of food crops for local consumption to the production of cash crops for sale in Northern markets. As the value of the cash crop that a landlord could raise on a given plot of land comes to exceed the return he receives form tenants growing crops for local consumption, landlords begin evicting their tenants. Smallholders can be pressured through more indirect means, such as stringent credit terms, higher taxes, and the withdrawal of other services essential to their margin of financial solvency. In this manner, they are compelled to sell off their land, usually to a local landlord, who alone has the capital to convert it to commercial production of export crops. As a result, the nation's entry into world markets for these crops is usually accompanied by the concentration of landholdings and, concomitantly, the disruption of the traditional patron-client social ties that held together the fabric of rural society.

The opportunities for profit combine with the production characteristics of the particular commodities in demand (e.g., sugar, cattle, cotton, coffee) to create additional pressures for the concentration of landholdings into large commercial estates. Often, the concentration of landownership occurs with the public blessing and active assistance of the national government and its foreign benefactors. In parts of Latin America during the nineteenth century, laws were passed to mandate the subdivision of communal lands into smallholdings. Individual peasant households could then be pushed off the land through various devices, thus making their land available for absorption into neighboring commercial estates. Some export crops require substantial capital outlays to begin or maintain production. Others (e.g., coffee) require a year or more before they produce a marketable crop. Many of these crops require large landholdings in order to achieve the economies of scale necessary to compete in world markets. These and related considerations serve to guarantee that entry into these markets will be restricted to the small, local economic elite who can afford the price of admission.

The major structural consequence of this transformation of land tenure and land usage patterns is a shift in the distribution of the rural population among the various land tenure categories: as people are displaced from the land as tenants and smallholders, the peasant population becomes increasingly concentrated in the landless-seasonal-laborer category of the rural labor force. Usually, even the size of the permanent labor force on the commercial estates is reduced as a result of the nation's entry into world markets. With the growth in the size of the landless work force, the wage rate for seasonal workers is depressed. Assuming that the amount of arable land is fixed, any increase in the number of landless peasants inevitably drives agricultural wages down because the supply of seasonal workers increases while the demand for labor remains relatively stable (because it is tied to the supply of arable land). Eventually, landlords begin replacing permanent workers with seasonal workers to whom they need not supply any other services beyond wages. Furthermore, discharging estate workers frees up for crop production lands that were previously cultivated by those peasants as a matter of usufruct. The permanent work force is cut to the minimum needed at the slowest time in the crop cycle; and any additional labor is contracted, as needed, from among the large and growing landless labor force. This deteriorating ratio of labor supply to demand is further exacerbated by the economies of scale that can be achieved on large commercial estates, as well as by the estates' tendency to shift to more capital-intensive modes of production.

The implications of these trends for the average peasant household is that fewer families are being supported by the agricultural economy than was the case when the land was subdivided into a *minifundia* of smallholdings and tenant plots. In short, demand for agricultural labor is generally reduced by the same shift in land use that so dramatically increased the supply of labor in the first place. Of course, the most significant consequence of this condition for peasant families is that wages are reduced and household income is reduced. Brewer (1983: 400) has noted that in El Salvador, among those employed in agriculture, agricultural wages are sufficient to provide only about 50 percent of the income needed for subsistence.

A further effect of these shifts in land use is a reduction in the supply and an increase in the price of basic food commodities and other subsistence goods. The same process that pushes peasants off the land and denies them the wherewithal to grow their food also reduces the supply of food available in the local market. Food crop production is displaced by export crop production (see, e.g., Durham, 1979: 30–36). At the same time, the displacement of peasants from the land means that fewer households are able to produce all or even part of their own food needs. Thus, market demand for food crops increases at the same time that local supplies are diminishing. This results in high rates of inflation in the market for these basic commodities.

Many nations attempt to deal with this problem by importing large amounts of food. However, the importation of grain for sale in local markets by itself does nothing to put cash in hands of the households that are in most urgent need of the imported food. It does link peasant households directly to the global economy, as their well-being is now contingent on fluctuations in the world market price of basic food commodities. Food import policies consume valuable foreign exchange that otherwise could be invested in programs that create jobs outside of the agricultural sector and thereby relieve mounting pressures in local markets for land and labor. Furthermore, cheap food policies implemented through the import of food commodities serve to drive into insolvency the remaining smallholders and tenants producing food crops for local markets. Usually, they simply cannot compete with foreign producers.

The deteriorating economic plight of peasant households is further exacerbated by the rapid growth in population that normally accompanies the nation's entry into the global political economy. The dynamics of the demographic transition occurring in the Third World are well documented and extensively analyzed.[3] The major effect of this process is that annual population growth rates in the Third World often range from 2.5 percent to 3.5 percent, which means that the population is doubling every twenty to thirty years. The resulting pressures on the already-eroding economic conditions facing the rural and urban poor are devastating. Population growth intensifies competition for a limited (and shrinking) supply of tenant plots. In this manner, it creates further upward pressure on the value of land and downward pressure on the size of tenant plots. Landlords find that they can subdivide their rental lands into ever-smaller plots and still extract higher per-acre rents. These trends render tenant farmers ever more vulnerable to the risks of agriculture, the events in climate and market over which individual farmers have no control but that can seriously affect the size and value of their crop.

Population growth also accelerates the process by which permanent workers on commercial estates are replaced by seasonal workers. The growth in the landless rural labor force that was generated by displacement of peasant households from the land is simply intensified by the natural rate of growth in that same segment of the population. Thus, population growth creates further downward pressure on agricultural wages and increases the incentives for commercial estates to replace permanent workers with seasonal employees.

Even with these pressures mounting in the countryside, displaced peasants rarely respond with spontaneous uprisings. Instead, in the absence of organized opposition, the reflexive response is to pursue one of several more conventional "escape valves" by which displaced peasants have traditionally sought relief from immediate economic distress. These include migration to another region where unused lands, better terms of trade from landlords, or occupational alternatives to agriculture might exist. Occasionally, there may occur spontaneous eruptions such as food riots or land invasions. However, these are usually short-lived, limited to extremely short-term goals, and seldom successful in altering the underlying structural conditions that are the source of peasant distress. More often, peasants simply accept the status quo and attempt through whatever means are immediately available (including crime and other forms of what James Scott [1985] has termed "everyday resistance") to secure the means of subsistence.

However, the very trends that led to their declining economic conditions also serve to foreclose these traditional escape valves. With the value of land increasing, there is not likely to be much unused land available. The tendency for export crop production to become concentrated in one or two major crops means that the terms of employment available from landlords in different parts of the country are likely to become rather uniform. The same dependency ties that touched off these changes in the first place also serve to distort the economy and restrict the growth of other sectors that might hold the promise of providing displaced peasants with occupational alternatives to agriculture. First, the profits that accrue from export crops are seldom invested in local industries that could relieve pressures in the countryside by providing industrial jobs. Local economic elites usually prefer to devote their increased income either to consumption or to more lucrative (and safer) investments in the industrial North. Furthermore, local economic elites often fear that industrial growth will hurt export agriculture by driving up wages at the expense of profits. Besides, even if they were to invest in local industry, it is doubtful that the resulting rate of job creation would be sufficient to absorb the growth in the labor force that accompanies population growth rates of 2 percent to 3 percent annually. For example, Gendell (1986: 64–65) has estimated that an annual growth in GDP of 8 percent would be required to absorb the growth in the labor force of Latin America projected for the years 1975–2000.

Thus, the most likely response to land pressures in the countryside is for displaced peasants to migrate to urban areas, not because they are drawn by the prospects of economic opportunity but because they are compelled to do so by the lack of economic opportunity in the countryside (see Walton, 1984: 150). In the city, what employment they can find is usually in the service sector and in the informal sectors of the urban economy, where wages are lowest and unemployment or underemployment are a way of life.[4] Thus, migration to urban areas provides escape from the land pressures in the countryside, but it does not relieve the economic marginality plaguing displaced peasant households.

In the absence of government programs to remedy their economic distress, displaced urban and rural nonelites turn to alternative institutions in search of relief from their immediate fate. Often, these include traditional communal organizations, peasant associations, and (in Latin America) the Catholic Church.[5] These institutions serve as the organizational catalysts for grassroots collective action aimed at providing displaced peasants with relief from their immediate conditions of distress. Typically, grassroots activities focus initially on community self-help programs, such as child care cooperatives, health and hygiene clinics, food distribution networks, schools, adult literacy campaigns, and job information services. Such actions are less politically risky for the participants and address their needs with immediate action, not promised reform (see Chaffee, 1979).

As nonelites experience some measure of success in cooperating for economic self-help, their grassroots organizations begin expanding into political mobilization in support of policy change and reform. Activities include strikes, petition drives, demonstrations, and other forms of nonviolent political opposition. In these efforts, the grassroots organizations develop links to the more explicitly political opposition groups, such as federations of labor unions and peasant associations, as well as opposition political parties. Through this mechanism, the mass base of active supporters that opposition political organizations can call upon expands dramatically. Note that the previously politically inert nonelites are mobilized for political action not directly by conventional political parties but indirectly through parties cultivating ties with the emerging grassroots organizations. The initial raison d'être of these popular organizations was not political activism but immediate economic relief for the impoverished. Having succeeded in the former, the members of these organizations can afford to devote more of their time and resources to seeking permanent solutions to their plight. Opposition political parties can then assume the role of mobilizing popular associations for explicitly political activities aimed at policy reform.

Faced with a growing opposition challenge, the existing regime has two broad alternatives from which to choose in attempting to defuse the challenge to its policies, authority, and legitimacy. It can attempt through reform programs to relieve the immediate economic distress and the structural sources of the poverty for displaced masses. Such reforms represent an effort to preempt opposition victory by coopting their base of popular support. Alternatively, the state may choose to rely on repression and coercion to disrupt opposition organizations and intimidate their actual or potential supporters into withholding active support from the opposition. Regrettably, the very conditions that gave rise to opposition in the first place also reinforce the tendency of the state to respond with repression rather than reform.

REPRESSION AND THE INSTIGATION
OF REVOLUTIONARY VIOLENCE

When the opposition challenge mounts to the point that it can no longer be ignored by the regime, the state will attempt a variable mix of positive rewards (reforms) and negative sanctions (repression) in order to preserve its authority.[6] The particular mix of coercion and accommodation it adopts will depend upon the resources at its disposal and the difference in the expected marginal payoff (in terms of political stability) from investing marginal resources in coercion versus accommodation (Lichbach, 1984).

However, the same syndrome of dependent development that gave rise to the opposition challenge in the first place also reinforces the tendency of the regime to resort to repression rather than reform in response to that challenge. The highly skewed distribution of land, wealth, and income, as well as the high rates of unemployment and underemployment typical of national economies in peripheral societies restrict the tax base from which the state can extract the resources needed to finance reform programs. Given the low level of industrialization, the major form of taxable property or assets is farmland. With landownership concentrated in a few hands, the landed oligarchy has sufficient political clout to preclude the imposition of substantial new land taxes to finance reform programs, especially if the ultimate intent of those reforms is to redistribute income, wealth, and land at their expense. At any rate, farmland by itself is a rather unstable revenue base on which to build a more equitable and prosperous society. As recent evidence from our own farm sector has shown, land value is tied far too firmly to fluctuations in world markets for the crops that can be grown on it. For a Third World nation the revenue flows available for investment in economic reform and development programs are subject to the same cycles of boom and bust that characterize world markets for the crops that can be grown on the land.[7]

Likewise, total national income tends to flow into the hands of a small economic elite, leaving the vast majority of the population so impoverished as to have little beyond subsistence for the government to tax. As noted above, the economic elite (both local and foreign) has the political clout, through its ties to the military and to foreign benefactors, to preclude any government efforts to shift the tax burden onto their income. What industry there is is often foreign-owned and has ensured itself against higher taxes among the concessions that Third World governments must typically offer to attract foreign investment in the first place. Thus, any efforts by the government to shift the tax burden of reform programs onto the economic elite will be met with resistance. They can threaten to liquidate their assets and emigrate. Foreign benefactors, including private banks, foreign governments, and international agencies such as IMF and the World Bank, can (and typically do) manipulate the loans, foreign aid, and other resources they provide these nations in order to pressure them into moderating or abandoning redistributive policies. If a civilian regime persists in pursuing redistributive reforms that threaten the prerogatives of the economic elite, those elites may choose to activate their ties to the military in the form of a coup that brings to power a junta more amenable to the interests of the economic elite. In short, the state in dependent societies usually lacks the redistributable resources, institutional machinery, or political will to pursue more accommodative, as opposed to coercive, policies in response to mounting opposition challenges.[8]

Conversely, one of the central features of the authoritarian regime in dependent societies is that the coercive machinery of the state is the most longstanding and the most highly sophisticated of the institutional capabilities at the disposal of policymakers. The ideology of the military in these regimes is such that political tranquility is presumed to be a prerequisite for economic development (Lopez, 1986). On this basis, the military sees itself not just as a temporary caretaker in times of strife but as the exclusive guardian of political stability and the ultimate arbiter of political authority (see Seligson, 1987: 4–5; Pion-Berlin, 1984). These perceptions are reinforced by the generous military assistance that the United States and other metropolitan powers are usually willing to offer in order to preserve in power a regime that is not antagonistic to their economic and strategic interests. International financial agencies such as IMF and the World Bank, as well as private lenders and national governments in the metropolitan North, often require the adoption of stringent monetary and fiscal policies by the local government as a condition of their assistance. These policies can be expected to stimulate increased opposition activity in protest against the additional hardships imposed on the urban and rural poor by these policies. The state's response to this escalation in opposition activity will almost of necessity be repression. To accede to opposition demands would be to violate the conditionality of external assistance, thereby jeopardizing its continued provision (Pion-Berlin, 1984: 107–108).

Finally, regimes that have been successful in the past in suppressing opposition through violent repression are likely to resort to such tactics (as opposed to accommodative measures) in the future, regardless of the character of the opposition organizations, the nature of their demands, or the composition of their base of popular support (see Gurr, 1986). Hence, the almost-reflexive response to opposition challenges is to increase the level of officially sanctioned violence directed against the opposition leaders and their actual, suspected, or potential supporters (Mason and Krane, 1985).

The central question then becomes whether and under what conditions escalating levels of repression deter or, alternatively, stimulate nonelite support for the opposition. The evidence on this question is by no means conclusive. Theoretical arguments and empirical evidence have been offered in support of stimulative (Eckstein, 1965; Gurr, 1969: 579), deterrent (Hibbs, 1973: 82–93; Tilly, 1978; Snyder and Tilly, 1972: 527), and curvilinear (Gurr, 1968, 1970; Bwy, 1968; Feierabend and Feierabend, 1972; Muller, 1985) relationships between the level of repressive violence and the level of opposition support. In line with my central theme, I will attempt to sort out these conflicting findings by exploring how different levels of repressive violence affect the calculus by which individual nonelites choose between supporting the regime, its opposition, or neither.

REPRESSION AND THE
DIFFUSION OF REVOLUTIONARY SUPPORT

In general, we begin with the assumption that individual members of the urban and rural masses would prefer to remain uninvolved in political struggles and instead devote their time and energies to the more urgent tasks of securing subsistence for their families.[9] Nonetheless, as we have seen earlier, nonelites do become involved in organized collective action intended to provide immediate relief from their conditions of economic distress. Through the mechanism of grassroots communal organizations, they then enter into more explicitly political activity. How they choose between supporting the government, supporting the opposition, or remaining politically uninvolved can be seen as a function of the relative benefits and costs of these alternative courses of action or inaction (see Chaffee, 1979; Tullock, 1971; Ireland, 1967; Mason, 1987, 1989). I shall argue that at this point in the escalation of political tensions, it is the scope and intensity of the state's repressive violence that determines whether opposition will be quelled by repression or will escalate into revolutionary violence. In this sense, revolutionary violence is more of a tactical choice made by an opposition that sees alternative courses of action as ineffectual and dangerous. The state's role in the eruption of revolution is a proactive one, the state has foreclosed nonviolent alternatives through its application of repression.[10]

When the state and the opposition are locked in the conflict not just over policies but over authority and legitimacy as well, the central concern of individual citizens in choosing the best course of action is the threat of coercive sanctions by the regime or the rebels or both. This is so for several reasons; but the most obvious one is that no amount of benefits—public or private—could offset the risk of death in return for supporting the wrong group. Thus, the determining factor in a nonelite's decision to support the regime, support the opposition, or remain uninvolved is his or her estimate of the threat of death by one side in retaliation for support of the other.

Whether repressive violence by the state will deter one's support of the opposition then depends on the scope and intensity of such violence. More specifically, the impact of repressive violence on the distribution of popular support between the regime and its opposition will vary depending on whether the violence is targeted against the leadership of opposition organizations, the rank-and-file participants in those organizations and their activities, or randomly selected groups of the mass public who have little or no demonstrable affiliation with the opposition.[11]

The most restrictive targeting strategy for repressive violence is one confined to the leadership of opposition organizations. Usually, this is the earliest and most common form of repressive violence. It appears long before the political struggle has escalated into an intractable civil war. At this point, opposition activity is usually concentrated in legal organizations such as labor unions, peasant associations, and political parties. What regimes do as a first step in the escalation of repression is arrest, exile, or assassinate the leaders of these technically legal organizations. Laws can be enacted to restrict the bounds of what is defined as legitimate opposition activity. As these boundaries are progressively narrowed, the regime provides itself with the legal pretext to silence the leadership of opposition organizations.

Repressive violence targeted specifically at the leadership of opposition organizations may achieve its goal of reducing the level of active support for the opposition, at least temporarily. It does so not so much by intimidating peasants and other nonelites into withholding their support for fear of becoming victims themselves (so long as the victims are confined to the opposition elite, nonelites need not consider themselves likely targets) as by inducing a sense of futility. People support political organizations because they think they will receive some benefits, both private and collective, in return. The presence of skilled leadership and effective organizational infrastructure leads them to believe that their contributions will be aggregated with those of others so as to produce the flow of benefits the contributors desire and the leadership has promised (Frohlich and Oppenheimer, 1970; Frohlich, Oppenheimer, and Young, 1971). Repressive violence that silences or eliminates large portions of the opposition leadership disrupts the ability of opposition organizations to deliver benefits to their supporters. Leites and Wolf (1970) describe this as "disrupting the conversion process" by which insurgents convert the inputs they exact from their supporters into outputs of insurgent violence against the state and benefits for their supporters. Consequently, supporters withdraw into inactivity out of a sense of futility. Devoting time and other resources to the activities of the opposition no longer appears to them as a prudent investment of their family's scarce resources. Therefore, they withhold them for other, nonpolitical endeavors.

While in a narrow sense this strategy does achieve the desired effect of diminishing the level of opposition activity, the persistence of this effect over time cannot be assured. Repression of organizations seeking redress of grievances does not eliminate the grievances themselves. Indeed,the failure of the state to take positive measures to relieve the poverty confronting so many simply allows those conditions to intensify, as the dynamics that gave rise to them in the first place remain unaltered by government policy. In other words, repression of opposition leadership may reduce active support for the opposition; but it does not increase active support for the regime. If anything, it is likely to shift preferences toward the opposition and thereby increase latent support. The level of latent support may be conceived of as those who, given a choice, would prefer the opposition and its programs to those of the current regime but who, for fear of the consequences, are unwilling to express those preferences with overt support behaviors (Mason and Krane, 1989). Should any leaders arise who can restore the ability of the opposition to deliver benefits to its constituents, we would expect support levels to rebound accordingly. Indeed, support for the opposition may even reach higher levels than before the instigation of repression. The targeting of opposition leaders signals to their supporters that they can expect little in the way of positive benefits from the regime. All that the state expects from its repression is their neutrality, not their active support. In effect, then, the "price" of nonelite support for the opposition declines because of what amounts to a lack of "demand" for their support on the part of the government.

Thus, repression of opposition leaders does not eradicate the challenge to the regime's stability. Rather, as Lichbach (1984) has shown, the repression of nonviolent forms of opposition (e.g., demonstrations, strikes, electoral activity) will simply induce the new opposition leaders to adopt violent tactics of their own. Indeed, if the regime represses the more effective of the opposition's two tactical alternatives (i.e., violent or nonviolent action), not only will the level of the other form increase but the total amount of opposition activity (violent and nonviolent) can be expected to increase (Lichbach, 1987).

The choice of new tactics for the opposition will be influenced by a number of concerns. First, it will seek to avoid actions that leave its new leaders exposed to the current tactics of repression being practiced by the regime. Second, it may choose tactics that have some promise of overcoming the perception among erstwhile supporters that past action strategies were futile. For this reason, it is likely to engage in activities that are less costly and risky for the participants and that mobilize a different segment of the nonelite population (e.g., peasants as opposed to factory workers). For instance, it may begin organizing mass demonstrations involving a coalition of organizations and crowds large enough to render individual participants relatively anonymous. Conversely, it may avoid strikes in which participation is confined to the rather small number of union members, who, because they are known members, are less anonymous and more vulnerable to retribution (Mason and Krane, 1989). By shifting tactics in this manner, the opposition does not necessarily cease and desist in its agitation for reform. Instead, it simply shifts to new and more effective tactical alternatives.

What, then, does the regime do when its efforts to demobilize opposition support by targeting its leaders fail to preserve the desired political quiescence? As I argued earlier, the almost-reflexive response of the regime in dependent societies is to escalate the level of repressive violence. More specifically, the regime is likely to expand the range of targets for its violence to include rank-and-file participants in opposition organizations and activities. For instance, it may begin arresting, detaining, or "disappearing" known union members and not just their leaders. When this occurs, the membership of unions, peasant associations, and other organizations must now consider themselves likely targets of repressive violence and act accordingly. The regime may also escalate the use of force as a means of controlling or stopping mass demonstrations. Thus, participants in those events must now assume the risk of being beaten, arrested, and "disappeared" or even killed in the streets.

The escalation of repressive violence to include nonelite participants in opposition activities will have different effects on different segments of that population. First of all, those who are known members of opposition organizations will not necessarily be intimidated into refraining from further activity. After all, they must assume that as known members, they remain likely targets. Therefore, rather than cease their activity, they are likely to shift from participation in "legitimate" nonviolent forms of action to more covert, unconventional, illegal, and violent forms of activity. In short, they have little to lose by "going to the hills" and joining an insurgent organization, because to do otherwise is to leave themselves vulnerable to the current levels of repression being practiced by the regime.

On the other hand, those who have previously remained uninvolved or at most have served as anonymous participants in mass demonstrations may well be intimidated into withdrawing from political activity altogether. A peasant who sees neighbors who joined a peasant union "disappearing" is likely to refrain from joining or otherwise providing overt support to the targeted organizations. This is the effect that the regime wishes to achieve. To the extent that it can confine its targeting to known participants in opposition activities, it should be able to preempt any expansion in the scope of *overt* support for the opposition, at least for the short term. The previously uninvolved will be intimidated into remaining so, and past participants in opposition organizations will be forced into temporary retreat as they seek security in order to revise their tactical blueprint. However, *latent* support for the opposition should increase, as compliance through fear cannot be equated with positive support for the regime. Furthermore, following Lichbach (1987), the repression of participants in one (nonviolent) form of opposition activity will simply result in a shift to other (violent) forms of activity, not a complete dissipation of opposition. Should the reconstituted opposition later demonstrate the ability to secure its supporters against retribution by the regime, it may be able to mobilize the pool of latent support and thereby pose an even more severe threat to the stability of the existing regime.

Thus, in the absence of any efforts to remedy the conditions that give rise to grievances in the first place, the expansion of repressive violence will lead not to an end to opposition activity but to a shift in opposition tactics to more violent and covert strategies. At this point, the organized opposition is no longer simply calling for policy changes within the structure of the existing regime. Because they must now consider themselves targets of state-sanctioned violence, the opposition is likely to constitute itself as an insurgent organization challenging the legitimacy of the current regime's right to rule.[12] For any efforts at accommodative reforms to appear credible to an opposition that has been the victim of violent repression, a general amnesty and assurances of civilian control over the security forces would be required, at a minimum. Given the strength of the military in the regime, it is unlikely that such assurances would be offered by civilian officials (for fear of a coup) or believed by the opposition (for fear of deception). Therefore, unless divisions develop within the military and one faction seizes power from another (as in El Salvador in 1979), the more likely response of a regime faced with an emerging insurgent challenge is the further escalation of repressive violence, which at this point would mean random targeting of death squad violence with little if any regard for the victim's known or suspected involvement with the opposition.

When the struggle between regime and opposition has escalated to the point of insurgent violence, the regime's application of repressive violence is intended to induce in the otherwise uninvolved the fear that if they do offer aid to the insurgents, they face the risk of extreme sanctions. In so doing, the regime hopes to deny the insurgents the base of supporters who, through the covert provision of supplies, sanctuary, and intelligence, enable rebel units to operate in a given area. To the extent that the regime succeeds in this strategy of denial, it restricts the territory in which the rebels are able to operate. In this manner, repressive violence directed against civilians in a region is intended to complement more conventional counterinsurgent operations aimed at locating and defeating in battle the insurgents' combat units.

However, for repression of this sort to achieve its intended effect, its application must be precisely targeted in the sense that an individual must be relatively certain that so long as he or she withholds support from the insurgents, there is no need to fear coercive sanctions at the hands of the state. If repression in the countryside is applied harshly and arbitrarily, the regime risks the possibility of converting previously indifferent peasants into active supporters of the insurgents. When repressive violence becomes widespread and randomly targeted, a given peasant's chances of becoming a victim are no longer related to provision of support for the insurgents. If entire villages are being terrorized on the suspicion that a few residents may have supplied aid and sustenance to the rebels, individuals must conclude that their chances of becoming a victim are less a matter of their own actions than of the mere presence of rebel activity in their general vicinity. Such activity may be taken by the state's security forces as sufficient evidence of local support for the rebels. In retaliation, they may begin terrorizing local villages through the random targeting of coercive sanctions, including death. Under these conditions, remaining uninvolved is no longer a viable option for local peasants. Their choices are to emigrate from the regions in which there is rebel activity or to join the rebels in hopes of gaining some security from repressive violence. Because noninvolvement can no longer ensure them against death squad violence, peasants become susceptible to rebel recruitment appeals that if nothing else, promise sanctuary from this repressive violence. In this manner, a high level of repressive violence indiscriminately applied ceases to deter popular support for the rebel opposition and, indeed, actually stimulates an increase in such support.

The problem for the regime is that of distinguishing the guerrilla irregular and his or her covert supporters from the politically uninvolved. And the very conditions that gave rise to the crisis of legitimacy in the first place also serve to crowd the regime's ability to target its repression precisely. In particular, unrelieved economic distress and high rates of population growth will fuel an expansion in the numbers and proportions of economically distressed young adults in the population. These people will swell the ranks of grassroots popular organizations, from which the opposition draws its support. Hence, any attacks on the leadership, membership, or participants in these organizations and their programs will threaten a larger number of nonelites and push them toward support of the rebels. Increasing amounts of resources must be expended to maintain a given level of coercive control over this population. Identifying actual insurgents from among the large and growing population of displaced nonelites will become increasingly problematic. As a result, repressive violence will become less precisely targeted, rendering more and more young adults susceptible to insurgent appeals as the risk of death from indiscriminate repression approaches the risk of death from active participation in an insurgent organization.

Population growth has additional effects on the capacity of the regime to detect and punish support for the rebels. High rates of population growth shift the age distribution of the population: the number and proportion of young adults in the population increases dramatically (see, e.g., Gendell, 1986: 52–59). Since the vast majority of these young adults are added to the landless rural population and the underemployed urban population, it follows that the number of disaffected young adults (i.e., potential recruits for the opposition) will increase as well. It has been shown in a variety of contexts that young adults are more likely to participate in civil disturbances than their older counterparts and that the probability of civil disorders in a locale is positively related to the number and proportion of disaffected young adults in the local population.[13]

Finally, the need for a constant increase in coercive forces, combined with the limited financial resources at the disposal of the regime, means that the quality of the added troops will begin to decline at some point. The regime will be compelled to rely on ill-trained recruits and draftees, as well as paramilitary units, irregulars, and local death squads that are less subject to direct supervision and control by either the central military command or civilian political authorities. Furthermore, the troops that make up these units are themselves marginalized nonelites who behave according to the same calculus of fear that guides those they are supposed to control. Many joined the army in the first place not to contribute to any worldwide struggle against communism but to secure the benefits of army life while avoiding the risks of punishment for draft evasion. When they are sent out on patrol, their most salient goal is to survive the mission. If their mission is to identify and punish suspected supporters of the rebels, they will be more worried about letting guerrilla irregulars (who might later kill them) escape than about killing innocent bystanders: concern for their own safety makes them more likely to engage in overkill than in underkill. All nonelites are suspects, and any stores of resources are potential supplies for the rebels. As raw trainees and paramilitary death squads are unleashed on the countryside, their blunt, arbitrary application of force will exacerbate the process by which the otherwise uninvolved, motivated solely by the desire to survive the conflict and indifferent as to who wins, will look to the rebels as the one group that can offer them some protection from indiscriminate government violence (Mason, 1987). In the aggregate, the size and proportion of the nonelite population that actively or tacitly supports the insurgents will begin to expand when further escalation in repressive violence results in declining selectivity in the targeting of such violence. In this manner, the exclusive reliance on a coercive strategy will eventually contribute to, rather than retard, the growth in support for the insurgent opposition.

Eventually, the regime's financial resources will be strained by the cost of constantly expanding its coercive machinery. Fewer resources will remain for investment in what accommodative programs the state may be willing to attempt. The growing financial burden of coercive control will eventually be felt by the very elites (domestic and foreign) in whose interests the state is attempting, through repression, to maintain the political and economic status quo. These pressures may at some point create strains within the authoritarian alliance itself, leading to a coup (as in Guatemala in 1973 and El Salvador in 1979), loss of support of a significant segment of the economic or political elite (as in Brazil form the mid-1970s), or the exodus of that elite (as in Cuba in the late 1950s). Whatever the outcome, the consequences for the regime's stability are potentially devastating, as evidenced by the fall of the Somoza dynasty in Nicaragua in 1979.

CONCLUSION

My purpose has been to integrate the major contributions of a number of research traditions concerned with the indigenous sources of Third World revolutions. The common denominator with which I have linked diverse paradigmatic perspectives has been the individual peasant: How do the forces described by a particular theory affect the life conditions facing the individual and make him or her more or less inclined to participate in a revolutionary insurgency? I have traced the origins of mass discontent in the economic dislocations and social disruptions catalyzed by dependent modes of development. However, I have argued that the presence of large numbers of aggrieved individuals does not necessarily result in revolutionary violence. Rational individuals prefer other, less risky alternatives when they are available. And before collective action of any sort can be expected, there must be some organizational infrastructure capable of mobilizing mass support behind collective action aimed at remedying these conditions. Perhaps most importantly, the central theme of much of the recent work on revolutionary violence is the proactive role of the state in determining whether mass-based collective action will assume revolutionary or other, less violent forms. It is when regimes respond with repressive violence to opposition calls for reform that the calculus of fear induces otherwise risk-aversive nonelites to consider participation in revolutionary organizations. Repression can quell opposition activity temporarily, but the error in relying exclusively on this strategy is that repression does not relieve the conditions that fueled opposition in the first place. Unless those conditions are remedied, a regime can expect opposition to its rule to reappear in the future. As its own policies of repression foreclose nonrevolutionary channels of opposition activity, the regime can expect renewed opposition activity to assume increasingly violent forms of its own. In this respect, the calculus of fear induced by repression makes inevitable the very revolution that the state seeks to preempt.

NOTES

1. A number of recent works are available that present summaries and analytical critiques of this body of literature and its various paradigmatic roots. See, for instance, Salert (1976), Rule (1988), Goldstone (1986), Zimmerman (1983), to name but a few.

2. This image of premodern agrarian structure and the disruptions brought on by export agriculture is a central theme in the works of Migdal (1974), Paige (1975), Scott (1976), Kerkvliet (1977), Race (1972), and, with some variations, Popkin (1979). See also Wolf (1969).

3. Saunders (1986) and Choucri (1984) present especially interesting collections of essays on the relationship between various demographic trends and the problems of political instability and conflict.

4. Booth (1986: 34) notes that underemployment ("typically an inability to find full time work or taking wage labor because of insufficient land for family subsistence") is believed to be from one to five times the official unemployment rate in Central America.

5. On the role of the church in fostering grassroots organizations in Latin America, see Lernoux (1982; 1984), Montgomery (1983), and Dodson and Montgomery (1982).

6. The proactive role of violence by the state in the instigation of revolutionary conflict is a central theme in Lichbach (1984; 1987), Leites and Wolf (1970), DeNardo (1984), and Walton (1984), among others.

7. The author is indebted to Marty Wiseman of Mississippi State University for this argument.

8. Many authors have emphasized the concept of the "weak state" in discussing the emergence of revolution. By this they mean that the state often lacks the will or the institutional capacity to act with any degree of autonomy from either the nation's economic oligarchy or the military. See, e.g., Walton (1984: 159) and Migdal (1988).

9. This is consistent with the image of nonelite political participation (or the lack thereof) in several treatments of Third World revolutions. See, e.g., DeNardo (1984), Scott (1976; 1985), Chaffee (1979), and Leites and Wolf (1970). Scott (1985) points out further that even when they are mobilized for revolutionary action, nonelites seldom share the same goals that their revolutionary leaders espouse in their ideological pronouncements about the movement. Some interesting counterpoints on peasant participation are offered by Popkin (1979) and Booth (1979).

10. See n. 6 for a list of works that depict the state as a proactive force in the instigation of revolutionary conflict.

11. For a more detailed elaboration of this argument, see Mason and Krane (1989) and Mason (1987; 1989).

12. This is what Tilly (1978), Aya (1979), and Walton (1984) refer to as a condition of "dual sovereignty."

13. From a rational choice perspective, young adults are more willing to participate in civil violence because they have more to gain and less to lose than do their older counterparts. For instance, young adults may not yet have a family to support or a job or plot of land with which to support them. Thus, they have fewer assets to risk and fewer responsibilities to tie them down and prevent them from joining an insurgent organization. As the size of the young adult population grows and repressive violence becomes more indiscriminate, the risk of death from participating in an insurgency is offset by the growing risk of death for doing nothing. Furthermore, whatever costs young adults do risk will be discounted to present value over a longer remaining life span, and any collective benefits that might result from successful revolt will be compounded over a longer remaining life span. Thus, the expected lifetime benefits are greater and the expected costs are less for young adults as compared to their elders.

REFERENCES

Aya, Roderick (1979). "Theories of Revolution Reconsidered: Contrasting Models of Collective Violence." *Theory and Society* 8:39–100.

Booth, John A., and Mitchell A. Seligson (1979). "Peasants As Activists: A Reevaluation of Political Participation in the Countryside." *Comparative Political Studies* 12:29–59.

———— (1986). "Toward Explaining National Revolts in Central America: Socioeconomic and Political Roots of Rebellion." Unpublished manuscript, University of North Texas.

Brewer, Toy Helena (1983). "Women in El Salvador," in Stanford Central American Action Network, eds. *Revolution in Central America*. Boulder: Westview.

Bwy, Douglas P. (1968). "Political Instability in Latin America: The Cross-Cultural Test of a Causal Model." *Latin American Research Review* 3:17–66.

Chaffee, Wilber A., Jr. (1979). "Let Jorge Do It: A Rational Choice Model of Political Participation." In M. A. Seligson and John A. Booth, eds. (1979). *Politics and the Poor*, vol. 2. New York: Holmes and Meier.

Choucri, Nazli (1984). *Multidisciplinary Perspectives on Population and Conflict.* Syracuse, NY: Syracuse University Press.

Cuzan, Alfred (1980). "Authority, Scope, and Force: An Analysis of Five Central American Countries." *Public Choice* 35:363–369.

Davies, James C. (1962). "Toward a Theory of Revolution." *American Sociological Review* 27:5–19.

DeNardo, James (1984). *Power in Numbers: The Political Strategy of Protest and Rebellion.* Princeton: Princeton University Press.

Dodson, Michael, and Tommie Sue Montgomery (1982). "The Churches in the Nicaraguan Revolution." In Thomas Walker, ed., *Nicaragua in Revolution.* New York: Praeger.

Durham, William H. (1979). *Scarcity and Survival in Central America: Ecological Origins of the Soccer War.* Stanford: Stanford University Press.

Eckstein, Harry (1965). "On the Etiology of Internal Wars." *History and Theory* 4:133–163.

Feierabend, Ivo K., and Rosalind L. Feierabend (1972). "Systematic Conditions of Political Aggression: An Application of Frustration-Aggression Theory." In Ivo K. Feierabend, Rosalind L. Feierabend, and Ted R. Gurr, eds., *Anger, Violence, and Politics*. Englewood Cliffs: Prentice Hall.

Frohlich, Norman, and Joe A. Oppenheimer (1970). "I Get By with a Little Help from My Friends." *World Politics* 23:104–120.

Frohlich, Norman, Joe A. Oppenheimer, and Oran Young (1971). *Political Leadership and Collective Goods*. Princeton: Princeton University Press.

Gendell, Murray (1986). "Population Growth and Labor Force Absorption in Latin America, 1970–2000." In John Saunders, ed., *Population Growth in Latin America and U.S. National Security*. New York: Allen and Unwin.

Goldstone, Jack A., ed. (1986). *Revolutions: Theoretical, Comparative, and Historical Studies*. San Diego: Harcourt, Brace, Jovanovich.

Gurr, Ted R. (1968). "A Causal Model of Civil Strife: A Comparative Analysis Using New Indices." *American Political Science Review* 62:1104–1124.

———— (1969). "A Comparative Study of Civil Strife," in Hugh Davis Graham and Ted R. Gurr, *Violence in America: Historical and Comparative Perspectives*. New York: Signet.

———— (1970). *Why Men Rebel*. Princeton: Princeton University Pres.

———— (1986). "The Political Origins of State Violence and Terror: A Theoretical Analysis." In Michael Stohl and George A. Lopez, eds., *Government Violence and Repression*. Westport, CT: Greenwood.

Heggen, Richard, and A. G. Cuzan (1981). "Legitimacy, Coercion, and Scope: An Expansion Path Analysis Applied to Five Central American Countries and Cuba." *Behavioral Science* 28:143–152.

Hibbs, Douglas A., Jr. (1973). *Mass Political Violence: A Cross-National Causal Analysis*. New York: Wiley Interscience.

Huntington, Samuel P. (1968). *Political Order in Changing Societies*. New Haven: Yale University Press.

Ireland, Thomas (1967). "The Rationale of Revolt." *Papers on Non-Market Decision-Making*. 3:49–66.

Jackson, Steven, Bruce Russett, Duncan Snidal, and David Sylvan (1978). "Conflict and Coercion in Dependent States," *Journal of Conflict Resolution* 22:627–657.

Johnson, Chalmers (1982). *Revolutionary Change*. 2d ed. Stanford: Stanford University Press.

Kerkvliet, Benjamin J. (1977). *The Huk Rebellion: A Study of Peasant Revolts in the Philippines*. Berkeley: University of California Press.

Kidron, Michael, and Dan Smith (1983). *The War Atlas: Armed Conflict— Armed Peace*. New York: Pluto Press and Simon and Schuster.

Leites, Nathan, and Charles Wolf, Jr. (1970). *Rebellion and Authority*. Santa Barbara: Rand.

Lernoux, Penny (1982). *Cry of the People: The Struggle for Human Rights in Latin America—The Catholic Church in Conflict with U.S. Policy*. New York: Penguin.

———— (1984). "Revolution and Counterrevolution in the Central American

Church." In Donald E. Shulz and Douglas H. Graham, ed., *Revolution and Counterrevolution in Central America and the Caribbean.* Boulder: Westview.

Lichbach, Mark I. (1984). "An Economic Theory of Governability: Choosing Policy and Optimizing Performance." *Public Choice* 44:307–337.

——— (1987). "Deterrence or Escalation in Repression and Dissent." *Journal of Conflict Resolution* 31:266–297.

Lichbach, Mark I., and Ted R. Gurr (1981). "The Conflict Process: A Formal Model." *Journal of Conflict Resolution* 25:3–29.

Linehan, William J. (1980). "Political Instability and Economic Inequality: Some Conceptual Clarifications." *Journal of Peace Research* 4:187–198.

Lopez, George A. (1986). "National Security Ideology As an Impetus to State Violence and Terror." In Michael Stohl and George A. Lopez, eds., *Government Violence and Repression.* Westport, CT: Greenwood.

Mason, T. David (1987). "Insurgency, Counterinsurgency, and the Rational Peasant." Presented at the annual meeting of the American Political Science Association, Chicago.

——— (1989). "Nonelite Response to State-sanctioned Terror." *Western Political Quarterly* 42:476–492.

Mason, T. David, and Dale A. Krane (1989). "The Political Economy of Death Squads." *International Studies Quarterly* 33:175–198.

Midlarsky, Manus I. (1982). "Scarcity and Inequality: Prologue to the Onset of Mass Revolution." *Journal of Conflict Resolution* 26:3–38.

Midlarsky, Manus I., and Kenneth Roberts (1985). "Class, State, and Revolution in Central America: Nicaragua and El Salvador Compared." *Journal of Conflict Resolution* 29:163–193.

Migdal, Joel S. (1974). *Peasants, Politics, and Revolution: Pressures Towards Political and Social Change in the Third World.* Princeton: Princeton University Press.

——— (1988). *Strong Societies and Weak States: State-Society Relations and State Capabilities in the Third World.* Princeton: Princeton University Press.

Mitchell, Edward J. (1968). "Inequality and Insurgency: A Statistical Study of South Vietnam." *World Politics* 20:421–438.

Montgomery, Tommie Sue (1983). "Liberation and Revolution: Christianity As a Subversive Activity in Central America." In Martin Dishkin, ed., *Trouble in Our Backyard.* New York: Pantheon.

Moore, Barrington (1966). *Social Origins of Dictatorship and Democracy: Lord and Peasant in the Making of the Modern World.* Boston: Beacon.

Muller, Edward N. (1985). "Income Inequality, Regime Repressiveness, and Political Violence." *American Sociological Review* 50:47–61.

Muller, Edward N., and Mitchell Seligson (1987). "Inequality and Insurgency." *American Political Science Review* 81:425–451.

Paige, Jeffrey M. (1970). "Inequality and Insurgency in Vietnam: A Re-Analysis." *World Politics* 23:24–37.

——— (1975). *Agrarian Revolution: Social Movements and Export Agriculture in the Underdeveloped World.* New York: Free Press.

Paranzino, Dennis (1972). "Inequality and Insurgency in Vietnam: A Further Re-Analysis." *World Politics* 24:323–329.

Pion-Berlin, David (1984). "The Political Economy of State Repression in Argentina." In Michael Stohl and George A. Lopez, eds., *The State As Terrorist*. Westport, CT: Greenwood.

Popkin, Samuel L. (1979). *The Rational Peasant: The Political Economy of Rural Society in Vietnam*. Berkeley: University of California Press.

Race, Jeffrey (1972). *War Comes to Long An*. Berkeley: University of California Press.

Rule, James B. (1988). *Theories of Civil Violence*. Berkeley: University of California Press.

Russett, Bruce M. (1964). "Inequality and Instability: The Relation of Land Tenure to Politics." *World Politics* 16:442–454.

Salert, Barbara (1976). *Revolution and Revolutionaries: Four Theories*. New York: St. Elsevier.

Sampson, Anthony (1978). "Want To Start a War?" *Esquire*, 1 March, 58–69.

Saunders, John, ed. (1986). *Population Growth in Latin America and U.S. National Security*. New York: Allen and Unwin.

Scott, James C. (1976). *The Moral Economy of the Peasant: Rebellion and Subsistence in Southeast Asia*. New Haven: Yale University Press.

――― (1985). *Weapons of the Weak*. New Haven: Yale University Press.

Seligson, Mitchell A. (1987). "Democratization in Latin America: The Current Cycle," in James M. Malloy and Mitchell A. Seligson, eds., *Authoritarians and Democrats: Regime Transition in Latin America*. Pittsburgh: University of Pittsburgh.

Silver, Morris (1976). "Political Revolution and Repression: An Economic Approach." *Public Choice* 17:63–71.

Simon, L. R., and J. C. Stephens (1982). *El Salvador Land Reform 1980–1981: Impact Audit*. 2d ed. Boston: Oxfam America.

Skocpol, Theda (1979). *States and Social Revolutions: A Comparative Analysis of France, Russia, and China*. Cambridge: Cambridge University Press.

Snyder, D., and Charles Tilly (1972). "Hardship and Collective Violence in France, 1830 to 1960." *American Sociological Review* 37:520–532.

Starr, Harvey, and Benjamin A. Most (1985). "Patterns of Conflict: Quantitative Analysis and the Comparative Lessons of Third World Wars." In Robert E. Harkavy and Stephanie Neumann, eds., *Lessons of Recent Wars in the Third World*, vol. 1. Lexington, MA: Lexington.

Tilly, Charles (1978). *From Mobilization to Revolution*. Reading, MA: Addison-Wesley.

Tullock, Gordon (1971). "The Paradox of Revolution." *Public Choice* 11:69–99.

Walton, John (1984). *Reluctant Rebels: Comparative Studies of Revolution and Underdevelopment*. New York: Columbia University Press.

Wolf, Eric (1969). *Peasant Revolts of the Twentieth Century*. New York: Harper and Row.

Zimmerman, Ekkart (1983). *Political Violence, Crises, and Revolutions: Theories and Research*. Cambridge, MA: Schenkman.

External Causes

WILLIAM J. FOLTZ

It is fruitless to argue over whether contemporary Third World revolutions are better understood and explained as domestic or international phenomena. The internal and the external aspects are closely interwoven, both as causes and as consequences. The same, of course, was true for such classic revolutions as the U.S., the French, and the Russian, in which "the revolutionary crises developed when the old-regime states became unable to meet the challenges of evolving international situations" (Skocpol, 1979: 47).

However domestic their causes, revolutions affect the external world. Some are explicitly designed to have international impact. Anticolonial revolutions, for instance, change sovereignty over far-flung bits of territory. Their success is symbolized by the cartographers' need to employ new colors for their maps of Africa and Asia. Secessionist movements, like those of southern Sudan, Eritrea, and Corsica seek to redraw international boundaries, as do panethnic movements like those of the Kurds, the Armenians, the Palestininans, or the Irish. Other revolutionary movements that seek only a change in the domestic order are seen by others as historical facts and precedents. They change the perceptual universe of outsiders and increase the probabilities that some of them will take steps to emulate, isolate, or overthrow the revolution that has taken place. Whatever the pedigree or pretensions of their perpetrators, all revolutions worthy of the name are condemned to be international events.

This said, it remains no simple analytic task to isolate the external connections and ramifications of a given revolution, much less to derive useful generalizations applicable to a variety of possible revolutionary settings. Here I should like to concentrate on the external connections of Third World revolutions that pose the greatest policymaking dilemmas and stir public controversy, the mechanisms through which external agencies and events cause or stimulate revolutions or otherwise help make them happen. Four such mechanisms may come into play, two of them causative and two facilitative. Each of these is in turn affected by the larger structure of power in which the Third World state is situated.

INSTIGATION

The first of the causative mechanisms is conceptually the simplest and potentially provides the most powerful explanation: the direct and intentional *instigation* of revolutions by a central external source. In analyzing the first recorded revolt against legitimate authority, John Milton organizes his inquiry in *Paradise Lost* around the question, "Who first seduced them to that foul revolt?" (1981: book 1, line 14). The answer seems clear from the beginning—a truly Satanic outside Power who, clandestinely entering a tropical Eden, rouses the innocent and peaceable inhabitants to break their covenant with higher authority. It is characteristic that the outside Power acts with no regard for the interests or fate of the hapless innocents whom he makes his tools. His interest lies solely in undermining the supreme Power of the age, which had earlier defeated the Satanic hosts in a titanic war for control of the universe. The locals and their descendents end up perhaps wiser but in a permanently sorry and parlous state. Milton, of course, knew revolution and its consequences at first hand (Hill, 1977); and it should be no surprise that three centuries later his blunt question still provides the starting point for most public inquiry into revolution, particularly those in poor countries, where great powers are tempted to act out their rivalries.

Seen from the United States in modern times, the Soviet Union is the obvious candidate for the role of revolutionary instigator. Given the right audience, Ronald Reagan could be moved to quasi-Miltonic rhetoric in discussing the subject—most memorably in his remarks to the National Association of Evangelicals (8 March 1983):

> As good Marxist-Leninists, the Soviet leaders have openly and publicly declared that the only morality they recognize is that which will further their cause, which is world revolution. . . . Let us pray for the salvation of all those who live in that totalitarian darkness—pray that they will discover the joy of knowing God. But until they do, let us be aware that . . . they are the focus of evil in the modern world (*New York Times*, March 8, 1983).

While few Western leaders since John Foster Dulles would choose to match that rhetoric, the underlying premise is widespread. Caspar Weinberger, in opening a 1986 Department of Defense conference on "low-intensity warfare," declared, "Tonight, one out of four countries around the globe is at war. In virtually every case, there is a mask on the face of war. In virtually every case, behind the mask is the Soviet Union and those who do its bidding" (quoted in Shafer, 1988: 284). The same conference produced equivalent statements from officials like Jeane Kirkpatrick and Fred Ikle and defense intellectuals like Sir Robert Thompson and Sam Sarkesian.

While it is tempting to dismiss such views as oratorical flourishes, the train of thought that traces all Third World revolution to Soviet instigation runs deeply through postwar U.S. official thought (Shafer, 1988). Furthermore, it is anchored in popular U.S. views of the Third World, which appear particularly resistant to the blandishments of the new Soviet diplomacy under Gorbachev. Thus, in 1984 a national survey of U.S. opinion found 56 percent agreeing that "the Soviet Union is like Hitler's

Germany—an evil empire trying to rule the world" and the same percentage agreeing that "whenever there is trouble around the world—in the Middle East, Central America or anywhere else—the chances are the Soviets are behind it." In October 1987 the same statements were given to a comparable sample of U.S. citizens. In response to the first, more general statement, agreement declined dramatically from 56 percent to 38 percent. In response to the statement specifying Third World areas, agreement marginally *increased* to 58 percent (Doble, 1988: 4–6).

Such deep-seated convictions are not an exclusively U.S. phenomenon. French counterinsurgency doctrine developed in Vietnam and Algeria emphasized the presumed Soviet role behind the scene (Paret, 1964; Shafer, 1988: 135–165) and exhorted its soldiers in the Algerian *bled* that they were fighting to keep the Soviet fleet out of Mers-el-Kébir (Horne, 1977: 14). A contemporary French expert on terrorism can line up with Claire Sterling and write, "If the KGB is not under every stone . . . it nonetheless remains that there are few revolutionary movements or terrorist organizations, even ephemeral ones, that do not serve its interests throughout the world" (Jacquard, 1985: 260). The former head of the French intelligence services, Alexandre de Marenches, has a similar global view: "Anywhere there is a seed of discontent, and anywhere there is a possibility of troubles, [the Soviet empire] organizes them, it helps them and stirs them up. That is the case in [South Africa], in Central and South America, in Ireland, etc." (Ockrent and Marenches, 1986: 230).

British, French, Portuguese, and Dutch officials throughout the colonial world—and even more white settler minorities—were convinced that Soviet-backed agitators underlay "their natives'" restlessness. Historians of empire pay unconscious tribute to Milton in labeling this the "devil theory." The government of South Africa, characteristically, has codified the devil theory in extreme form by asserting that the country faces a total onslaught centrally directed from Moscow. In this formulation, "South Africa must stand united against the spirit of revolution incited against the country from abroad" (Botha, 1987). The African National Congress is seen as a conscious and controlled agent of the Soviet Union; other opponents, from rock-throwing schoolchildren, to opposition members of the white Parliament, to U.S. members of Congress are viewed as, at best, thoughtless dupes of Moscow's strategy (Jaster, 1985). The propaganda and psychological benefits of such doctrine are evident; but as even the South African government appears to be realizing, it explains little of what actually is happening and leads to policies that can only be ineffective.

Such suspicions are not confined to one side of the East-West conflict. One comparative study of superpower reactions to revolutionary threats found the similarities between U.S. and Soviet fears "truly impressive": "The U.S. fear of Communist subversion was matched by an equally salient Soviet fear of capitalist restoration" (Adelman, 1986: 289). Such suspicions operate independently of evidence for direct, superpower instigation of revolts and are best understood as normal (if not helpful) products of the psychology of group conflict (Jervis, 1976).

The Western analyst of revolution cannot leave it at that, however, but must separate the objective interest a competitor like the Soviet Union may be perceived to have in a particular revolutionary situation from the vague suspicion that it must be all their fault. The Soviets have done much evil and will doubtless do more, as even noncrusading superpowers sometimes do. They have assassinated leaders, as in Afghanistan, and then invaded. They have lined up with ongoing revolutions, as in Ethiopia, and encouraged some of their worst excesses. They have welcomed—though more selectively than we sometimes notice—troubles and upheavals in Western spheres of interest. As one student of Soviet foreign policy reminds us, however, "Welcoming an indigenous movement is not the same as causing it. It is imperative that domestic movements and revolutions that run counter to U.S. policy be analyzed carefully and not inappropriately attributed to Soviet instigation" (Herrmann, 1985).

CONTAGION

If searching for significant cases of direct superpower instigation seems a fruitless task, one should not overlook the possibility that meddlers closer to the scene may play an important role. Revolutions can be spread by neighborly contact. *Contagion*, the intentional transmittal of revolution by a Third World revolutionary regime provides our second causative mechanism.

While a new revolutionary regime may lack the massive troublemaking resources of a superpower, it also likely lacks many of the internal and external constraints that frustrate an established superpower's initiatives. Furthermore, a committed Third World regime has some clear advantages over a superpower in spreading revolution in its neighborhood. Simple propinquity—the ability to slip across the border, to broadcast propaganda and instructions, to offer a secure rear base—is a major advantage. So, too, is cultural and ecological similarity with those one would enflame. At least as important, a Third World regime is likely to be a fresh one; and such new regimes are characteristically filled with revolutionary ardor and missionary zeal.

There are ideological and practical, as well as psychological, reasons why a Third World state would want to turn such ardor outward. Leninist proletarian internationalism provides the most consistent and elaborated ideological base for active revolutionary contagion. Lenin's formula is both simple and grand: *Weltklasse, Weltpartei, Weltrevolution* (world class, world party, world revolutionary movement). In this variety of revolutionary thought "there is a presumption *in favor* of intervention, and exceptions have to be found for abstention" (Halliday, 1988: 196). But formal adherence to Leninist ideology does not inhibit finding exceptions, nor is it necessary for spreading the revolutionary gospel. Whatever else may have moved them, it was not Leninist ideology that encouraged U.S. hotheads to set off to liberate Canada from its imperialist yoke in 1812, the armies of the French revolution to spread their cause in Europe, or the Ayatollah Khomeini to call for the overthrow of the Saudi monarchy. In these cases, something in the dynamic of a recent revolution is at work.

Any revolution worthy of the name mobilizes masses of people, and that mobilization does not end abruptly when a new regime is established. As the French revolution dramatically displayed, such mobilization produces an excess capacity most easily turned to military purposes, whose external deployment may in turn cement the spiritual union between the new revolutionary regime and old-fashioned national patriotism. As Skocpol has argued, "Whether 'communist' or not . . . revolutionary elites have been able to build the strongest states in those countries whose geopolitical circumstances allowed or required the emerging new regimes to become engaged in protracted and labor-intensive international warfare" (Skocpol, 1988: 150). In the contemporary Third World, Cuba, Vietnam, and Iran have all carried the revolutionary flame abroad *manu militarii*.

The excess revolutionary capacity need not be of the labor-intensive variety; elite specialists may also find themselves redundant at home. Not all professional conspirators and agitators will easily be absorbed by the apparatus of bureaucratic routine in a new revolutionary regime. The Guevaras and Trotskys of this world may be encouraged or obliged to pursue their calling outside their homelands, like the less-notorious ambassadors, sent to lie abroad for the good of their country.

External revolutionary adventure likewise provides a mobilized population with distractions from internal divisions and gives the government excuses for material deprivations. If forced to backtrack from promises of an abundant future or quietly to cut a thoroughly capitalist deal with international creditors, a new regime can nonetheless attempt to cover itself with revolutionary glory by acting abroad. As U.S. presidents all know, a well-timed dramatic initiative abroad can rally folks around the flag and produce a surge of political support when it is needed at home. Ayatollah Khomeini's call for Salman Rushdie's assassination is a savagely pointed example of such an initiative (Ashraf, 1989).

Whether bidden to initiate action or not, a Third World regime may use its revolutionary missionary activities as a way of attracting or maintaining a superpower's help. As in the matched case of Cuban and South African interventions in Angola in 1975, confluence of interest between the Third World regime and its superpower patron usually makes it impossible—and perhaps meaningless—to determine whose initiative was responsible for a particular foreign engagement. As when nonrevolutionary Third World regimes, like those in Pakistan, Zaire, and Honduras, undertake or facilitate intervention in a neighbor's affairs, material and political support from a superpower patron is a legitimate expectation.

A final reason for a new regime to infect its neighbors thoroughly with compatible ideological germs is that of protecting the new revolutionary *foco* from hegemonic reprisals by establishing a protective *glacis*. Precisely because intervention (counterrevolutionary as well as revolutionary) is best carried out from a neighboring country, the specter of being a revolutionary beacon all alone in a region is as scary as it might be exhilarating. Purely defensive considerations would have to rank high on the list of reasons why the Nicaragua Sandinistas might take an interest in supporting the Farabundo Marti National Liberation Front in neighboring El Salvador.

Even though newly established Third World regimes may have various incentives to share their revolution, the evidence suggests that the metaphor of an insidiously spreading ideological contagion is no more appropriate than the metaphor of falling dominoes. Revolutions in the Third World have typically been spread to neighbors not through ideological subversion but through the consequences of military action. These actions have ranged from provision of arms and sanctuary to preexisting revolutionary movements (e.g., Nicaraguan support for Salvadoran rebels and Mozambican support for Zimbabwe's Patriotic Front) to direct military conquest of immediate neighbors previously destabilized by war (e.g., Vietnam's occupation of Cambodia and Laos). The efforts of zealous new regimes to spread revolution through the export of activist cadres typically proves inconsequential in the face of a larger and autonomous revolutionary process, as was the case of the Soviet agents sent to China in the 1920s (Wilbur and How, 1988). When the local conditions are simply not ripe for the particular revolution's being exported, as was the case with Che Guevara's attempts to establish *foco* first in Congo, then in Bolivia, the effort simply goes nowhere.

IMITATION

Instigation and contagion both presume that the revolutionary initiative comes from the outside. By contrast, a third external factor involving the outside world is *imitation*, where no intentional act by an external force is required. Rather, an indigenous movement or clique reaches out of its own national context in search of inspiration, guidance—if possible a surefire formula—to overthrow the existing order. Under the right circumstances (and such circumstances may vary greatly) a single revolutionary success can change the perceptual universe of unhappy and ambitious groups throughout a region and inspire them to action if only by providing a demonstration that something can be done. If the successful revolution proclaims a liberatory doctrine that speaks in comprehensible terms to the situation of its neighbors, the demonstration effect will be enhanced. Nasser's Egypt took no direct steps to overthrow King Idriss in Libya or the Hashimite monarchy in Iraq. Rather, ambitious young officers in those countries heard Nasser's message of Arab empowerment, took inspiration from what the Egyptian Free Officers had done, and seized their chance (Brown, 1984: 170; Harris, 1986: 15).

Beyond the simple *ah hah!* effect of inspiration, activist groups will find that revolutionary ideology is not covered by copyright. It can be readily imitated, borrowed, and reproduced. At the most basic level, this can provide a common language for an elite group, to bind them together and give tongue to common purpose. In time, a simplified version can be developed to bring in mass supporters. This is very much a first organizational step, but it may be essential. Like a common colonial language, something may be needed to bridge domestic social cleavages of ethnicity, religion, region, caste, and the like and to symbolize a new revolutionary identity. In the poorly integrated societies of tropical Africa, revolutionary language has been an important common bond for nationalist and rebel movements; and seizure of power has sometimes enshrined a new political vocabulary (Whiteley, 1961; Laitin, 1977). Perhaps the most common use of borrowed revolutionary vocabulary in independent African regimes, however, is to maintain the outward facade of revolutionary change long after the reality has disappeared.

For borrowed ideology to survive and produce truly revolutionary consequences, it must become anchored in domestic social and organizational reality. Failure to do so will produce no more than jacqueries, putsches, or the countercultural posturing that the Western world affected in the late 1960s. Such anchoring, however, often produces substantial doctrinal distortions. Peru's Sendero Luminoso (Shining Path) claims Maoist inspiration; but the Maoism is mixed with Andean Indian mysticism and ritual and with the worldview of its charismatic leader and organizer, Abimaél Guzmán. Far from being a tool of China's policy, Sendero statements denounce the PRC's leadership for betraying "true" Maoism. Indeed, Sendero's "only known foreign contact" was established during the 1970s with Albania, which did not spare Enver Hoxa from being subsequently denounced by Guzmán for "revisionism" (McCormick, 1988: 121).

Mao's own borrowing from Lenin and Marx, of course, involved major changes—not least a fundamental redefinition of the role of the peasantry, a neo-Confucian understanding of the role of the intellectual, and the addition of military precepts from Sun Tzu. Mao's creative synthesis of revolutionary traditions pales beside that of the leader of China's Taiping Rebellion a century earlier. Hung Xinchuan's doctrine mixed fundamentalist Protestantism with the ancient rituals of Chou, an amalgam that gave Hung status as Jesus' younger brother. The doctine made him anathema to the missionaries and suspect to most Chinese yet helped gain him control of half that vast country for five years (Fairbank, 1987: 257).

Whatever adaptations may be made by late-twentieth-century revolutionary movements, one complex of ideas typically provides the theme on which local variations are based. The core of the complex is Leninist organizational form and strategy. The form includes a vanguard party inspired by middle-class intellectuals, cell structure, democratic centralism, a base in the exploited classes (urban or rural, depending on the situation), and the firm injunction to stick close to that base. The strategy emphasizes the national struggle against foreign imperialism and its local agents through at least an initial common front with the patriotic national bourgeoisie, destined to be brought under the firm control of the vanguard. This set of now-banal ideas has been borrowed, imitated, and embroidered primarily because it fits most contemporary Third World situations. It provides a superior organizational strategy for most revolutionary purposes. Anyone who wants to overthrow a government, especially a minority-based, exploitative government beholden to foreign interests, would be foolish not to make use of it. One need not assume active instigation or contagion from external sources, merely that would-be revolutionaries search for models and exercise some discrimination in choosing among them. The model can as well be used in the 1980s by a Jonas Savimbi, attempting with U.S. and South African aid to overthrow an Angolan regime dependent on Cuban and Soviet support as it was previously by Savimbi's opponents in their erstwhile fight against Portuguese rule (Marcum, 1986).

There is nothing magic about the Leninist–national front organizational model, and in specific circumstances other models may be far more effective. The Shi'a militarism demonstrated so effectively in Iran may provide a more appropriate basic model for other Muslim contexts—including some that are formally Sunni and in no way directly beholden to the ayatollahs. Similarly, Martin Luther King's successful use of church organization and Christian doctrine has provided a model for men like Desmond Tutu, trying to overthrow a racist order in another nominally Christian context. No direct missionary instigation was required, merely intelligent imitation with variations imposed to suit the change in circumstances.

Imitation can be used with manipulative intent through the public declaration of fealty to extract resources from the original model country. Such manipulative expressions of fealty are likely to come forth when the imitative revolution has had its initial success but then runs into trouble with its neighbors or just has difficulty making ends meet. Fidel Castro's declaration of allegiance to Marxism-Leninism in 1960 locked in Soviet economic and military support. As Kwame Nkrumah's regime in Ghana used up its initial resource base and its diplomatic credit in the West, it similarly attempted to assure Soviet support by proclaiming a devotion to "scientific socialism," a devotion far more apparent in rhetoric than in policy (Thompson, 1969). By hosting a well-publicized convention of "freedom fighters" from Nicaragua, Afghanistan, and other hot spots of concern to United States foreign policy, Jonas Savimbi employed a similar form of coercive ingratiation.

Revolutionary movements with an ethnic or religious base can attempt to use such identity to appeal to susceptible groups abroad. One of the first modern instances was the Greek Revolt of 1822–1829, which brought in ultimately decisive support from Western Europe, aided by romantic appeal to the image of ancient Greece as the cradle of Western thought. For purposes of assuring European support, the Greek revolutionaries embraced a nationalism borrowed from European images of what Greek democracy should be—which had little relation, of course, to the realities on the ground (Brown, 1984: 46–62). In our own time the Tamil Tigers of Sri Lanka, the Irish Republican Army, and the PLO are among those who shape their formal ideology in imitative terms designed to appeal to crucial external supporters.

Any competent analyst of revolutionary movements quickly learns to distinguish the symbols borrowed for purposes of external consumption from their internal realities. The IRA's Noraid appeals in the bars and parish halls of Boston's South End no more reflect accurately the origins or actions of Sinn Fein than the revolutionary protestations of the Benin and Burkinabe representatives at Libyan public ceremonies reflect what goes on in those impoverished West African client states.

Revolutionary posturing, however imitative and hollow, can have real consequences in international affairs if the imitation is in turn imitated by others to produce a bandwagon effect. Any great power can take comfort from imitative efforts that suggest that that power's ideology represents the "wave of the future" that new, dynamic forces throughout the Third World seek to ride. Opponents of that power may understandably be alarmed. The prime limitation on this is simply the willingness of the patron to pay the price— not just the cost of hostility from opposing powers but also the cost of supporting a mass of penurious clients. Sloughing off such clients is easiest early in a new regime. Thus, in the mid-1960s Brezhnev cut down support for many of the would-be African revolutionary states and movements that Khrushchev had cultivated, only to acquire his own set of penurious African clients a decade later (Foltz, 1969; Legvold, 1970). Gorbachev has taken steps to cut loose from the Brezhnev legacy of clients by echoing Lenin's words to the effect that "a revolution must be able to defend itself" and, in Havana, by opposing "doctrines that endorse the export of revolution or counterrevolution" (*New York Times*, 1989). With less oratorical flourish the Bush administration has taken steps to eliminate military support for the contras and has laid the groundwork for doing the same in Angola. It remains to be seen whether the two administrations will acquire new sets of revolutionary clients of their very own later in their mandates.

HISTORIC CHANGE

The fourth set of external factors contributing to revolution are the most removed and indirect; they encompass the great *historic structural changes* that provide the background against which all collective human action is carried out. Most fundamentally, these take the form of slow, secular trends in demography, technology, economics, religion, and worldly beliefs that set the stage for the rise and decline of core hegemonic orders, which in turn create opportunities for peripheral and small groups to gather situational advantage and revolt. These trends are typically punctuated by intense and dramatic moments of upheaval (such as the two world wars of this century) that both reflect the cumulated tensions of secular change among the powers and abruptly create conditions for spreading that change among the distant and the hitherto weak. While the importance of such trends cannot be doubted, the levels of interaction between them and any given revolution are so many—and the complexity of possible interaction so great—that accurate prediction or even contemporaneous understanding of a specific revolutionary path is virtually impossible. In retrospect one can see that the Japanese invasion of China created the conditions both for the Chinese Communist party to seize leadership of the long-simmering revolution (itself a product of changes in the world power balance a century earlier) and for Mao to wrest control of the CCP from the twenty-eight Bolsheviks (Fairbank, 1987: 247). Such was hardly Japan's purpose, nor were the connections clear to any but the most astute analysts at the time. Likewise, in retrospect one can see that great power pressure on the Ottoman Empire, interacting with the rise of nationalism in the Porte's European dominions, produced in 1908 an emulatively nationalist Turkification of the empire's core that created the conditions for revolutionary Arab nationalism to rise in the place of a broader and more tolerant Muslim solidarity (Brown, 1984: 95).

HEGEMONIC STRUCTURE

The reader can be spared a parade of examples of similarly complex historical connections with revolutionary outcomes, examples that in their bewildering accumulation reinforce the commonsense warning against monocausal explanations of events as complicated as revolutions. More usefully, such examples direct the analyst's attention to a factor lying between the vast, historical, secular trends and the local realities internal to a potentially revolutionary situation, a factor that will influence the shape, impact, and ideology of a revolution, whatever its genesis. This factor is the *hegemonic structure*, the international distribution of power and domination over a particular Third World area at a given time. This structure, while never static or determinate, nonetheless powerfully conditions the degree to which instigation, contagion, and imitation of revolutions can take place and the form that such efforts will adopt.

The simplest case is a regional structure dominated by a single hegemon. Central America provides the closest example—in the words of the Mexican nationalist, Porfirio Diaz, "so far from God, so close to the United States." Under such a structure a revolutionary movement, above all, must define itself in relation to the hegemon; and the hegemon cannot avoid taking a position. Indifference on the part of the hegemon is never perceived by outsiders as neutrality; nor, in the real world, can policy be so finely administered that it has no effect on the outcome. The internal dynamics of the revolutionary movement will consist in good part of disputes about confronting, neutralizing, or coopting the hegemon and the degree of risk to take in pursuit of any of these. Most likely antihegemonism, even if kept secret initially, will be a strong link among revolutionaries and will be reinforced as a way of maintaining revolutionary solidarity. Where, however, a movement, as well as the society from which it springs, is thoroughly penetrated by hegemonic power so that unity against the hegemon is impossible, the most likely result is paralysis or a multiplicity of meaningless coups and regime changes. Honduras may be the extreme example: it has endured "126 changes of government, 16 constitutions and 385 coups since gaining independence" (La Feber, 1984: 298). The succession of coups and government changes in Afghanistan under Soviet domination may be roughly comparable and may be perpetuated by fights among the Mujahadeen now that the Soviet army has withdrawn across the border, while no other major power is in a position to replace or balance Soviet influence.

A contrasting regional structure, one characterized by multiple shifting and competitive outside centers of power, is that of the Arab Middle East, the surprisingly durable Middle East of the "Eastern Question," so effectively analyzed by L. Carl Brown (1984). Great powers here involve themselves principally as a function of their mutual rivalries, embracing a regional "friend," stigmatizing an "enemy" of the moment by virtue of its alliances of the moment. As their rivalries shift, so does the pattern of their intervention in regional affairs. The effect on regional actors, governmental, revolutionary, and counterrevolutionary alike, is a political approach emphasizing factionalism and shifting alliance within the region. Attempts at resolving issues eventually bring in all possible outsiders, which in turn reinforces a pattern of shifting, kaleidoscopic politics and totalist patterns of demands in which everything is related to everything else and no issue is so minor that its resolution can possibly be delayed. Such a structure is conducive to much revolutionary posturing but little in the way of permanent change. It is significant that the one Middle East revolution, peripheral to the Arab world, that has escaped this pattern is the Iranian, a revolution that derived its force in part from its determination radically to exclude all great power influence and participation.

Competition between outside powers for patronage of revolutionary movements is a hallmark of situations where overall hegemonic power has decayed badly and the situation looks ripe for the picking. The result is typically to increase the flow of revolutionary resources but to augment factionalism among revolutionaries. The virulent Sino-Soviet competition in Africa in the mid-1960s produced a legacy of divided liberation movements in southern Africa. The divisions between ZAPU and ZANU in Rhodesia, ANC and PAC in South Africa, SWAPO and SWANU in Namibia, and the MPLA and FNLA–UNITA in Angola flourished as ambitious men found external investors willing to support their striking out on their own, with ethnic brothers to provide the troops. Again, such divisions are not created by the outside power; but efforts to overcome them must fight an uphill battle against the support available to those who would maintain them. The short-term result is to weaken the revolutionary effort. In the longer run, the result, as seen in Angola and, for that matter, in Kampuchea, may be bloody civil war long after the old imperial power has left the scene.

What might the pattern of influences be in a region that attracted no significant great-power interest? Such a hypothetical case could be realized in Middle Africa (south of the Sahara and north of the Zambezi) in the event that détente progresses between the United States and the Soviet Union and that both powers continue to feel it important to reassure one another that they have no vital interests in the area. In theory, at least, an Africa free from great-power pressures has long been a goal highly desired by the states in the region. The norms of the African state system enshrined in the Organization of African Unity's charter (and to some extent in its practice) enjoin its members to seek "African solutions" to their problems by attempting to resolve conflicts close to home, without outside power intervention (el-Ayouty and Zartman, 1984). This has not prevented the two superpowers from intervening themselves or sponsoring the intervention of allies and clients on behalf of central governments besieged by revolts (the United States in Zaire and Haile Selassie's Ethiopia; the USSR in Angola and Mengistu's Ethiopia) and on behalf of insurgent movements (the United States in Angola and in Chad, 1981–1982; the USSR in a variety of anticolonial struggles).

However desirable superpower restraint might be in itself, it would hardly put an end to domestic insurgencies or external intervention. In Africa, at least as much as elsewhere, insurgencies arise from internal cleavages and strains, which frequently cross state borders to draw in neighbors and kinsmen. Even if France, a frequent outside intervener, were to give up its role of *gendarme de l'Afrique*, outsiders closer to hand would not be lacking to advance their own interests by supporting one side or the other. Morocco, Libya, Zaire, Nigeria, Tanzania, Zimbabwe, and South Africa are among the states that have intervened militarily in support of one side or another in a neighbor's internal disputes. Sudan and Ethiopia play host to one another's regional independence movements and from time to time get drawn into more active roles in one another's affairs.

Such involvement in pursuit of presumed state interest is likely to continue, whether outside great powers are concerned or not. If the powers truly keep their distance, however, local revolutionaries and their opposing governments would presumably have fewer incentives to wrap themselves in imitative ideological banners appropriate to the Cold War in order to attract or coerce support. Other banners might serve equivalent purpose, however; the green flag of Islam has been known to attract Libyan support for movements of otherwise quite different ideological coloration. At the least, however, this sort of coercive imitation is likely to avoid the division of the continent into blocs of movements and regimes claiming ideological affinity as "radicals" or "moderates" of the sort that in the early 1980s paralyzed the OAU's abilities to contain disputes involving Chad and the Western Sahara.

Vows of superpower abstention will in any case be difficult to keep. While the superpowers may earnestly desire to avoid direct competition, they likely will continue to have interests in the survival and success of specific countries or regimes with which they have been associated. Conflicts between such African regimes, particularly if each side is busy supporting a revolutionary or separatist movement on its opponent's home ground, could draw their distant patrons back onto the scene, whatever their initial intentions. Whatever the theoretical attractions of declaring Middle Africa (or any other region of the world) a "superpower-free zone," many groups and governments in such a zone will have compelling reasons to draw the powers in on their side. If they appeal in terms of historic obligation, linked to higher ideological goals, such as "socialism," "racial equality," or "human rights," these efforts will be hard for the superpowers to resist.

CONCLUSION

I must conclude where I began, with the analytic impossibility of making a neat separation between internal and external factors in the genesis of revolutions in the Third World or elsewhere or of giving clear analytic precedence to one or the other. The four categories of external factors discussed here—instigation by a common source, contagion from other Third World countries, international imitation by revolutionaries, and historic structural changes—are arrayed in ascending order of their explanatory power. But as each factor broadens its explanatory base, it loses precision and particularity. These must come from careful consideration of internal factors, including the analysis of what makes a *specific* group of men and women, in a *specific* time and place, alert to *specific* external cues and receptive to the opportunities they suggest. Any model of a revolutionary situation must be one in which the external and the internal interact in an indeterminant field with neither the internal nor the external predominating and in which the external entanglements and enticements of both revolutionaries and the regime in power play a role.

The most difficult part of such analysis is understanding the exploratory, searching behavior of revolutionary actors who reach to take or wrest something—an idea, an arms shipment—from the external world for purposes that are being discovered in the course of action. Such analysis is intrinsically difficult; and the difficulty is compounded by the human tendency to look first and foremost to the external instigator—to ask, as did Milton, "Who first seduced them to that foul revolt?" As his analysis developed, Milton, too, concluded that this question missed the essentials of the explanation, which were to be found in his protagonists' very nature— noble and at the same time base, curious, loving, and ambitious—and in the hegemonic structure of their world in which independent action had to appear directed against the single Power that oversaw and judged their actions.

REFERENCES

Adelman, Jonathan R. (1986). *Superpowers and Revolution*. New York: Praeger.

Ashraf, Ahmad (1989). "Religion? No. Politics." *New York Times,* ·25 March, 27.

el-Ayouty, Yassin, and I. William Zartman (1984). *The OAU after Twenty Years*. New York: Praeger.

Botha, P. W. (1987). *Statement by His Excellency the State President at the Opening of Parliament*. Cape Town: Union of South Africa.

Brown, L. Carl (1984). *International Politics and the Middle East: Old Rules, Dangerous Game*. Princeton: Princeton University Press.

Doble, John (1988). *U.S.-Soviet Relations in the Year 2010*. Report of the Public Agenda Foundation and the Center for Foreign Policy Development. Providence: Brown University.

Fairbank, John King (1987). *The Great Chinese Revolution 1800–1985*. New York: Harper and Row.

Foltz, William J. (1969). "Le parti africain de l'independance: Les dilemmes d'un mouvement communiste en Afrique occidentale." *Revue francaise d'etudes politiques africaines* 45 (September): 8–35.

Halliday, Fred (1988). "Three Concepts of Internationalism." *International Affairs* (London) 64, no. 2, (Spring): 189–198.

Harris, Lillian Craig (1986). *Libya: Qadhafi's Revolution and the Modern State*. Boulder: Westview.

Herrmann, Richard K. (1985). *Perceptions and Behavior in Soviet Foreign Policy*. Pittsburgh: University of Pittsburgh Press.

Hill, Christopher (1977). *Milton and the English Revolution*. London: Faber and Faber.

Horne, Alastair (1977). *A Savage War of Peace: Algeria 1954–62*. New York: Penguin.

Jacquard, Roland (1985). *Les dossiers secrets du terrorisme: Tueurs sans frontieres*. Paris: A. Michel.

Jaster, Robert (1985). "South African Defense Strategy and the Growing Influence of the Military." In William J. Foltz and Henry S. Bienen, eds. *Arms and the African*. New Haven: Yale University Press.

Jervis, Robert (1976). *Perception and Misperception in International Politics*. Princeton: Princeton University Press.

La Feber, Walter (1984). *Inevitable Revolutions: the United States in Central America*. New York: W. W. Norton.

Laitin, David D. (1977). *Politics, Language, and Thought: The Somali Experience*. Chicago: University of Chicago.

Legvold, Robert (1970). *Soviet Policy in West Africa*. Cambridge: Harvard University Press.

McCormick, Gordon H. (1988). "The Shining Path and Peruvian Terrorism." In David C. Rapoport, ed. *Inside Terrorist Organizations*. New York: Columbia University Press.

Marcum, John A. (1986). "Bipolar Dependency: The People's Republic of Angola." In Michael Clough, ed. *Reassessing the Soviet Challenge in Africa*. Berkeley: University of California.

Milton, John (1981). *Paradise Lost*. New York: New American Library.

New York Times (1983). 8 March.

New York Times (1989). 6 April.

Ockrent, Christine, and Alexandre de Marenches (1986). *Dans le secret des princes*. Paris: Stock.

Paret, Peter (1964). *French Revolutionary Warfare from Indochina to Algeria: The Analysis of a Political and Military Doctrine*. (New York: Praeger).

Shafer, D. Michael (1988). *Deadly Paradigms: The Failure of U.S. Counterinsurgency Policy*. Princeton: Princeton University Press.

Skocpol, Theda (1979). *States and Social Revolutions: A Comparative Analysis of France, Russia, and China* (New York: Cambridge University Press.

———— (1988). "Social Revolutions and Mass Military Mobilization." *World Politics* 40, no. 2 (January): 147–168.

Thompson, W. Scott (1969). *Ghana's Foreign Policy 1957–1960*. Princeton: Princeton University Press.

Whiteley, Wilfred H. (1961). "Political Concepts and Connotations: Observations on the Use of Some Political Terms in Swahili," in Kenneth Kirkwood (ed.) *African Affairs*, No. 1 London, England: Chatto and Windus (St. Antony's Papers, no. 10).

Wilbur, C. Martin, and Julie Lien-ying How 1988. *Missionaries of Revolution: Soviet Advisors and Nationalist China, 1920–1927*. Cambridge: Harvard University Press.

East-West Relations

ZAKI LAIDI

A ttempts to investigate the strategies and political choices of Third World actors frequently run up against insurmountable analytical obstacles. One of the most problematic of these is considering the nature of the East-West "conflict" in the context of Third World politics. A major constraint is found in analyzing the entangled relationships between internal processes and external dynamics. Analysts frequently confer privileged status to a particular set of external circumstances at the expense of more fundamental regional or local determining factors that are often so basic to the situation.

Contemporary international politics is replete with such examples. The tactical rapprochement between Syria and the PLO is more the result of Damascus' intention to neutralize the Palestinians prior to presidential voting than anything else. The Iran-Iraq conflict, originating in the context of the East-West rivalry, seems independent of the normalization of Soviet-U.S. relations. In South Africa, the relative lack of influence of U.S. diplomacy results from the autonomy of South African initiatives and from its ambivalence within the dynamic of East and West. In some ways South Africa exacerbates this dynamic, but in others it circumvents and goes beyond it (see Laidi, 1986a). In Central America, the influence of the United States is brought into question in light of the capacity of local actors to engage in a productive dialogue.

The lack of appropriate analytic tools for understanding the dynamics of Third World politics is attributable to a number of factors. Western studies of the Soviets have been content, for the most part, to analyze the USSR position without posing questions about the "correspondence" between prevailing polices in Moscow and their actual application in local Third World settings. Ignorance of the concrete meaning and social functions that clothe, for example, Angolan or Ethiopian Marxism is overwhelming; while in contrast certain evident rites are held to be "irrefutable proof" of belonging to the communist worlds (use of the Marxist vulgate, the formal constitution of an avant-garde party, etc.). Even more serious is the fact that "tropical Sovietologists" have not thought much about the discrepancy between the USSR's principles of actions and its actual practices. It is interesting to observe in a country such as the Congo the gulf that can exist between official USSR appraisals of Marxism-Leninism and the remarks on the Congolese economy formulated by Soviet planners. The Congolese Workers' party has nothing "avant-garde" about it other than the name. Its control over civilian society is weak. In reality, the assimilation of Congolese Marxism is as absurd as the identification of Mexican multipartyism with U.S. liberalism.

It would, however, be unfair to blame Sovietologists alone. Students of Third World politics, for example, suffer form the opposite malaise. They often underestimate the weight of external determining factors. Rather paradoxically, emphasis on "dependency" seems to free the analyst from demonstrating its concrete mechanics. A recent analysis of Mozambique, to use a case in point, never raises the question of the relationship with the USSR (see *Politique africaine*, 1988). By not investigating the mechanisms of ideological dependency the authors imply that they are not important. As a general rule, the study of U.S. influence seems easier. U.S. politics may be perceived from a multitude of perspectives. The difficulties are less the result of the availability of sources than of the definition of the object to be studied.

My purpose, then, is to investigate the "double process" by which Third World states experience, but also weaken and transform, international constraints. To accomplish this, three levels of analysis that are too often confused must, in my opinion, be clearly defined. The first level concerns what I will call the *instrumentalization* of the East-West conflict. The second level is the *interiorization* of constraints but also of the sociocultural values of East-West relations. Finally, the third level concerns *double coding*, that is, the simultaneous use of references borrowed from East-West relations and of strictly internal referents originating in a stock of ethnic, cultural, and historic references.

THE MECHANISMS OF INSTRUMENTALIZATION

Instrumentalization may be defined as the process by which Third World actors draw references from East or West. Importantly, this does not imply any diplomatic or ideological allegiance to either superpower. The "register" on which instrumentalization has most frequently occurred is that of the diplomatic-strategic alliance. The Soviet-Egyptian alliance of the sixties and the Soviet-Indian alliance, especially since the 1971 treaty, are good illustrations of this first kind of pattern. Within a well-defined regional context, alliances are forged on the basis of the principle, *The enemy (USSR) of the friend (United States) of my enemy (Pakistan, Israel) will always be my friend.* This type of alliance most often remains unaffected by internal policy choices. In other words, a country may make a lasting alliance with the USSR without believing in socialism.

While the impermeability of the separation between the diplomatic alliance and internal decisions may be challenged by certain "pro-Soviet" economic decisions made by India or Egypt, the motive underlying their relations with the USSR has always been military even though the problematic nature of national construction operations in Egypt has benefited from Leninist contributions. Despite the Soviet role in the development of the Bhilai or Helouan steel works, the Indian model is socialist only to the same minimal extent that Zairean liberalism is capitalist. An observer of India writes with accuracy that "Indian socialism has only state management in common with socialism; the mixed economy represents the juxtaposition of a sizable and largely unproductive public sector and a private sector which continually outperforms it" (Hurtig, 1986: 813).

In inverse fashion, "socialist discourse" has served more to provide an ideological alibi for "protobourgeois" groups than to prepare the way for Sovietization. Thus, it has been observed that in Africa the contribution of public-sector enterprises to the gross national product was two times higher in Zambia than in Tanzania even though the first country is considered "pro-Western" and the second "socialist."

In the 1960s the imperative of national construction in the new countries made fashionable the Soviet-type "party state," independent of any ideological considerations. The Rassemblement du Peuple Togolais (Gathering of the Togolese People), the single party of a pro-Western country, was structured by the North Koreans on Leninist principles. As Jean Copans (1988: 35) wrote, "Recourse to the USSR is neither a last resort nor an illusion: it is a powerful instrument of learning about state power of the bourgeois nation-state. Ideological coherence, the articulation between control of the masses, the administrative apparatus and police repression have, so its seems, a greater historical efficacy than the bourgeois tradition of the colonial apparatus."

The Third World is characterized by the capacity to use several references and to take advantage of multiple alliances. Furthermore the instrumentalization of external models is not necessarily stabilizing. It depends on the evolution of the *demand for* external resources on the part of the Third World and the *supply* of these resources (i.e., of the capacity of the external actors to satisfy demand) and on the general configuration of the worldwide ideological marketplace that Theda Skocpol (1985) has termed the "worldwide climate." The structure of the *demand* for resources hinges classically on the need to consolidate the state's supreme authority (weapons) and promote its development (economic assistance)—but also to benefit from ideological resources capable of strengthening the political regime's moorings to a universal category (i.e., "free world," "socialist country," etc.). The sale of arms, as it is commonly known, represents one of the principal means by which the Soviets propagate their influence. Long after the expulsion of Soviet advisers, Egypt is still in the position of renegotiating its military debt with Moscow. The list of countries to which the USSR refuses to sell arms diminishes constantly. Even Saudi Arabia has received Chinese missiles, perhaps a first step toward the purchase of Soviet equipment. In the Middle East this military factor in the equation of Soviet-Arabic relations is especially basic to the situation, due to the United States' unconditional support of Israel.

The example of the Middle East demonstrates that the military factor cannot by itself determine the nature of the relationship forged with either of the superpowers since were this the case, Kuwait, Jordan, and Saudi Arabia would long ago have entered the East's camp. Despite the Iran scandal and the U.S. support of Israel, the oil monarchies remain attached to Washington. This is especially the case since apart from arms, the USSR's means of influence remain limited. The era of the large dams and steel works has passed. The USSR is not only short of financial resources (given the magnitude of its internal constraints and its support of the COMECON countries) but also of human resources adapted to the requirements of structural adjustment and of privatization.

On the ideological level also, current developments are not necessarily favorable to the USSR. Although the merits of single parties still seem rather substantial to many political regimes, the Marxist doctrine often associated with it in Africa and the Middle East has lost its attraction. Secularly inspired leftist ideological discourse is losing its impetus. Through the middle of the 1970s, this discourse allowed the establishment of coherence uniting economic nationalization (assimilated to socialism), political control (single party), and alliance with the USSR against U.S. support for Israel. Today the context is very different. The creation of a progressive discourse for the purpose of neutralizing the radical Left is no longer necessary. In the Arab countries the local Communist parties are breaking up. In Africa communist cells have for the most part disappeared. In Angola, Mozambique, and the Congo, Marxist ideology survives "by default," that is, in the absence of a substitute discourse. In Algeria references to socialism are to an increasing extent being eliminated. *Evolution*, not *revolution*, is the watchword. References to the establishing texts (such as the national charter) are becoming less and less frequent. It must also be added that the Arabs' or Africans' perceptions of the economic and cultural failure of the authoritarian brand of modernization is such that it forces the rulers of these states to seek new references, without encouraging criticism of their rule.

Compared to the Soviets, the United States holds solid winning cards. These should not, however, be overestimated. On a global scale U.S. economic resources used to promote Third World development are constantly diminishing. The United States and Japan are today in the rear guard of those providing assistance to developing countries. Military aid is becoming a decreasingly effective component of the U.S. resource arsenal: only a tight core of allied countries (Israel, Egypt, Pakistan) benefit from it. Finally, despite the ideological ebbing of Marxism, economic nationalism remains strong. Furthermore, most of the liberal Third World regimes have relied on a strong state-controlled sector. They show no strong impetus to dismantle it except when they possess the means to be the ongoing beneficiaries of economic privatization.

The U.S. advantage over the USSR results less from the large amount of intrinsic resources the United States possesses than from the structure of influence. Soviet influence stops at the frontiers of the Soviet state. The cultural and economic values that the Soviet Union advances are *indissociable* from preexisting political decisions. Outside of the state, the USSR possesses no resource to bear the burden. The pro-Sovietism of some groups is a short-lived value, having the character of refuge, which is particularly vulnerable to the hazards of Soviet policy.

The structure of U.S. influence is radically different: the state represents only one of the available instruments of propagation of that influence. The influence of Wall Street, of the Chicago Stock Exchange, or of U.S. television can be more significant than that of U.S. aid, the Marine Corps, or the Sixth Fleet. Furthermore, the IMF and the World Bank operate according to a neoliberal perspective that conforms to U.S. objectives.

Finally, it should be understood that the structure of the worldwide ideological marketplace has changed. In the 1960s and 1970s, the Third World existed in an international ideological context that emphasized national construction and nonalignment. The first objective led to submitting the issue of democracy to the criterion of profits and losses, to believing that this was a luxury that only rich countries could afford. The second objective emphasized the formal acts of sovereignty rather than high economic performance. This period was characterized, for example, by Algerian and Iranian technocrats who understood economic development as the sum of scarce products available on the market, made accessible by oil resources (see Billers, 1985: 28–43).

This relatively simplified conception of the international stakes broke apart rapidly in the 1980s. Political voluntarism led to a double dilemma. At the internal level it ran up against economic constraints and cultural and social points of resistance. A landless peasant is not transformed overnight into an industrial worker. The beneficial breakup of conventional patterns that access to industrial modernism was supposed to introduce became a nightmare. On the international level results were even more deceiving. The ability of some Third World states to be major players on the world scene was not accompanied by any change in North-South relations. Paradoxically, the countries that have proved themselves economic competitors of the West have never fought the West ideologically and have demonstrated substantial diplomatic *servility*. This line of reasoning holds, of course, for the four "Asian dragons" but also for Thailand, Malaysia, and Turkey. The necessity for "structural adjustment" thus mandated new values and a new hierarchy.

This political or diplomatic instrumentalization is, very naturally, the province of the states. But its consequences in civil society are substantial. In what may be termed the "public opinions" of the Third World, ideological and cultural images of East and West are extremely ambivalent. In much of the East, pro-Sovietism and anti-Sovietism generally involve only a small group of intellectuals or politicians. "The "Solzhenitsyn effect," which has aroused the European, especially the French, intelligentsia to such a degree, had almost no impact in the Third World. Similarly, the "Gorbachev effect" barely arouses the interest of the media of the countries of the periphery. Most of the time the USSR leaves populations indifferent. At most, Africans are surprised to see Soviet assistance personnel traveling on foot and not in private automobiles. They are scornfully referred to as "capitalists without dollars." In the Arab world atheism constitutes the strongest cultural objective to USSR cultural penetration.

Pro- and anti-Americanism form part of a much more complex matrix. In Latin America, where the U.S. image is the most pronounced, pro and anti attitudes are equally strong. Most often, these attitudes are held by the same individuals and the same social groups for whom the apparent contradiction does not raise any real problems. On the whole it seems that nationalist and political anti-Americanism (concerning Washington's interventions in Central America) is in harmony with a cultural pro-Americanism. For the Latin American middle classes "the American way of life" is certainly the model that inspires all efforts. This ambivalence also occurs in other parts of the world. The extent to which the Zaireans had been offended by U.S. medical authorities' claims that they were the principal causes of AIDS in the world is a case in point. Kinshasa woke up the next day permeated by spontaneous rumors that AIDs had been propagated by the CIA. Thus, as a result of its power, the United States is quickly seen as the source of all evils—and the remedy for all problems.

INTERIORIZATION AND THE DOUBLE CODE

The instrumentalization of external references rests on the hypothesis that actors may ultimately change references at will according to their needs and to varying circumstances. In Africa, for example, known for the fluidity of international relations, Ghana, the Sudan, Somalia, and Guinea have nimbly gone from the East to the West camp. Mozambique and possibly Angola are also on the verge of changing protector. But this movement most often remains superficial and illusory: to the extent that it is extremely rare for a state to align itself completely with one bloc, it also appears difficult truly to change one's logic. In Ghana, for example, the fall of the Nkrumah regime did not change the regime's internal structure or the connection between wealth and political power. The true break occurred much later, with the ascendancy of the "Marxist" Rawlings. But far from resuming faithfulness to a rationale based on the power of investors, he laid the foundation for a market-based economy, in accordance with the recommendations of the IMF and the World Bank. In reality, changes of camp often are limited to arms supply or votes in international bodies. At the internal level the impact is limited. Countries that pronounced themselves yesterday to be socialist and have entered the West camp through opportunism have not converted to economic liberalism despite the change.

In addition, by instrumentalizing (or simply using) external references, some politicians end up interiorizing them. External powers quickly end up classifying a particular regime as in the Western camp despite its "flaws" and consider another as being "pro-Soviet." In Angola, for example, Marxism is a waning ideological value. The Marxist Old Guard is being swept away. But in order to solidify its authority, the group in power in Luanda still requires Marxism as a source of *legitimacy*: Marxism still provides the structure for internal politics. Thus, a growing discrepancy exists between the incorporation of an excessively ideological context into political discourse and increasingly pragmatic practice. This same evolution could be observed in the neighboring Congo, where mastery of the Marxist ideological code is indispensable in all factional disputes (see Ossebi, 1982: 197). The USSR has understood that the constraints provided by ideology are the best guarantee of its influence in these countries even though actual practice contradicts discourse on a daily basis.

In order to illustrate the movement from instrumentalization to interiorization, let us compare the case of Algeria to that of Morocco. Historically, the Algerian political system rests on a double base: the refusal to belong to any bloc whatever and the demand for a particular form of socialism. This lack of connection between the internal and the external is not, however, easy to implement. On the ideological level, for example, the definition of socialism has always been problematical. To demand a scientific socialism signifies moving in opposition to a political culture that is profoundly nationalist and Islamic, since behind the concept of scientific socialism looms the image of atheism and of the Soviet Union. But the specific idea of socialism is not attractive, first, because it has been compromised and second, because it introduces a tendency to blur distinctions and a relativity that makes the invalidation of internal opponents of socialism more difficult. The 1975 national charter establishes a compromise between the imperative for political irreversibility and the requirements of the Algerian political culture; but a lot has changed since 1975. Algerian president Chadli likes to remind listeners that the Koran is intangible. This has two meanings: first, the irreversibility of socialism is no longer taken for granted; second, the Koran represents the ultimate rationale for the political system. Does this mean that the Algerian political regime has been transformed? Probably not. Although the nature of political discourse has changed, and the invalidation of certain social groups has been removed, the mode of internal political control remains identical. A single party remains, and all initiatives aimed at creating openings or introducing flexibility are carefully controlled by the leadership. The political culture continues to be unanimist. In spite of its efforts to assume responsibility for specific social needs that had been poorly provided for, Chadli's government has encountered problems in attempting to install a new structure of legitimacy. Although the problematic nature of "pure and uncompromising socialism" no longer signifies socialism's success, finding a substitute still appears to be difficult.

The problems are comparable as regards external relations. Algerian diplomacy has always demonstrated great pragmatism; and although always striving to deal tactfully with the Soviet Union, Algeria has marked its opposition to the USSR whenever its interests ran counter to those of the "socialist fatherland" (see Laidi, 1984: 129). While maintaining excellent relations with Moscow, Chadli has made unmistakable attempts to introduce balance into its relations with Washington. The crucial role played by Algiers in the liberation of the U.S. citizens held hostage in Teheran probably changed Washington's perceptions of Algeria, and Chadli's trip to the United States was meant to complete the process of reestablishing an equilibrium. However, the nature of U.S.-Algerian relations has not changed. The Algerians understood that the United States would never side with them against Morocco. The development of military cooperation with the United States is not always well regarded within the army; and while the diversification of military relations remains a desired goal, it has not necessarily threatened Algeria's privileged relations with Moscow. Within the single party, antiimperialist ideology remains very strong. For example, Algeria still does not have diplomatic relations with South Korea in spite of the Ministry of Foreign Affair's exhortations to move in that direction.

The situation in Morocco is, in many respects, different from that of Algeria. Rabat has always sought a place in the Western bloc. This membership in the West has been affirmed with special emphasis because the Moroccan monarchy, which is dependent for its survival on Western economic benefits to a considerable extent, has no need to borrow its ideological resources from the West to strengthen its claim to legitimacy.

In spite of everything, the Alid monarchy has undergone some tense moments. Through the middle 1970s it had to combat the ideological discredit that attached to monarchies in the Arab world. In international affairs, Algerian diplomacy for a long time overshadowed its Moroccan counterpart. In addition to the low level of professionalism of its diplomats, Morocco had difficulty participating in the creation of a specifically Third World ideology. The nature of its relations with the United States prevented it from playing this role. The decade of the 1970s was a turbulent decade for Rabat because of two putsch attempts and the murderous Western Sahara conflict: one only has to recall the U.S. intelligence community's forecasting a six-month life expectancy for Hassan II after the fall of the shah.

Today, in spite of the seriousness of the economic situation, the monarchy's position appears more stable than ever. The explanation for this reversal of course derives from neither strictly internal nor strictly external factors but from the combination of the two and the handling of "double codes." Internationally, Morocco has undeniably benefited from the ideological weakening of "Third-Worldism" and from the value placed on alignment with the external powers. Morocco's loyalty has been reciprocated: it appears on the U.S. list for debt relief. It also benefits from Washington's substantial military support, which has enabled it to hold the Polisario Front in check. With strong U.S. support, Rabat takes full advantage of rivalries among the Western countries. The French, in order to justify their support of Morocco, explain quite simply that by retreating they would leave the field open to the United States. In all of the maneuvering, the Soviets have not been left out entirely: they participate in the development of the Meskallah phosphate operation.

THE REVENGE OF HISTORY—AND OF THE ECONOMY

The political societies of the Third World are today being pressed by two fundamental movements that are partially contradictory. On the one hand, undergoing a process of economic restructuring tends to substitute the logic of the marketplace for client-based and patrimonial systems. Ultimately, the goal is to make the sphere of wealth production coincide with that of social redistribution. In Latin America, Africa, and the Middle East this undertaking bears a strong resemblance to social revolution because it entails modification of the principle stating that access to political power opens the way to the accumulation of wealth. This movement works undeniably in favor of the West and to the disadvantage of the Soviet Union. Even though liberalism may be strongly opposed, absolute economic state control no longer has any real defenders. The *perestroika* of Gorbachev tends more to hasten disaffection with the Soviet model than to stress the value of modernizing it.

This movement toward adjustment and economic modernization is developing in conjunction with the reactivation of internal processes of organization and of the creation of legitimacy, processes that have been repressed or masked by the politics of authoritarian modernization. The best-known form is, of course, Islam, which has a multiple reality. But it is not the only form. The Syrian government, labeled as secular, is today founded less on a single party of the traditional type than on the *acabiya*, the tribal mobilization of the Alids. The degeneration of a conflict at the highest level of the South Yeminite Communist party into an authentic civil war illustrates the symbiosis uniting a modern code (Marxist ideology) to a traditional code (tribal allegiance). In the absence of the ability to resolve an internal conflict through the offices of the political bureau, each clan mobilizes its tribe for the purpose of gaining the advantage over the other (see Roy, 1986: 857). The method for resolution of conflicts has been a major surprise for specialists studying the communist world. But for the Yemenites, even those who are not communist, all of this is very natural. Tribalism is not the only form of organization or representation capable of associating itself with Marxism. In the Congo, Marxism and sorcery live comfortably together. For example, the day before one particular major party meeting, all of the sorcerers in Brazzaville were mobilized. In the Eastern camp, things occur in the same fashion, as indicated by the case of Morocco.

All of this should lead us to shift the significance of our observations and reflections. Rather than tiring ourselves out classifying the membership of this or that state in one or the other camp, we should give consideration to the internal significance of external references.

REFERENCES

Copans, Jean (1988). "The U.S.S.R.: Alibi or Instrument for Black African States?" In Zaki Laidi, ed., *The Third World and the Soviet Union*. London: Zed.

Hurtig, Charles (1986). "Capitalisme d'état et influence sovietique en Inde." *Revue francaise de science politique*, December.

Laidi, Zaki (1986a). *Les constraints d'une rivalité: Les superpuissances et l'Afrique*. Paris: la Decouverte.

────── (1986b). "Stability and Partnership in the Mahgreb." *Annals of the American Academy of Political and Social Science*.

Ossebi, H. (1982). *Affirmation éthique et discours ideologique au Congo*. Ph.D. Dis.

Politique africaine (1988). "Mozambique." April.

Roy, Olivier (1986). "Le double code afghan: Marxism et tribalism." *Revue francaise de science politique*, December.

Skocpol, Theda (1985). *States and Social Revolutions: The Revolution in France, Russia, and China*. Paris: Fayard.

Villers, G. de. (1985). "Acheter le developpement: Le cas algérien." *Politique africaine* 18 (June).

PART TWO

CASE STUDIES

CHAPTER FOUR

Revolution and the Collapse of Traditional Monarchies: Ethiopia

Edmond J. Keller

The case of Ethiopia provides an important study of the demise of the traditional monarchical regime type. Moreover, not only does Ethiopia exhibit the characteristics of the classical "Western-type" revolution, but it manifests as well the attributes of the dependency state syndrome associated more closely with the Third World experience. Further, Ethiopia provides an ideal case of analyzing the models of indigenous revolutionary change discussed by Mason in Chapter 3 and the external factors impinging on the revolutionary process illuminated by Foltz and Laidi, also in Chapter 3.

The legitimacy that disappeared with the passing of the Ethiopian traditional monarchy has not been successfully transformed into a revolutionary consensus by the military regime, which has failed to consolidate its own authority. Complicating and contributing to this crisis of legitimacy has been the persistent ethnonationalist revolutionary movement of the Eritrean Peoples' Liberation Front—a "revolution within a revolution."—THE EDITORS

The regime of Emperor Haile Selassie was toppled in September 1974. The act of deposing the emperor was the first watershed of a revolutionary process that continues today. Other major benchmarks include the ascension of Mengistu Haile Mariam between 1977 and 1978 as the preeminent leader of the revolution, the formation of the Workers' Party of Ethiopia (WPE) in 1984, and the inauguration of the People's Democratic Republic of Ethiopia (PDRE) in 1987.

The Ethiopian Revolution, like all revolutions, must be considered as a process rather than an event. The mere disposal of an ancien régime is no guarantee that a revolution is complete. Once an old order is rejected, society must be established on new ideological or mythical foundations. In most if not all cases this does not happen overnight. A fundamental revolutionary transformation of any society takes time and is likely to be fraught with civil conflict at every step along the way.

In order to provide a full understanding of any revolution, an analysis must be firmly grounded in the historical context that gave rise to that revolution. This is necessary to understand not just the long-term and immediate causes of the revolution but also its consequences. My purpose is to analyze the Ethiopian Revolution critically in order to understand the processes that led to the formation and perpetuation of the historical bureaucratic empire, as well as the forces that continue to contribute to protracted civil unrest in the aftermath of the initial act of revolution.

Several fundamental questions guide this analysis: What factors enabled Haile Selassie's anachronistic bureaucratic empire to survive as long as it did, given the long-standing worldwide trends away from such forms of political organization? What factors contributed to the timing and structure of the revolution? How can we explain Ethiopia's protracted civil unrest? What lessons about the revolutionary phenomenon can be learned from the Ethiopian case?

There are no simple answers to any of these questions. Traditional Ethiopian society was extremely complex, and Haile Selassie's modernization policies added further complexities. Authoritarian, feudalistic rule and widespread social inequality were always considered potential sources of conflict. Yet it was generally agreed by observers of Ethiopian politics that as long as the church, the aristocracy, the bureaucracy, the military, and existing foreign military and diplomatic alliances remained intact, the empire would survive (see Perham, 1948; Huntington, 1968; 140–191). Some observers link the collapse of the Haile Selassie regime to the immediate socioeconomic effects of widespread drought, famine, and inflation.[1] Without question, these were all precipitating crises; but to focus only on such catastrophes would be a mistake. The underlying determinants of revolution must also be considered. An analysis that considers underlying, precipitating, and facilitating causes of a revolution is essential to understanding the new regime's efforts to consolidate itself.

The primary thesis of this analysis is that there was a dialectical relationship between, on the one hand, the multiple contradictions that were products of Haile Selassie's attempt to centralize and modernize Ethiopia while only marginally changing traditional institutions and authority relationships and on the other the timing and structure of the revolution.[2] My subsidiary thesis is that the protracted period of widespread civil unrest over the past decade can be explained, as it has been elsewhere, as a natural outgrowth of the revolutionary process. Once the old order has been deposed, revolutionaries must be able to establish themselves as a legitimate new government in the eyes of the majority of the population by means of a new, viable, and legitimate social myth. Until this happens, multiple, competing power blocs persist; and the "period of no government" is protracted (see Petee, 1971: 1–56). This is what happened in nineteenth-century France, twentieth-century Angola, and elsewhere. It also happened in Ethiopia. The political aspects of the revolution predominate until the state's monopoly of power is reestablished. During the "period of no government" intellectuals continue to fight over the appropriate ideological character of the new society, including the structure of the regime.

THE ORIGINS OF THE ETHIOPIAN REVOLUTION

A Model of Revolution

The factors that trigger revolution vary from one society to the next. However, the objectives of all revolutions are generally the same: radically to transform a given society to make it better conform to the changed values and aspirations of significant segments of society. Revolutions differ from other types of social change in that they result in the sudden, radical reordering of fundamental political values and relationships and the ideology or social myth on which society is based.

The causes of revolution can be grouped into two basic categories: underlying causes and precipitating and facilitating causes. Underlying causes might include, among other things, historic inequalities and exploitation, cultural cleavages, disputes over land, and intraclass hostilities among dominant classes (see Green, 1984; Skocpol, 1979). Any of these types of factors could cause segments of a population to feel deprived or indignant enough to challenge existing authorities. When disaffected groups are large and powerful enough, they possess a genuine revolutionary potential. However, there must be precipitating events and facilitating factors before a revolution can occur.

Possible precipitating factors include recent military defeat, widespread domestic political unrest, domestic or international economic crisis, and the contagious effect of other revolutions. Precipitating causes are highly situational or idiosyncratic variables and largely depend on conditions in the immediate political environment.

Facilitating factors are what give revolution its particular character. Revolutions are distinct from other types of violent rebellion. Inspired revolutionary leadership, an explicitly revolutionary organization, a revolutionary ideology, and support of aggrieved members of society are facilitating factors, any combination of which makes a rebellion a revolution.

The success of any revolution is highly dependent on environmental factors, not the least of which is the military strength of the ancien régime. Even when underlying, precipitating, and facilitating factors would seem to dictate revolution, a strong state might well thwart a revolutionary movement. By the same token, a militarily weak state could prove an easy prey for the forces of revolution.

A master symptom of revolution is a regime's loss of intellectual support for its policies. When the discontent of intellectuals becomes sharper—more public and more bitter—the regime usually resorts to force and violence. When this occurs, the efficiency and loyalty of the state military is critical. When the military is inefficient, disloyal, or otherwise incapacitated, not only is the potential for revolution much greater, but its chances of success are also much greater. Revolutions that take place without counterrevolutionary activity on the part of the state military or that involve the military as a revolutionary actor are the most likely to succeed (see Tilly, 1978; 210). The Egyptian and Turkish revolutions are classic examples of revolution involving the military itself. We might now also include in this category the Ethiopian military as it existed in 1974. In each case soldiers came to dominate coalitions comprised of dissident civilian intellectuals and other corporate movements.

A diachronic view of a society in the midst of revolution can provide only a partial understanding of the revolutionary phenomenon. For complete understanding a revolution must be placed in its historical context. Only then can the interaction between underlying, precipitating, and facilitating factors be appreciated.

Background to Revolution

Ethiopia is a multiethnic society of more than forty million people and forty different ethnic groups. The politically dominant Amhara-Tigre people trace the origins of the state of Ethiopia back some three thousand years, but the modern state did not begin to take shape until the mid-nineteenth century.

The distinctive character of the Ethiopian state can be traced to its Abyssinian origins and the adoption of Christianity in the mid–fourth century. The Abyssinian state remained a conquest state, expanding and contracting over the ages depending on the military strength and political cohesiveness of ruling groups. After having ceased to exist in all but name between the mid–eighteenth century and the mid–nineteenth century, the Ethiopian state began its most recent phase of consolidation under the leadership of emperors Tewdros, Yohannes IV, Menelik II, and eventually Haile Selassie I, who assumed the throne in 1930. These men were in large measure responsible for consolidating and secularizing the modern Ethiopian Empire. Significantly, the consolidation of the modern state coincided with the European "scramble for Africa." Consequently, a number of ethnic groups subjugated by the Amharas and Tigres during this period look on the whole process as nothing more than colonial conquest.

By the time he died in 1913, Menelik II had laid a good foundation on which Haile Selassie could continue the modernization process. He had begun to organize the central government along the lines of other secularly based governments of the time. He also introduced modern schools and other social amenities, which had heretofore been foreign to Ethiopia. Menelik was clearly responding to the challenge being posed by the heightened interest of the European powers in colonizing Africa. He was dedicated to maintaining

Ethiopian independence through its modernization. This principle was also followed by Haile Selassie.

Despite Haile Selassie's efforts to modernize Ethiopia—temporarily delayed by events related to World War II, including the Italian occupation between 1936 and 1941—his strategy was doomed to fail. There were many reasons for this, not the least of which was his failure to realize that conditions were not right in Ethiopia for a modernization of royal absolutism. He attempted to present a facade of national unity and economic progress, but his policies merely sharpened the contradictions already existing in society. The state provided subordinated groups with only meager social services and even fewer opportunities to improve their life chances. More than anything else, emphasis was placed on the control and exploitation of the majority of the population (see Baxter, 1978). The land issue was perhaps the most critical underlying factor contributing to the revolution.

Traditional patterns of land tenure have been described as, if not feudal, protofeudal (see Gamst, 1970). The emperor used three different categories of land tenure—kinship and village tenure, private tenure, and government tenure—to maintain the loyalty of public servants and members of the clergy. Eventually landlord-tenant relations developed, as more and more peripheral land was privatized in the push to commercialize agriculture. In the process a complex system of dominance and exploitation based upon political and economic, as well as cultural, hegemony was established (see Keller, 1981).

The process of economic and political modernization gave rise to the formation of new classes, which came into open conflict with traditional values. By the mid-1960s elements of these new classes were far more radical in their modernist orientations than the emperor himself and eventually challenged his rule.

In his role as emperor, Haile Selassie would occasionally pay visits to dissident areas of the periphery to give symbolic assurances of being concerned with the welfare of the residents, but such visits were seldom followed by significant policy changes. As a result, in many parts of the periphery, resentment of "Amhara colonialists" was long-standing. This was as true in areas of the periphery inhabited by the Somali and Oromo and incorporated into Ethiopia between the late 1800s and mid-1900s as it was in Eritrea, which was annexed only in 1962.

Ethnic consciousness began to rise in urban areas in the early 1960s and quickly spread to the countryside. This consciousness coincided with the government's growing exploitative and oppressive policies and the loss of land security among peasants and tenants because of the trends toward land privatization and the commercialization of agriculture. Armed opposition to the state surfaced in the 1960s in Eritrea, the Ogaden, and parts of the South dominated by the Oromo people (see Keller, 1981). Rather than responding with social reforms to accommodate ethnic opponents of the regime, Haile

Selassie responded with force and continued to pursue his own misguided development strategy. Multiple contradictions rooted in Ethiopian history exposed the weakness of the imperial system, making society ripe for revolution.

The Precipitating and Facilitating Factors of Revolution

Drought and famine were two of the primary precipitants of the Ethiopian Revolution (see Keller, 1988). Between 1973 and 1974 drought and famine plagued large areas of the periphery and even parts of the highland core. Around a hundred thousand people died of disease, malnutrition, and starvation, a catastrophe to which the regime appeared oblivious despite growing public concern expressed by students and faculty at Haile Selassie University.

The problems created by this natural catastrophe were compounded by the fact that the number of landless peasants had increased dramatically due to the trends toward freehold tenure and the commercialization of agriculture. As landlords became capitalist entrepreneurs, they purchased more land for mechanized commercialization; and they evicted tenants, who were rendered obsolete in the process.

In the cities industrialization was slow—too slow to absorb the labor being rapidly displaced from the land. In addition, inflation was fueled by a worldwide economic crisis inspired by the OPEC oil embargo. Shortage of gasoline, fuel oil, and food commodities became commonplace. Corporate groups ranging from teachers and students to clergymen, prostitutes, taxi drivers, and industrial workers took to the streets in protest. However, the regime either ignored them or dealt irresponsibly with their grievance.

The open protest of teachers and students was a clear indication that the emperor's support among the intellectuals so critical to his regime's survival was in serious jeopardy. These groups were opposed to recently announced educational reforms that promised to deemphasize formal education in favor of vocational schooling. To leverage their protest, students and teachers entered into informal alliances with a variety of urban protesters. In the process they provided the intellectual guidance to what was to become a "creeping revolution."

Intellectuals' disaffection with the regime was apparent elsewhere as well. For example, many members of the national assembly were becoming increasingly critical of Haile Selassie's development strategy and alleged government corruption.

Perhaps most significant was discontent within the military (see Legum, 1975). The revolution began unpredictably in February 1974 as mutinies occurred at military installations throughout the country. Junior officers and enlisted men arrested their superiors, demanding reforms in the system in which they worked. They called for better working conditions as well as salary increases. The government gave in to a number of the demands of the mutineers, but for the most part they remained unsatisfied. Amid widespread social discontent, the government of Prime Minister Aklilu Habte-Wold resigned. He was replaced by a nobleman, Endelkachew Makonnen. The new prime minister eventually negotiated an end to the mutinies, but a residue of discontent remained within the military. In fact, some elements within the military became more and more politically oriented and formed themselves into the Armed Forces Coordinating Committee (AFCC). This group was comprised of three representatives from each of the units of Ethiopia's armed forces and the police (see Erlich, 1986: 241–242). It was clear by the summer of 1974 that the emperor's support within the armed forces was diminishing.

Disaffection with the regime among the educated classes seemed to crystallize in a committee that was set up in 1974 to revise the Constitution of 1955. The emperor himself was willing to give up some of his absolute power, but "monarchists" on the committee opposed a radical alteration of the existing system of government. They had already lost many of their traditional privileges as modernization took hold, and they seemed bent on preserving what was left. "Progressives," on the other hand, wanted what amounted to revolutionary changes. They proposed the abolition of royal absolutism and the introduction of genuine parliamentary democracy, with separation of powers among the branches of government, universal suffrage, and guaranteed civil rights. In addition, they demanded the complete separation of church and state. When this struggle was resolved in August 1974, the "progressives" emerged triumphant. The recommendations of the constitution-drafting committee were liberal in tone and called for more democracy than had ever before been witnessed in Ethiopia (see Legum, 1975: 44).

By the summer of 1974, the AFCC—or the Derg, as it was now known—was exerting a great deal of influence over government policy, although it seemed reluctant to seize power directly. However, this entry into politics by "men in uniform" inspired the germination of a revolutionary ideal. This vision was not clear at the time the emperor was physically deposed on 12 September 1974. It was not even clear when the Derg issued its first political manifesto, *Ethiopia tikdem* (*Ethiopia First*). But an ideology rapidly crystallized, and by spring 1976 the Derg announced its commitment to the principles of scientific socialism and a noncapitalist road to development.

CONSOLIDATING THE REVOLUTION

Revolution on the Cheap

In order to be considered a success, a revolution must consolidate itself on new structural and ideological foundations. Rather than being the product of a protracted armed struggle waged by revolutionaries guided by a "correct" ideology, the Ethiopian Revolution resulted from a coup made by soldiers who had no clear-cut ideology. Initially, they attempted to win popular support through their promises and their deeds.

The first hint of an ideology was contained in a proclamation issued some three months after the Derg seized power, *Ethiopia tikdem*. This statement resembled the utopian, populist, nationalist tenets of such varieties of "African" socialism as Ujamaa socialism and humanism. Although this statement alluded to the need for an all-embracing, single party, the absence of even the barest beginnings of such a party was obvious.

The initial aims of the Derg were twofold: to preserve the territorial integrity of the country and to establish its own legitimacy. By stepping up the military campaign in Eritrea, its served notice that Ethiopia's internationally accepted boundaries were sacrosanct. To enhance popular support in the short run, the Derg launched the National Development Campaign Through Cooperation, the Zemache. This campaign, involving some sixty thousand high school and college students, was intended to explain the aims of the revolution to peasants. It was hoped that the diverse ethnic groups that make up Ethiopia would be instilled with a common political and social orientation. Since the Derg had no clear notion of the kind of society it wanted to create and no coherent and cohesive vanguard party to lead the campaign and was being offered a multiplicity of competing political ideas by civilian leftists about how to build the New Ethiopia, the youthful campaigners were free to define the ideological essence of the new society on their own. The result was confusion and conflict between campaigners and peasants and even campaigners and representatives of the state.

In the earliest days of the revolution, the substance of what came to be regarded as Ethiopian socialism was represented in the Derg's economic strategy. Within months of seizing power, it nationalized all banks and other financial institutions and most large-scale manufacturing industries. All rural property became state property and most urban property was also nationalized. The initial rural lands proclamation was followed by several decrees that led to the creation of peasant associations and cooperatives. In the cities, urban dwellers' associations were established. In both urban and rural areas, these new institutions were originally intended to empower those who had suffered most under the old system. Social programs were started to improve health care, broaden educational opportunities, and provide city dwellers with adequate, affordable housing. Over the first decade of the revolution, the quality of life did improve for most of those who had been most oppressed under the old system; but it worsened for others (see International Labour Organisation, 1983).

In addition to the tangible objectives of the Derg's economic and social policies in this period, the policies were also intended to win the Derg the support of the civilian Left and the population at large. Most leftist groups adhered to varying strands of Marxism-Leninism. Among them, the best organized and most active were the Ethiopian People's Revolutionary party (EPRP) and the All-Ethiopian Socialist movement (Meison) (see Keller, 1985a: 1–17). Pressures from the civilian Left seem to have encouraged movement away from populist socialism and toward scientific socialism. Another important variable was the recognition by the Derg that the country was on the verge of anarchy and that it had to reassert central control. The goal of grassroots empowerment had been qualified by early 1976; and the vanguard role of the "men in uniform" was now emphasized, at least until a vanguard workers' party could be established.

On 20 April 1976, the Derg announced the Program for the National Democratic Revolution (PNDR).[3] In the document of this name the principles of Marxist-Leninist scientific socialism are declared the most appropriate guide to development for Ethiopia. In the absence of a mature capitalist economy, a national democratic revolution led by a coalition of "revolutionary democrats" is declared to be a prerequisite for socialist transformation. This would allow the normal capitalist phase of economic development to be skipped and provide a bridge to socialism. In this approach, dialectical materialism, the essence of the orthodox Marxist methodology, is maintained.

The National Democratic Revolution

The inauguration of the PNDR marked the entry of the revolution into a second, more decisive phase of consolidation. The Derg seemed determined to define the fundamentals of Ethiopia's brand of scientific socialism on its own. It continued to consult with civilian leftist groups, but only to keep them in check. The Derg tried at the time to create the illusion of openness and free exchange of ideas by allowing selected political groups to operate in a semilegitimate fashion. Among these were the military-based Revolutionary Flame (founded in 1976) and civilian-based groups such as Meison, the EPRP, the Labor League, and the Revolutionary Struggle of the Oppressed Ethiopian Masses (ECHAAT). These groups were formed into an advisory political bureau to counsel the Derg on political as well as policy matters (see Ottaway, 1987: 25–42).

When it became apparent that the Derg had no interest in actually sharing power with civilian groups—let alone surrendering power to them— violent ideological disputes erupted among the groups, particularly EPRP and Meison, the best organized civilian movements. Meison believed in controlled democracy and was willing, at least in the short run, to accept the vanguard role of the Derg. The EPRP advocated unlimited people's democracy (Ottaway, 1978: 1–18).

By late 1976, the EPRP had initiated a clandestine movement to undermine the credibility and effectiveness of the Derg. It infiltrated mass organizations like peasant and urban dwellers' associations, labor unions, and even the Zemache. Sporadic bloody encounters, assassinations, and counterassassinations involving the EPRP and Meison began to occur in urban areas. By that time, Meison had become the most influential civilian group in the political bureau, and the EPRP was driven underground. At the same time, Revolutionary Flame, having become more ideologically sophisticated, felt compelled to counter the growing influence of Meison in the political bureau.

The Derg labeled the tactics of the EPRP "white terror" and countered with its own "red terror." The aim of the "red terror" was to wipe out all enemies of the revolution by any means. By January 1978, it was estimated that between three thousand and ten thousand suspected members of the EPRP had been eliminated in the Red Terror Campaign. This period coincided with the Derg's growing estrangement from all civilian groups. By early 1979, Revolutionary Flame was the only officially recognized political organization.

In addition to the political challenges the Derg faced at the center, groups on the periphery also arose to question its vision of the new order. Opposition movements in the north in Eritrea and Tigre and in Somali and Oromo areas of the South, attempted to capitalize on the apparently vulnerable, exceedingly "soft" character of the new regime's authority. By late 1977, three Eritrean movements controlled the whole region except the major urban centers. A combined force of Ogadeni irredentists and regular Somali troops captured large portions of the Ogaden. Oromo movements also recorded some gains during this period (see Keller, 1985b).

The Derg's vulnerability was highlighted by the breakdown of Ethiopia's relations with the United States in April 1977. This resulted in the ouster of U.S. military advisors from the country and the curtailment of U.S. military aid. The Soviet Union cautiously seized the opportunity to replace the United States as Ethiopia's superpower patron. With the assistance of the USSR and its allies (Cuba, East Germany, South Yemen, and others), the Derg was able to stem the tide of opposition by early 1978.

Over the first fourteen years of the revolution, key elements in the Derg's quest to build the New Ethiopia were bureaucratic reform, party formation, and the inauguration of a new Marxist-Leninist constitution. There is no doubt that the Soviet Union and its allies have influenced the character of the new regime as it has emerged so far. However, in large measure, these developments can be attributed to the regime's own efforts to ensure its survival through tighter control. Legitimacy has seemed a secondary priority.

To enhance its bureaucratic control, it reorganized the central bureaucracy and politicized its cadre. This was seen as a major step in dismantling feudal privilege. All new appointees to regional, subregional, and district posts since these reforms have been military men or university-educated supporters of the Derg, all of whom are perceived to be committed communists.

Peasant associations and urban dwellers' associations were also a part of this scheme. Currently, there are about twenty thousand peasant associations throughout the country. They represent the lowest level of central administration and are responsible for processing and interpreting policies from the center, maintaining law and order, facilitating party formation and ideological indoctrination at the local level, and leading economic development. In the cities, urban dwellers' associations serve similar functions (see Rahmato, 1985).

In the industrial sector, Working People's Control Committees, created in 1981, have come to serve a somewhat threatening "watchdog" role over productive activities. The committees are supposed to be involved in monitoring and promoting worker productivity. The regime claims that people's control committees have uncovered numerous incidents of fraud, corruption, and wastefulness in the workplace. The tight surveillance that characterizes the workplace in Ethiopia today has been facilitated by the training provided committee members by Soviet and East German security advisors. It is now evident that the government's capacity to project its authority to remote corners of society is steadily increasing.

The expansion of the central bureaucracy was clearly an effort to shore up the coercive capacity of the state and to lay the groundwork for the establishment of an all-embracing vanguard party. In 1979 the Derg announced the establishment of the Commission To Organize the Party of the Working People of Ethiopia (COPWE) (see Wilson, 1983: 18–19). However, the real work of the commission did not begin until its second congress in 1983. Simultaneously with the creation of COPWE, the Derg set about creating new mass organizations such as Revolutionary Ethiopia Youth, women's associations, and various professional associations. It also strengthened already-existing mass organizations such as peasant associations, urban dwellers' associations, and the All-Ethiopia Trade Union. The function of mass organizations is to represent the interests of their memberships not only at party congresses but also on an everyday basis. They are assumed to have active educational and developmental roles.

COPWE finished its work in September 1984, and the Worker's Party of Ethiopia was inaugurated. An eleven-member politburo was ostensibly named to replace the Derg, but the entire seven-person executive committee of the Provisional Military Administrative Council was included in this new body. Of the 134 members of the WPE central committee, 29 are members of the armed forces, and at least another 45 are ex-soldiers. This contrasts with only 22 positions held by representatives of mass organizations. Counting full and alternate members of the WPE central committee, military people make up over 60 percent (see Korn, 1986).

More significant and striking than the predominance of Derg members in the politbureau and WPE central committee is the fact that the party is far from being democratic in its representation. Although mass organizations such as labor unions and peasant associations are represented at party congresses, few of their representatives are on the WPE central committee. In fact, fewer than 35 percent of the central committee was civilian in 1987. One in five civilians was a technocrat (see *Africa Confidential*, 1984).

The primary task of the WPE, following its formation, was to devise a new national constitution that would inaugurate the People's Democratic Republic of Ethiopia (PDRE). In the process the regime hoped to enhance the twin goals of control and legitimacy. A 143-person constitutional drafting committee was appointed by the party. The drafting committee labored at hammering out the details of a socialist constitution for more than a year. In June 1986 it issued a 120-article draft constitution.

One million copies of the draft constitution were distributed throughout the country. For the next two months the document was discussed at more than twenty thousand locations (see *Africa Confidential*, 1986). The regime apparently used this approach in an effort to legitimize the process of constitution-making and to test the mood of the general population. In some areas people attended local constitutional discussions only after pressure from the local party cadre, but in others they attended voluntarily. Generally, people were disinterested in the new constitution. They seemed willing to concede a process they knew they could not control or influence.

After two months of deliberations at the grass roots level, the drafting committee was reconvened to consider proposed amendments. Ninety-five separate amendments were proposed, but only cosmetic changes were made. The referendum on the new constitution was held on 1 February 1987. The results of the vote were announced by WPE general secretary Mengistu Haile Mariam three weeks later. It was reported that 96 percent of the fourteen million people eligible to participate actually voted. It was said that 81 percent of the electorate endorsed the constitution, while 18 percent opposed it.

The PDRE was officially proclaimed on 22 February 1987, making Ethiopia the sixth black African regime subscribing to the designation *People's Republic* (see Keller and Rothchild, 1987). The constitution resembles a hybrid of the Soviet and pre-1990 Romanian constitutions. The original draft was closely patterned on the Soviet model, but the final version departs from that model in two critical respects. First, the office of the presidency is strengthened and elevated above the authority of the Council of State. This change creates a presidency with powers similar to that of the pre-1990 Romanian chief executive. Second, the Soviet model of self-determination is consciously not endorsed. It was reported that the problem of nationalities was hotly debated in the drafting committee as well as in the WPE central committee, but nothing immediately changed in this regard (see *Africa Confidential*, 1987a).

Ethiopia is declared by the constitution to be a unitary state with Amharic as the national language. However, the language, religion, and culture of all legally constituent nationality groups are said to be protected. Article 9 of the document declares that "administrative and autonomous regions" are to be created in order to "give a democratic expression to the rights of nationalities and a Marxist-Leninist solution to the nationalities issue." "Narrow nationalism" is deemed counterrevolutionary and therefore is not tolerated. Regional autonomy is assumed in certain cases to encourage class unity and is thus theoretically able to neutralize the negative aspects of nationalist affinities.

The responsibility for spelling out the legal basis for autonomous and administrative regions was assigned to the 835-member National Assembly, or Shengo. That body meets once a year. Day-to-day operations of the central government are handled by the Council of State, seven permanent commissions, and various ministries.

The first session of the National Assembly was convened in early September 1987. One of its first items of business was to enact the government's plan for administrative reorganization of regional government. The plan was rapidly endorsed by the assembly. As a result, twenty-four administrative regions and five autonomous regions were created. The autonomous regions are Tigre, Dire Dawa, Ogaden, Assab, and Eritrea. Among the autonomous regions, Eritrea seems to have the most autonomy. In particular, its regional government has broader powers in the areas of industrial development and education. In contrast to the governments of other autonomous regions, the Eritrean government can independently establish any type of industry, and it controls education up to the junior college level. Other autonomous regional governments are limited to independently setting up medium-sized industries and controlling education only to the secondary level (see *Africa Confidential*, 1987b).

Eritrea also differs from other autonomous regions in that it has three administrative regions of its own: the North, made up of what were once Barka, Karen, and Sahel provinces; the south-central part of historic Eritrea; and the West. The northern administrative region is an area that was for years totally under the control of the Eritrean People's Liberation Front (EPLF). Some observers suggest that the regime may consider giving up at least that region to the EPLF in a future political settlement. On the other hand, the creation of a new Assab autonomous region seems a clear attempt to foreclose any Eritrean claims to that area. It also guarantees Ethiopia's access to the Red Sea. Significantly, the Assab region includes portions of what were once districts in eastern Tigre and Wollo provinces.

The latest round of administrative reorganization is a reality only on paper. The party and administrative infrastructure necessary to implement the policy are only slowly being put into place. Moreover, the regime has encountered considerable resistance from the various liberation movements and other opposition movements who universally reject the plan. The EPLF, for example, now controls almost all of Eritrea except major urban areas to the south.

The EPLF has called for a UN-sponsored referendum so that the Eritrean people themselves can decide their fate. It is not insignificant that the EPLF sees no role for the Organization of African Unity (OAU) in the resolution of this problem, since that body has consistently rejected Eritrea's claim to self-determination. By the time the OAU was formed, Ethiopia had already annexed Eritrea, and it was considered by the OAU to be a province of that country. The Tigre People's Liberation Front (TPLF) regards the new constitution as irrelevant to its own movement for social justice in Ethiopia.

The regime's efforts to consolidate its rule have largely failed. It lacks the legitimacy and the political and economic power to ensure citizen compliance with its policies. Consequently, it seems compelled to rely on brute force and authoritarian control to ensure its survival. In the long run, this very approach is the largest obstacle to revolutionary consolidation.

THE ETHIOPIAN REVOLUTION IN PERSPECTIVE

The Ethiopian Revolution at this stage is an ongoing linear process. However, for analytical purposes we can divide it into two distinct phases: the political phase and the phase of consolidation. The political phase of the revolution predominated up to the overthrow of the Haile Selassie regime. This is not to say that politics ended with the removal of the emperor but only that the political struggle largely defined the revolution in its initial phase.

The Ethiopian Revolution is now in the midst of the phase of consolidation. In this phase, the revolution is consumed with social reconstruction in all its aspects. This involves radically altering the cultural and institutional fabric of society. The remaking of society and reestablishing it on new ideological foundations will not take place overnight, or even over a mere few decades. Yet it must happen if the Ethiopian Revolution is to be considered complete.

In many ways the Ethiopian Revolution resembles the classic social revolutions of the modern era (the French of the late eighteenth century and the Russian and Chinese of the early twentieth century) more than it resembles other Third World social revolutions. The "great revolutions" resulted from contradictions that emerged and became unmanageable for "well established imperial states with proven capacities to protect their own hegemony and that of the dominant classes against revolts from below" (see Skocpol, 1979). This characterization could well be applied to the Ethiopian empire-state that consolidated itself after 1855 and matured over the next century. Under the weight of internal social contradictions, the authoritative apparatus of the state collapsed. As revolt transformed naturally into revolutionary movements, revolutionary leadership spontaneously emerged. In the case of Ethiopia, this leadership was represented in the Derg. Revolutionary leaders were ultimately faced with the challenges of resolving societal contradictions and building a new society. All of these features were common to the Russian, French, and Chinese revolutions, as well.

While the Ethiopian Revolution resembles the "great revolutions," it could be argued that except for the fact that it emerged from the breakdown of a moribund imperial system, the Ethiopian Revolution has more in common with the modern social revolutions of the Third World (e.g., Cuba, Vietnam, Mexico), particularly in Africa (e.g., Algeria, Guinea-Bissau, Angola, Mozambique). The Ethiopian Revolution, like revolutions in other parts of Africa, took place in a country that was in a relatively weak and dependent position in the world economic and political order. Structurally, it was organized much as were the colonial systems found in the rest of Africa. Furthermore, the imperial state was constrained from asserting its unquestioned autonomy in making domestic policy by its limited resource capacity. This is a fundamental difference between modern Third World revolutions and the "great revolutions."

The Ethiopian state's pursuit of autonomous decisionmaking must be analyzed in the context of dependency. Despite the fact that new states of the Third World that are products of revolutions like Ethiopia's are dependent and thus constrained from autonomous decisionmaking, there are opportunities for some state autonomy, depending on the circumstances and the relative strength of the state. These regimes are highly dependent on economic and military aid from abroad for their very survival. Yet they do tend to be relatively stronger and more autonomous than the regimes they displaced, as in the case of Cuba and Ethiopia itself.

Although Ethiopia continues to be dependent and lacks absolute autonomy, it does possess some leverage and political power, depending on the circumstance. Like the imperial regime, the current regime has diligently worked to strengthen its autonomy relative to domestic, as well as international, actors.

The introduction of a scientific socialist ideology to replace the myth of the divine right of the monarchical absolutist state was a conscious effort on the part of the Derg to enhance its legitimacy to enable it to pursue its statist development strategy. Social policies and economic reform were also a part of this design. Bureaucratic restructuring, expansion, and consolidation were all intended to strengthen the hand of the state center. Indeed, the planning and coercive capacity of the state improved, but its capacity for effective policy implementation did not. For example, the state's lack of hard currency has forced it to be heavily dependent on foreign capital, most of which comes from the West—despite the regime's public disdain for Western imperialism.

The state's autonomy in domestic policymaking is further compromised because it has failed to recognize the importance of satisfactorily resolving the "national question" in the course of building a new order. Rather than emphasizing a negotiated, political solution to this problem, the regime has responded with force and bureaucratic centralism. Force and cooptation, however, have not worked. The central authorities continue to lack legitimacy among most intellectuals of either rightist or leftist persuasion. Furthermore, large segments of the non-Amhara ethnic population question the regime's sincerity in addressing their interests. This is clearly manifested in the widespread civil unrest involving opposition movements like the EPLF, TPLF, and Oromo Liberation Front (OLF).

The continued opposition to the regime's policies has resulted in a strengthening, rather than a lessening, of its military and economic dependence. It has found it necessary to expand the size of the armed forces dramatically in order to cope with stepped-up armed opposition and provide itself some limited freedom to pursue its development strategy. The armed forces now number more than three hundred thousand, and military expenditures are more than four hundred million dollars annually (see U.S. Arms Control and Disarmament Agency, 1987; Press, 1988: 11). Most of Ethiopia's military aid now comes from the Soviet Union and its allies. However, the regime has been able to leverage its military dependence on the Eastern bloc against its economic dependence on the West, thus creating for itself a measure of autonomy from both sets of patrons. Because Eastern bloc countries in general, and the USSR in particular, cannot provide the level of economic aid that would be necessary to energize Ethiopia's economy adequately, the door has remained open for Western capital and, to a certain extent, Western influence.

The phase of revolutionary consolidation in Ethiopia has encountered false starts and pitfalls. Yet there is little doubt that a new society based on a variant of state socialism and the principles of Marxism-Leninism is being created. The development strategy the new regime has chosen, as well as its new social myth, is valued most because of the amount of control the state is afforded. Ethiopia today is characterized by a form of what might best be called "dependent autonomy." Although the state does possess some limited autonomy in decisionmaking, that autonomy is often circumscribed by its external dependence. Ethiopia's endemic resource scarcity is destined to ensure that this condition will remain for the foreseeable future.

NOTES

1. See Shepard (1975), Legum (1975), and Ottaway and Ottaway (1978).
2. This is not to suggest that traditions *must* give way to the forces of modernization but only that the coexistence between the two forces is dependent upon the minimization of divisive contradictions.

3. See "Program for the National Democratic Revolution of Ethiopia," Addis Ababa, 20 April 1976.

REFERENCES

Africa Confidential (1984). "Ethiopia: Last Tango in Addis." Vol. 25, no. 20, 15 October.

——— (1986). "Ethiopia: Some Constitution." Vol. 27, no. 13, 18 June.

——— (1987a). "Ethiopia: Timetable." Vol. 27, no. 20, 1 October.

——— (1987b). "Ethiopia: Redrawing the Map." Vol. 28, no. 23, 18 November.

Baxter, P. T. W. (1978). "Ethiopia's Unacknowledged Problem, the Oromo." *African Affairs* 77:283-299.

Erlich, Haggai (1986). *Ethiopia and the Challenge of Independence.* Boulder: Lynne Rienner.

Gamst, Frederick C. (1970). "Peasantries and Elites without Urbanization: the Civilization of Ethiopia." *Comparative Studies in Society and History* 12:373–392.

Green, Thomas H. (1984). *Comparative Revolutionary Movements: Search for Theory and Justice.* Englewood Cliffs: Prentice-Hall.

Huntington, Samuel P. (1968). *Political Order in Changing Societies.* New Haven: Yale University Press.

International Labor Organization (1983). *Socialism from the Grassroots: Accumulation, Employment, and Equity in Ethiopia."* Addis Ababa: ILO.

——— (1985a). "State, Party, and Revolution in Ethiopia." *African Studies Review* 28, no. 1, 1–17.

——— (1985b). "United States Policy in the Horn of Africa: Policymaking with Blinders On." In Richard Sklar et al., eds., *African Crisis Areas and United States Foreign Policy.* Berkeley: University of California Press.

Keller, Edmond J. (1981). "Ethiopia: Revolution, Class, and the National Question." *African Affairs* 80:519–550.

——— (1988). *Revolutionary Ethiopia: From Empire to People's Republic.* Bloomington: Indiana University Press.

Keller, Edmond J., and Donald Rothchild, eds. (1987). *Afro-Marxist Regimes: Ideology and Public Policy.* Boulder: Lynne Rienner.

Korn, David (1986). *Ethiopia, the United States, and the Soviet Union.* London: Croom Helm.

Legum, Colin (1975). *The Fall of Haile Selassie's Empire.* New York: Africana.

Ottaway, Marina (1978). "Democracy and New Democracy: The Ideological Debate in the Ethiopian Revolution." *Ethiopianist Notes* 1, no. 3, 1–18.

——— (1987.) "State Power Consolidation in Ethiopia." In Keller and Rothchild, eds., *Afro-Marxist Regimes.* Boulder: Lynne Rienner.

Ottaway, Marina, and David Ottaway (1978). *Ethiopia: Empire in Revolution.* New York: Holmes and Meier.

Perham, Margery (1984). *The Government of Ethiopia.* London: Faber and Faber.

Petee, George (1971). "The Process of Revolution." In Clifford T. Paynton and Robert Blackey, eds., *Why Revolution?* New York: Cambridge University Press.

Press, Robert M. (1988). "Famine and War Put Ethiopia on Superpower Summit Agenda." *Christian Science Monitor* (Boston), 31 May, p. 11.

Rahmato, Dessalegn (1985). *Agrarian Reform in Ethiopia*. Trenton: Red Sea.

Shephard, Jack (1975). *The Politics of Starvation*. New York: Carnegie Endowment.

Skocpol, Theda (1979). *States and Social Revolutions: A Comparative Analysis of France, Russia, and China*. Cambridge: Cambridge University Press.

Tilly, Charles (1978). *From Mobilization to Revolution*. Reading, MA: Addison-Wesley.

U.S. Arms Control and Disarmament Agency (1987). *World Military Expenditures and Arms Transfers*. Washington, DC: GPO.

Wilson, Roberto Correa (1983). "On the Eve of the Establishment of the Party." *Verde olive* (Havana), 13 October.

CHAPTER FIVE

Religious Resurgence
and Revolution: Islam

JOHN VOLL
FRED R. VON DER MEHDEN

The phenomenon of Islamic resurgence brings together a new form of revolutionary ideology—new in that it points toward a regime- and legitimacy-transforming process. As Chaliand indicates in Chapter 2, Western conceptions of revolution have had difficulty in comprehending Islamic resurgence. It requires a more eclectic, predominantly non-Western conceptual approach, capable of accommodating the modernizing phenomenon of revolutionary state transformation with the societal reaction to Western values—liberal and Marxist—and the return to a religion-sanctioned mythic past.

The significance of Islamic resurgence for our understanding of Third World revolutionary movements is that it presents a new path for political change, one that evinces diverse impact in different regime contexts and presents a viable threat to a regime lacking a degree of legitimacy. This dynamic and complex process exists, actually or potentially, in every state with a Muslim majority or significant minority.—THE EDITORS

The role that Islam plays in contemporary politics and society is a multifaceted one that defies simplistic analysis. For its part, the Islamic resurgence presents many faces and any effort to define its programs and manifestations necessitates a review of a complex set of patterns that have arisen within the Muslim world. We attempt to assess the extent to which the programs, goals, and manifestations of the resurgence can be defined as "revolutionary." We will first forward a definition of revolution against which to analyze the resurgence and then establish a somewhat arbitrary categorization of Islamic movements. On this basis, it is possible to assess the extent to which these facets of the resurgence can be classified as revolutionary.

For the sake of this analysis, we wish to employ a version of Samuel Huntington's now classic definition of revolution. In his *Political Order in Changing Societies*, he called revolution "a rapid and violent domestic change in the dominant values and myths of a society, in its political institutions, social structure, leadership, and government activity and politics" (1968: 264).

We would revise this definition along two lines. Revolutions need not be violent in terms of mass death and injury, particularly if it comes from the top. Thus, the Burmese Revolution of 1962 meets all of Huntington's criteria and resulted in only one death. Secondly, it is useful to note that *rapid* need not mean immediate and that a variety of events over a relatively short period of time may culminate in fundamental change in the society.

Our analysis of the character and impact of the resurgence in the Islamic world is formulated within three rather arbitrary categories. We will initially assess two states that we consider to have experienced a revolutionary change in the name of Islam: Iran and Libya. The second type, which will be very briefly reviewed, includes states in which Islam has long played major political and social roles. Islam may even have provided the basis for changes in political institutions and societal leadership that were of a revolutionary character. However, these "revolutions" took place long before the contemporary resurgence and the current leadership cannot be considered revolutionary. Examples would include Saudi Arabia and Morocco.

Finally, we will analyze countries where Islam is in competition or confrontation. These would include countries in which Muslim minorities have sought secession, autonomy, or special religious rights (exemplified by the Philippines and West Africa) and countries in which Muslims are the majority but elements of that community seek to strengthen the role of their religion against secular or "un-Islamic" forces. (Examples of this pattern would be found in Egypt, Malaysia, and Indonesia.)

At the outset, it must be underscored that the present revitalization of Islam is a highly complex phenomenon that has taken on a wide variety of manifestations. It ranges from greater attention to religious practices, such as prayer, to the more publicized acts of violence by radical groups seeking the immediate formation of a society based upon Islamic principles. It is difficult to generalize with confidence about the resurgence because of this diversity. The crucial analytical questions produce different answers in different places. In this situation it is very important to distinguish between the more general experiences of Islamic resurgence and those that are explicitly revolutionary. To treat every manifestation of the contemporary resurgence as if it were revolutionary in the more limited definition used here could create the basis for major errors of interpretation and policy.

THE HISTORICAL CONTEXT

All of the Islamic movements of resurgence and revolution share some common historical background. This is included in the main lines of global history since the sixteenth century. At that time there was an era of Islamic dynamism and power, reflected in the successes of great states like the

Ottoman, Moghal, and Safavid empires. However, by the eighteenth century this dynamism appears to have weakened at the same time that Western European states were emerging in powerful and expansive forms. In less than two hundred years, virtually all of the Islamic world had come under the direct or indirect control of Western powers; and in most areas Muslim leaders were actively engaged in Westernizing or modernizing their societies. While there was little formal rejection of Islam, there was a significant questioning of traditional Islamic formulations and a major effort to create a synthesis of Islamic and Western ideas. These resulted in the development of Islamic modernism in a variety of forms.

In the two decades after World War II, most Muslim communities gained formal political independence. During these years, nationalism provided the basic programmatic ideology. Then, in the 1960s various ideologies of development, some radical and some ostensibly conservative but all essentially modernizing, emerged as the basis for policy and governmental identity. Although there were many achievements, by the 1970s, a sense of dissatisfaction began to be expressed with varying degrees of vigor. Somehow, "imported" ideologies, programs, and concepts were seen as having failed—or at least as not having achieved their expected goals.

Many scholars feel that this is the basic background for the resurgence of Islam in general and the emergence of Islamically oriented revolutionary groups in particular. The resurgence has, in this context, important negative and positive dimensions. It is, on the one hand, a rejection of "foreign" ideologies and, on the other hand, an affirmation of an authentically Islamic alternative. In some areas, this has meant some tensions but primarily an increase in visible adherence to Islamic practices. However, in other areas it has led to real conflicts and even (as in Iran) revolution.

At this point the diversity of experience becomes apparent, and we need to look at specific cases. The task here is to focus on experiences where the resurgence has a revolutionary impact. It is, however, important to recognize that the resurgence has been regime-supporting in certain situations, as well as the basis for opposition. Thus, Islamization programs have been part of attempts, not always successful, to provide legitimacy for regimes. The program led by Zia ul-Haq in Pakistan has had some success, while the Islamization efforts of Ja'far Numayri in the Sudan helped to increase the opposition that led to his overthrow in 1985.

ISLAMIC RESURGENCE AS REVOLUTION

The Islamic resurgence has a clear revolutionary impact in at least two contemporary states, Iran and Libya. These two states provide cases for analysis of the Islamic resurgence as revolution.

Iran

It is clear that what happened in Iran during 1978–1980 was by any definition a revolution. What needs to be examined is the nature of that revolution. Certain classic expectations regarding revolutions in the Third World are possible to test on the basis of what is known about the Iranian experience. This can be seen in a number of the discussions of the causes of the Iranian Revolution.

It has been assumed by some thinkers—possibly as far back as Aristotle—that a very unequal distribution of wealth is an important cause of political violence and revolution. However, in the Iranian case it has been argued that while there was substantial inequality in the distribution of wealth and income in Iran, the level of this inequality was no more than (and sometimes less than) distribution inequalities in many other middle-income countries that have not had revolutions (Momayezi, 1986: 68–76).

This type of analysis has been done for many often-cited causal factors for revolutions. A basic question has been, Why did an Islamic revolution take place in Iran and not elsewhere? Asked in this way, the answer is very difficult to find because it leads to isolating and rejecting factors on an individual basis. It is possible to argue that the factors of rapid economic growth, disruptive modernizing education, demands for broader political participation, economic growth and frustrated expectations, and even resentment against foreign domination all existed in Iran; but they also existed in countries that did not experience major revolutions. In this line of analysis, these are seen as elements in the Iranian situation, not as the major "cause" of the revolution.[1]

One analysis of causes starting from some common assumptions about modern revolutions came to a very frank conclusion: "If the Shah's regime collapsed despite the fact that his army was intact, despite the fact that there was no defeat in war, and despite the fact that the state faced no financial crisis and no peasant insurrections, where does all this leave the usual generalizations about revolutions? Mostly in the pits" (Arjomand, 1986: 387).

It is, in this context, tempting to define the Iranian Revolution primarily in terms of what it is not. It is not a peasant revolution. The traditional population in the countryside was not mobilized until the revolution was well along and they had little to do with setting the priorities or the mood of the revolution as it developed. It is also not a Luddite-style of revolution with the primary motive being the destruction of an intrusive modern technology. In fact, it seems clear that the revolutionaries were both willing to utilize modern technology and able to manage it effectively.

In defining the nature of the revolution, it is necessary not to become too involved in the search for the theoretically perfect causal factor. It is possible for something that does not lead to a revolution in one place, combined with other factors, to be part of the "cause" of the revolution in another place. Discontent with unequal distribution of income and wealth, for example, did exist in Iran and provided some basis for the appeal of a revolutionary message that called for greater equality and economic justice. Other governments have been seen as puppets of a foreign superpower and have survived. However, Iranian resentment against the shah's identification with the United States certainly helped to create an audience for a revolutionary opposition to the shah calling for a state that was subservient to neither the West nor the East.

The Iranian experience involves a number of familiar revolutionary themes. However, that experience also appears to go beyond them. The whole of the Iranian Revolution is more than simply the sum of its parts. The special character of the Iranian Revolution is increasingly being recognized by analysts. Marvin Zonis has spoken of it as being the most impressive and important revolution in world history since the Bolshevik Revolution in Russia. Arjomand believes that it "is theoretically the most interesting of modern revolutions."[2]

In the Iranian Revolution we can see leadership and organization coming from a transformed and mobilized group with foundations in the premodern society. The revolution ultimately did not reflect the victory of the modern elements of labor, secularism, and modern-style nationalism. Instead, the Iranian Revolution and the Islamic Republic that it created represent the victory of the preservers of premodern and non-European values, concentrated among the Shi'ite religious leaders and their sociopolitical allies. Their victory does not, however, represent a rejection of all things modern or European. It is the product of a successful adaptation to the contemporary world while affirming an authentically Islamic identity. The revolutionary synthesis is new both within the Shi'i tradition and in modern experience. The closest parallel in modern world history is probably the transformation of the imperial tradition in Japan, which began with the Meiji Restoration in the nineteenth century.

As a result, it would be ineffective to deal with the Islamic Revolution in Iran as if it were simply another Third World nationalist revolution or a reactionary nativism that will soon be undermined by the continuing process of modernization. Instead, it might be useful to see the Iranian Revolution as part of a new type of revolution in the world combining a rigorous adherence to a continuing tradition of values and beliefs with an ability to manage the factors of power and technology in the contemporary world.

Through the Iranian experience, the Islamic resurgence has at least one aspect that is revolutionary. It is revolutionary in that it is a drastic change in political institutions and social structures in Iran. It may also be revolutionary in the even broader sense that it reflects a revolution in the mode of revolution itself in the modern world. This new mode appeals to many in the Islamic world even if those people do not accept the specific leadership or direction of Khomeini or the Iranian government.

Libya

The other clearly revolutionary experience with some relationship to the Islamic resurgence is in Libya. The Libyan revolutionary regime spans two eras. It was born in the last days of Arab socialist enthusiasms in the Middle East and has extended into the era of the clearly visible Islamic resurgence. When Mu'ammar Qaddafi led his fellow military officers in overthrowing Idris I and the Libyan monarchy in 1969, the event was observed with almost a sense of déjà vu. Jaded analysts had seen so many military coups led by young officers that they assumed they already knew the script.

In some ways the new government in Libya conformed to the pattern of radical Arab socialist movements. Arab unity was a high priority and Gamal Abd al-Nasir (Nasser) was the ideal and the model for Qaddafi and his men. Qaddafi was active in promoting unity projects among Arab states and also instituted a single-party government along the lines of Nasser's Arab Socialist Union and Egyptian state.

There were, however, actions taken by Qaddafi from the very beginning that indicated that Islam was going to play a more important role in the new Libya than it had played in the other military-socialist states in the Arab world. Almost immediately, a prohibition of alcoholic drinks was announced; and soon Qaddafi made it clear that implementation of the Sharia was one of his high priorities. At first, this was in the context of a relatively traditional interpretation of the Koran and Islamic law. Qaddafi's concept of Islamization was not especially distinctive in the early 1970s.

Gradually, Qaddafi came to develop a special interpretation of the fundamentals of Islam. In the late 1970s his ideas were presented in the three volumes of the *Green Book*. In these volumes Qaddafi defined a third universal theory, which he contrasted with capitalism and communism. With the implementation of principles of the *Green Book*, Libya experienced a second revolution. The first, in 1969, had overthrown the conservative monarchy and established an Islamically oriented Arab Socialist Republic. The second, which was the product of the *Green Book* program, created the Libyan Arab Jamahiriyyah. *Jamahiriyyah*, spoken of as the "state of the masses" or "peopledom," was chosen in "an effort to convey the suggestion that the people rule themselves without the intervention of a state administration" (Anderson, 1986a: 264).

Over the years, Qaddafi's developing radicalism has aroused a variety of opposition. However, these groups have lacked effective unity. At the same time, the longevity of the revolution and its special emphasis on equality have created a constituency for the continuing revolution. Lisa Anderson has pointed out that more than half of the Libyan population has been born since the 1969 revolution and that although "there is considerable popular skepticism about the Third International Theory on which Qadhdhafi bases his revolution, particularly among the older generations and the social elite, it is regularly taught in schools and it finds adherents there, especially among rebellious youths and children of the disadvantaged" (1986b: 227). Anderson notes further that the ideal of the Jamahiriyyah and Qaddafi's radically egalitarian policies "have politicized segments of the population which were previously quiescent, especially the relatively underprivileged: the young and the low-born" (pp. 228–229). These newly mobilized Libyans provide a basis for support, which means that the Qaddafi revolution has survived for two decades.

As it evolved, the Libyan revolution has changed from a familiar type of revolution into a radically new one. At least part of the distinctiveness of the new revolution is its strong emphasis on Islam. In this it is a part of the resurgence of Islam. It is revolutionary both in transforming a political and social order and also in that, like Iran, it seems to have adopted a different revolutionary style.

Despite the differences in specifics, the Libyan revolution is similar to the Iranian in that it is based not on Western forms and modern organizational concepts but rather on a transformed premodern organizational style that has been significantly adapted to make it an effective operator within the contemporary global context. "Qadhdhafi has translated past legacies into revolutionary foreign and domestic policies, expressing a highly radicalized version of Libyan character" (Roumani, 1983: 164).

The futures of the revolutionary regimes in Iran and Libya are difficult to predict. There are some aspects that have a high degree of probability. The revolutions have irreversibly transformed their societies. There is virtually no potential for a reversion to a conservative, Western-allied regime in either country. Whatever may be reasons for opposition or change of contemporary polices, almost all sectors of the political spectrum support the rejection of an apparent subordination of Libyan or Iranian interests to foreign ones. Similarly, the old aristocratic cliques associated with the monarchies have virtually disappeared, and the old power elites have no chance of recreating themselves and regaining power.

It would also seem highly improbable that either Qaddafi or Khomeini's successors will be replaced by governments that are not actively committed to visibly Islamic foundations for policies. The chief opponents of Khomeini before his death were in the Iranian National Front. They do not reject the principles of Islamic revolution. They argue, rather, that Khomeini and his followers deviated from those basic principles. Even in a situation like the Sudan, where the legislation that was the key to Numayri's Islamization program was widely opposed as not properly Islamic, it has been hard, even after the overthrow of Numayri, to reverse those "September Laws." An ideological reversal in Iran or Libya, where there is much general support for the principles of the revolutions, would be even more difficult.

The Libyan and Iranian revolutions are important parts of the Islamic resurgence. However, as revolutions, they have gone beyond the basic efforts to reaffirm the authenticity of the Islamic message in contemporary life. This affirmation can be, and has been, made in many different ways in Islamic communities from Chicago to Cairo to Jakarta. The revolutionary dimension of the resurgence, as reflected in the Iranian and Libyan cases, goes beyond this to a radical restatement of Islam that has brought about the significant transformation of social and political orders, not simply a replacement of one political elite by another within the context of a state system similar to that conceptualized by people in the West.

OLDER ISLAMIC STATES

Our second category for looking at the relationship between the Islamic resurgence and revolution includes states in which Islam has long played a major political and social role but whose governments, even in the context of the Islamic resurgence, cannot be considered revolutionary. It is helpful to consider one special type of case in this category where the existing government was in some way established by an Islamically oriented revolution that took place some time before the current resurgence. Good examples of this are Saudi Arabia and Morocco. Only a brief account of Saudi Arabia can be given here, but the implications of the Saudi experience are important for understanding our topic.

Saudi Arabia

Saudi Arabia is clearly identifiable as an Islamic sociopolitical order. The current state was, in fact, created by what was an Islamic revolution at the beginning of the twentieth century. The development of this "fundamentalist Islamic state" is an important part of the modern history of Islam.[3] Saudi Arabia in the twentieth century is the third in a series of states created in the Arabian Peninsula by the combination of Saud family leadership skills with Islamic fundamentalism. The particular Islamic inspiration was defined originally by Muhammad ibn Abd al-Wahhab in the eighteenth century and has continued as the Wahhabi tradition of puritanical Islam in Arabia since then.

A young prince of the Saud family acted to reestablish Saudi fortunes after the family had been defeated at the end of the nineteenth century. This prince was Abd al-Aziz "Ibn Saud," who began a long career of conquest and state building that resulted in the establishment of the twentieth-century Kingdom of Saudi Arabia. This represented a major political and social revolution in the Arabian Peninsula. In his efforts to establish Saudi rule, Abd al-Aziz "reaffirmed Wahhabism as a state ideology and established religiously inspired institutions to promote and implement his policies. . . . The challenge that confronted Ibn Saud and his successors was to continue the use of Wahhabism as a state ideology while developing a modern state as well" (al-Yassini, 1985: 57).

Saudi Arabia became an important representative of an Islamically committed state in the years before the Islamic resurgence of the 1970s and 1980s. By the 1960s, however, Saudi Arabia had come to represent a conservative opposition to the revolutionary Arab socialism of that time and ceased to be, in any significant way, a revolutionary regime. It had become an established or routinized revolution that was now a conservative force.

In this context, although Saudi Arabia has played a role in supporting many of the nonrevolutionary aspects of the recent resurgence, the revolutionary dimensions of the resurgence are a challenge to the Saudis. The regime's legitimacy and its fundamental worldview remains Wahhabism, but it is important to note that the articulation of Wahhabi principles has not changed significantly since the writings of Ibn Abd al-Wahhab. As a result, the "continuous use of Wahhabi ideology without seriously modifying its content to suit reality has contributed to the weakening of the regime's legitimacy" (al-Yassini, 1985: 130).

As long as the challenges in intellectual terms were from Western-based ideologies like Arab socialism, standing firm on the unadapted principles of Wahhabism was a relatively sound position. However, the Islamic resurgence has brought forward new modes of affirming Islamic authenticity that also recognize the current world conditions. In this sense, the Islamic resurgence provides the basis for a revolutionary challenge to the old Islamic revolutionary movement in Saudi Arabia. The real strength of this Islamic challenge to the Saudi government can be debated, but the takeover of the Grand Mosque in Mecca in 1979 shows that it exists.

Other Old Islamic States

There are a number of states in the Islamic world whose legitimacy is based, at least to some degree, on a long-standing identification with Islam. We might mention the Gulf states and Oman in this, as well as the monarchy in Morocco (which, similar to the Saudi kingdom is based on a revolutionary movement that is now conservative). In these cases there is a tendency to maintain the Islamic identity in its old form and thus open the way for a challenge to come from the new forms of Islamic assertion that have been developed as a result of the Islamic resurgence. To the extent that the resurgence is a reaffirmation of Islam in nonrevolutionary forms, it provides support for these regimes. However, revolutionary resurgence Islam may threaten the very basis of the regime in a way that modernist secularism could not.

In our second category, then, we see the Islamic resurgence to have different types of impacts. It can be regime-supporting in countries where Islam has long played a major political and social role. However, it can also be regime-threatening if it challenges a conservative position by providing a new vehicle for affirmation of Islam that is both adapted to contemporary conditions and clearly Islamic.

ISLAM IN CONFRONTATION

Our third general category of situations for analyzing the relationship between the Islamic resurgence and revolution includes countries where Islam is in some way in competition or confrontation. This confrontation is with forces or elements that are in some way non-Islamic as opposed to the possible competition between modes of Islam that we have suggested may be part of the scene in places like Saudi Arabia.

In this aspect of the subject, we continue to assess the extent to which the Islamic resurgence is revolutionary. In the third category of situations we will examine two patterns: where Muslims are a minority seeking secession, autonomy, or special rights and where they are a majority seeking to strengthen the role of their religion among the faithful or throughout society as a whole.

Muslims As Minorities

Efforts of Muslims to achieve a greater role in self-governance relate to a wide range of goals. However, prior to assessing the "revolutionary" character of these goals, it should be noted that in many cases these movements are both religious and ethnic in character, that is, they arise among groups that differ from the dominant powers in the society in both their Islamic and their racial-ethnic identities. Examples would include the "Moros" of the southern Philippines, Malay Muslims of southern Thailand, Arakanese of Burma, Palestinians in Israel and the Occupied Territories, and tribal elements in the northern parts of West African states. In these cases Islam may provide part of the ideological basis for action, but ethnicity is also a driving force.

The Asian and African examples noted above are illustrative of long-standing conflicts, although exacerbated by the end of colonialism and development of better communications. The former factor lifted European controls over internal disputes and the latter brought the dominant and minority groups into closer contact. It can also be argued that the worldwide Islamic resurgence has given added religious impetus to these movements. First, it has reinforced religious pride and a sense of identity among these peoples. They see themselves as part of an expanding and revitalized Islamic community. Secondly, other countries have become increasingly involved in trying to influence these peoples. In particular, Iran and Libya have been accused of attempting to aid secessionist elements in Southeast Asia and Africa through monetary, intellectual, and even military support.[4] Finally, intellectual currents from the outside have provided much of the ideological foundation for these movements. No longer do we witness isolated, somewhat atavistic rhetoric almost entirely based upon parochial ideas. Now self-governance demands have become peppered with the concepts of well-known contemporary Islamic spokespersons, many of them radical.

The question that now arises is, To what extent are these movements revolutionary in nature? Obviously, we are assessing cases that vary markedly in terms of goals and actions even within a given example. However, we can rather arbitrarily divide movements into three types, two of which do not appear to be revolutionary in nature. The first would include cases where Muslims seek autonomy or independence from the dominant polity in order to follow basically traditional religious or religioethnic goals. These would include efforts by the Arakanese in Burma and sectors of the Muslim populations of the Philippines and Thailand. In these cases neither the rhetoric nor the programs of the leadership can be described as demands for fundamental changes in the values and social fabric of those who are to be "liberated." These people primarily seek independence or greater autonomy from the central authorities but wish to retain or rebuild traditional authority and values.

A second and somewhat overlapping type involves efforts to obtain the right to practice Islam and particularly to live within a juridical system based upon the Sharia. The goal is not independence but recognition of the special needs of the Muslim community. Such requests and demands have been made by Muslims in India, the Philippines, Thailand, and parts of West Africa. While such demands may appear to be "revolutionary" to the dominant elements of the society, they are not perceived as such by those proclaiming the need to institutionalize their Islamic identity and do not normally call for other types of fundamental changes.

Finally, there are both movements and leaders within these Muslim groups who either support revolutionary goals or ally themselves with organizations or causes generally recognized as revolutionary in nature. In the latter case, sectors of Muslim separatist organizations in both the Philippines and Thailand have allied themselves with the local communists. Generally, this can be defined as a marriage of convenience against the government and, as in Iran, the relationship would probably deteriorate quickly if success were to be achieved in ousting those in power. It should also be noted that the majority of Muslim leaders in these communities do not accept the basic premises of Marxism-Leninism. Of course, in the Soviet Union, this marriage of communism and Islam is anything but revolutionary and the Soviet system is often buttressed by Islamic religious teachings and leaders (see Voll, 1987: 125–151).

Of greater interest to us here are those cases where Islamic movements proclaim goals that include fundamental changes in values, power, and structure within an Islamic context. Among secessionist movements this pattern is best exemplified by the so-called "fundamentalists" now apparently increasing in numbers among the Palestinians in Israel and the Occupied Territories. Although there have been earlier signs of Islamic influence on the politics of the area, the most recent developments arose at the end of the 1970s. Factors responsible were the rise of the Likud party's role in Israeli politics and growing frustration with the peace process, the seeming success of Muslim groups in forcing the Israelis out of much of Lebanon, the rise of Khomeini's Iran, and, according to one commentator, reactions to growing Marxist influence on Gaza and the West Bank and possible support from both Israel and Jordan in an effort to counter the PLO (Sahliyeh, 1988: 88–100). While allied to the secularist PLO, many of the representatives of this section of the Palestinians appear to reflect the views of religious radicals such as Qutb, Hasan al-Banna, and Mawdudi. Given the dominance of the more secularist PLO among Palestinians and the relatively recent nature of the fundamentalist strength in Gaza and the West Bank, it is difficult to see religious leadership gaining an upper hand sufficient to move the Palestinians in a different direction from that proposed by the PLO. At the same time there are strong Islamic roots in Palestinian nationalism and Yasir Arafat has employed the unity of Muslims and religious imperative to free Jerusalem and Palestine to reinforce his position. Thus, on his 1978 pilgrimage to Mecca he proclaimed "I declare from here, from the land of the Prophet, from the cradle of Islam, the opening of the gate of holy war for the liberation of Palestine and the recovery of Jerusalem."[5] Without overemphasizing its intellectual content, the extranational religious currents of this movement are, perhaps, almost unique among secessionist Islamic cases. Most other groups have been more isolated geographically and less influenced by external radical Islamic thinkers, and their causes have been more parochial in goals.

Confrontation in Muslim Societies

The second aspect of the resurgence in which Islam is in competition or confrontation is within states where Muslims are the formal majority. The elements with which the forces of the resurgence see themselves in conflict may be secularism or a weakening of belief and practice (necessitating the need to reinstill the faith into the society) or false or un-Islamic elements (necessitating better understanding of the faith and cleansing the society). Obviously, these perceptions and goals may overlap. There are numerous examples of these patterns. In Indonesia, Muslim activists see themselves in confrontation with a government proposing what they believe are un-Islamic policies. In Egypt, we see Muslim spokespersons pressing for an increased role for Islam in the society and, certainly during the Sadat years, questioning the religious credentials of the secular leadership. Muslims in Malaysia, while they form a slight majority, see themselves in competition with a non-Muslim minority in a modernizing society. In Lebanon, another bare majority of Muslims war among themselves and with the Christians over religious and political issues. In Sudan, the government of al-Numayri attempted to maintain itself by a formal implementation of its version of the Sharia. In Tunisia, fundamentalists disagreed with what they perceived to be President Bourguiba's break with Islamic traditions and law. Finally, in Syria, conflicts between the Muslim Brotherhood and President Hafiz al-Asad's government led to large-scale bloodshed.

We cannot analyze each of these cases in detail. Rather, we will focus on elements of this aspect of the resurgence in terms of their revolutionary programs and potential. It should be underscored initially that most advocates of the Islamic resurgence have not demanded those immediate and fundamental changes in society that could be readily defined as revolutionary. The core to this movement throughout the Islamic world has been to encourage Muslims to develop a deeper understanding of, and commitment to, their religion. It seeks to reinforce the religious identity of the populace and to provide an Islamic alternative to the Western-secular challenge that has arisen with the confrontation with modernization and intrusion of Western values. The representatives of this sector of the resurgence include many of the *dahwah* organizations of Afro-Asia, groups such as the Muhammadijah in Indonesia, important less radical elements in the contemporary Muslim Brotherhoods in the Middle East and North Africa, and government-led efforts to strengthen Islam in the Sudan under Numayri, Pakistan under Zia, and Malaysia's Islamization attempts.

Yet while these groups and individuals do not appear to be inherently revolutionary in their demands and programs, they do uphold one position that lies at the heart of the issue of the revolutionary potential of the Islamic resurgence. In almost every case, at the foundation of each movement has been a demand that the state and society should return to the Sharia, the God-given "path."[6] General agreement exists that the ultimate aim of all Muslims should be to recognize God's sovereignty on earth, to find in the practice of early Muslims a more authentically Islamic experience, and to end the separation of religion and the state (see Dekmejian, 1988: 10–12). There are obvious variations in the specifics of how this is to be done, what such an Islamic society would look like, and the speed with which it should be instituted. However, relevant to the issue before us is the extent to which the establishment of such a society would be revolutionary in terms of fundamentally changing the values, myths, politics, and economy of any system developed under the Sharia. The difficulty of answering this question is due to the previously noted variations in interpretation and the often vague nature of statements by revivalist advocates as to what this new society would look like. At one level there is not very much that is revolutionary among those who argue that the resurgence means that Muslims should understand and practice their religion better and who interpret the core of

Islam in terms of social justice and equity.[7] At the other extreme of the spectrum are those who demand the end of the secular state, immediate establishment of rule under the Sharia, and the abandonment of the Western-influenced values of the present society. In various forms, this is the Islamic revolution as envisioned by men such as Ayatollah Khomeini, Sayyid Qutb, and Abul Ala Mawdudi (see Esposito, 1983). While noting these differences, it is also important to underscore the point that within any modern secular state a demand for a substantial "return" to a system based on the Sharia may be inherently revolutionary. It would seemingly necessitate fundamental changes in contemporary values, the need for a different legal system and religious leaders capable of interpreting the law, and (according to some, like Khurshid Ahmad) a new economic framework. However, again it must be underscored that those proclaiming the desirability of a state following the "path" are often unclear as to what it would ultimately mean in reality.

If the revitalization of Islam has its advocates for gradual change or, as in the cases of Pakistan and Malaysia, even the reinforcement of state power in the name of Islam, it also has its more explicit revolutionaries. We can divide this group into two types: the "fathers" of the revival and more contemporary leaders and organizations. Whenever the intellectual roots of the present Islamic revival are explored, the names of four men normally come to the fore, Sayyid Qutb, Abul Ala Mawdudi, Hasan al-Banna, and Ali Shariati. These men are often referred to by both the gradualists and the revolutionaries, as well as by contemporary Islamic Studies departments throughout the world, which often include their writings in their curricula. Thus Qutb's ideas reach from the Nigerian resurgence in West Africa (see Clarke and Linden, 1984: 100-102) to the reading list in Islamic Studies departments in Malaysia. Each of these men preached doctrines that have revolutionary connotations—or at least have been perceived as such by many of their followers and government authorities.

While the ideas proposed by these men differed in specifics, there is a bedrock of agreement in several critical areas. They viewed the political and social systems derived from the West as inappropriate and sought Islamic alternatives. In order to cast off the unacceptable accretions of Western thought and practice, they argued that it was necessary to return to the Koran and to Muhammad as the great example. The new Islamic society must be based on certain eternal verities, acknowledging the sovereignty of God and the unity of state and society under that sovereignty. They presented to Muslims the imperative of struggling to achieve this vision, and radical interpretations of that imperative have provided an intellectual foundation to modern revolutionary Islam.[8]

In the past two decades we have also seen a plethora of small revolutionary organizations—at times formed around a particular personality—arise in the name of Islam. While their specific goals may differ, they have a number of elements in common. They are prepared to employ violence to achieve their ends, including bombings, assassination, and kidnapping. They seek immediate change in the political and social structure. They appear to consider that many of those in authority do not lead acceptable religious lives and are, in fact, apostates. In sum, they seem to accept the view that jihad, in terms of violent struggle to protect and expand Islam, is the "sixth pillar" of Islam. The list of such organizations is long and includes al-Tahrir al-Islami (which fought Egyptian security forces in 1974), al-Jihad (responsible for the murder of Sadat), and al-Takfir wa-al-Hijrah (all from Egypt); Kommando Jihad and the Islamic Youth Movement (Indonesian organizations accused of an airline hijacking and bombing shopping centers); various groups in Lebanon such as Islamic Jihad, the Islamic Liberation Movement, and Hizbullah; Maitatsine, and his followers in West Africa (those responsible for the seizure of the Meccan sanctuary in Saudi Arabia in 1979); and a variety of small Syrian militant groups.[9]

There have been many cases where this type of organization has employed violent means in an effort to overthrow regimes or murder major leaders; and to the extent that this may destabilize the government, they can lay the groundwork for revolution. However, generally these groups have lacked the organization and broad base necessary for successful revolution. Often their programs and goals have been obscure and their membership and leadership necessarily unknown; and due to internal fragmentation and external pressure, their period of existence has often been relatively short. Rarely have they been able to develop a mass base. It can even be argued that in many cases these groups have provided governments with the tools of even greater control. Thus, the Malaysian authorities have employed radical movements as a means of warning the populace of "deviant" religious behavior, and the Indonesian and several Middle Eastern governments have used the specter of radical Islam to clamp down on a broad range of critics of the regime.

To sum up our analysis of this third pattern of Islamic resurgence, it would not be accurate to describe most activists within these movements, either among majority or minority communities, as revolutionary in program, goals, or actions. At the same time there is a strong, radical intellectual foundation, as well as contemporary groups and their leaders who can be defined as revolutionary, particularly among the small radical elements who seek the immediate formation of an Islamic society and are prepared to utilize violence to achieve their goals. However, at this point, most of them are too small, fragmented, and endangered by government suppression to have much hope for immediate success. This does not mean that the potential does not exist for fundamental change in the future as alienation and frustration continue at high levels.

CONCLUSION

The general issue of the relationship between the Islamic resurgence and revolution is both broad and complex. It is clear that not every experience of contemporary Islamic resurgence is revolutionary. In certain cases, the resurgence may be a support for existing political systems or may provide an avenue for expression of opposition that can be fulfilled in a relatively stable, reformist program.

It is clear, however, that the Islamic resurgence is a context for significant revolutionary activity. In our analysis we have looked at three types of situations to explore the potential revolutionary impact of the resurgence. In two major cases, Iran and Libya, the resurgence and revolution have become joined. The result is a new style of Third World revolution different from earlier nationalist or radical socialist models. This new revolutionary style can be a challenge to states in our second category, those where there has been a long-standing identification with Islam. Thus, the resurgence in these states can be both state-supporting and revolutionary. In our third category of countries, where Islam is in a competitive position, we can see this same duality. The Islamic resurgence can be, but is not necessarily, revolutionary.

The Islamic resurgence provides a variety of cases and is not a single, monolithic movement. It presents a challenge to analysts and policymakers because it represents a joining of traditional and contemporary issues in ways that are new. As a potential revolutionary force, it may reflect a new mode of action in the world.

NOTES

1. A comprehensive presentation of this factor-by-factor analysis can be found in Munson (1988).

2. See Arjomand (1986: 395). For the views of Zonis, see Wright (1986: 31) and his comments in the television special *The Sword of Islam*.

3. Useful discussions that help to point up the Islamic and "revolutionary" character of the early Saudi state are al-Yassini (1985), Safran (1985), and Edens (1984).

4. There is extensive literature on Libyan attempts to influence secessionist movements in the Philippines and Africa, at times clandestinely and, as in the Philippine case, at times through diplomatic channels. See Noble. (1987: 97–124), Gowing and McAmis (1974), and Madele (1986: 282–314).

5. Quoted in Johnson (1982: 75). This book has a very interesting section on the Islamic content of the Palestinian nationalist movement.

6. In the words of one observer, "The Shariah is the core of the world-view of Islam. It is the body of knowledge which provides the Muslim civilization with its unchanging bearings as well as its major means of

adjusting to change. Theoretically, the Shariah covers all aspect of human life; personal, social, political and intellectual. Practically, it gives meaning and content to behavior to Muslims in their earthly endeavors. Normally, the Shariah is described as 'Islamic Law.' But the boundaries of the Shariah extend beyond the limited horizons of law" (Sardar, 1985: 106).

7. This is one element in the views of men like Anwar Ibrahim, former head of the *dahwah* movement Ang Katen Belia Islam Malaysia (ABIM) and now minister of education in Malaysia.

8. For a good summation of the thoughts of these men see Esposito (1983: 67–68, 191–214).

9. There has been a great deal written on these groups, much of it journalistic or emotional. Among recent discussions of these groups, the more extensive and analytical include Wright (1986), Dekmejian (1985), Taheri (1987), Dietl (1984), Jansen (1986), and Dawisha (1986).

REFERENCES

Anderson, Lisa (1986a). *The State and Social Transformation in Tunisia and Libya, 1830–1980*. Princeton: Princeton University Press.
——— (1986b) "Qadhdafi and His Opposition." *Middle East Journal* 40, no. 2 (Spring): 225–237.
Arjomand, Said (1986). "Iran's Islamic Revolution in Comparative Perspective." *World Politics* 38, no. 3 (April): 383–414.
Clarke, Peter, and Ian Linden (1984). *Islam in Modern Nigeria*. Mainz: Kaiser-Gruenwald.
Dawisha, Adeed (1986). *The Arab Radicals*. New York: Council on Foreign Relations.
Dekmejian, Richard H. (1985). *Islam in Revolution*. Syracuse: Syracuse University Press.
——— (1988). "Islamic Revival Catalysts, Categories, and Consequences." in Shireen Hunter, ed., *The Politics of Islamic Revivalism*. Bloomington: Indiana University Press.
Dietl, Wilhelm (1984). *Holy War*. New York: Macmillan.
Edens, David G. (1974). "The Anatomy of the Saudi Revolution." *International Journal of Middle East Studies* 5, No. 1 (January): 50–64.
Esposito, John, ed. (1983). *Voices of Resurgent Islam*. New York: Oxford University Press.
Gowing, Peter, and Robert McAmis (1974). *The Muslim Filipinos: Their History, Society, and Contemporary Problems*. Manila: Solidaridad.
Huntington, Samuel (1968). *Political Order in Changing Societies*. New Haven: Yale University Press.
Jansen, Johannes (1986). *The Neglected Duty*. New York: Macmillan.
Johnson, Nels (1982). *Islam and the Politics of Meaning in Palestine Nationalism*. London: KPI.
Madele, Nagasursa (1986). "The Resurgence of Islam and Nationalism in the Philippines." In T. Abdullah and S. Siddique, eds., *Islam and Society in Southeast Asia*. Singapore: Institute of Southeast Asian Studies.

Momayezi, Nasser (1986). "Economic Correlates of Political Violence: The Case of Iran." *Middle East Journal* 40, no. 1 (Winter): 68–76.

Munson, Henry, Jr. (1988). *Islam and Revolution in the Middle East*. New Haven: Yale University Press.

Noble, L. (1987). "The Philippines: Autonomy for the Muslims." In John Esposito, ed., *Islam in Asia*. New York: Oxford University Press.

Roumani, Jacques (1983). "From Republic to Jamahiriya: Libya's Search for Political Community." *Middle East Journal* 37, no. 2 (Spring): 154–163.

Safran, Nadav (1985). *Saudi Arabia: The Ceaseless Quest for Security*. Cambridge, MA: Belknap.

Sahliyeh, Emile (1988). "The West Bank and the Gaza Strip." In Shireen Hunter, ed., *The Politics of Islamic Revivalism*. Bloomington: University of Indiana Press.

Sardar, Ziauddin (1985). *Islamic Futures*. London: Mansell.

Taheri, Amir (1987). *Holy Terror*. London: Hutchinson.

Voll, John (1987). "Soviet Central Asia and China." In John Esposito, ed., *Islam in Asia*. New York: Oxford University Press.

Wright, Robin (1986). *Sacred Rage*. New York: Simon and Schuster.

al-Yassini, Ayman (1985). *Religion and State in the Kingdom of Saudi Arabia*. Boulder: Westview.

CHAPTER SIX

Revolutionary Organization in the Countryside: Peru

HENRY DIETZ

More than any other revolutionary regime or movement, Peru's Sendero Luminoso is shaped by internal forces unique to the Peruvian rural environment. This case of an atypical, dogmatic movement based primarily on Maoist principles, threatens to emerge as a bona fide threat to the existing government. Sendero's uniqueness if self-evident; its proclamations of independence and violence and its disdain for any process separate it from every other movement inside and outside Peru.

*This said, Sendero Luminoso remains identifiably comparable to other rural- or peasant-based revolutionary movements. Both the economic and social preconditions for revolutions discussed by Mason and the characteristic of "emulation" of the Chinese model developed by Foltz resonate the growth of the Sendero movement in Peru. As in the eclecticism of resurgent Islam (discussed in Chapter 5), Sendero Luminoso synthesizes the modernizing Maoist tenets of Marxism-Leninism with the traditional image of a mythic Indian past. The ruthless pursuit of revolutionary objectives with tight organizational discipline give Sendero Luminoso increasing opportunities to effect changes amid the disintegrating legitimacy of the Peruvian government.—*THE EDITORS

T he question why one revolutionary movement achieves some or complete success while another one dies stillborn or is smothered early on has long fascinated social scientists (not to mention practitioners of revolution).[1] The pragmatic limitations that constrain inquiry into the topic are severe: revolutionary movements are, after all, relatively rare occurrences anywhere in the world; many of them are clandestine or are led by elites who are inaccessible; and the great majority of them disappear after only a short period of time.

I examine a specific revolutionary movement in Latin America, Sendero Luminoso in Peru, which has had, by almost any standard except its own, quite remarkable success. *Except its own* is appropriate here because Sendero's own goal is the forcible overthrow of the political, economic, and social systems that exist in Peru today and the imposition of a vaguely defined Maoist-precapitalist society that has recently been labeled a República

Popular de Nueva Democracia (New Democratic Popular Republic). Such a goal has not been achieved, and the probabilities are that it will not. Yet Sendero has forced Peru's civilian and military elites to focus much of their attention and resources on repressing the movement; caused violence and bloodshed sufficient to bring about at least twelve to fifteen thousand deaths since 1980; at least for certain periods of time forcibly occupied certain areas of Peru's poverty-stricken rural southern highlands; and carried its fight into the capital of Lima, where it has caused extreme concern and unrest and been able to penetrate into low-income areas and universities in the city.

Given these achievements, the question that rather naturally occurs to its adherents and its opponents equally is to what extent Sendero's successes are idiosyncratic and sui generis and to what extent they depend on general circumstances that might bring about a Sendero-like movement in another country. Such a question cannot lead to a solid prediction or anything like one but at best a highly conditional and probabilistic estimate of what factors appear to have been most important in allowing Sendero to emerge in Peru in the first place. In order to identify such factors, I have divided the discussion into eight parts or questions.

1. What is the history of Sendero Luminoso? What might it have in common with other movements of the past?
2. What social, economic, and political conditions have been especially conducive to the appearance of Sendero? What level of legitimacy did previous regimes have?
3. What is the ideology of Sendero?
4. What is the nature of leadership within Sendero? Does a single leader dominate, or is leadership diffuse? Is the leadership issue-oriented or ideologically driven?
5. How is Sendero organized? What are its sources of recruitment?
6. What global influences and connections are linked to Sendero?
7. What has been the response of the government to Sendero? What options have been tried and have failed? What has not been tried?
8. What are Sendero's goals and what are the chances that they will be achieved?

Such questions will provide a framework for much of the descriptive material that follows. However, to go beyond this descriptive material and to offer some analytic conclusions of more generalizable utility, it will be useful here to put forth a number of propositions and hypotheses to be tested using Sendero as a case study and also to serve as guideposts for the analysis of Sendero as a revolutionary movement.

Palmer's (1985) claim that Sendero is largely a sui generis movement has validity, as we shall see. But there are also certain features of the movement and its interactions with the Peruvian state that can be generalized and offered as testable propositions and hypotheses. For example, many revolutionary movements have tried to take advantage of existing, massive social inequalities in the form of maldistributions in wealth, income, land, or power (see, e.g., Midlarsky, 1988; Muller, Seligson, and Fu, 1989; Midlarsky, 1989). If such inequalities are exacerbated by ethnic or racial divisions, political violence may become more likely or intense. Such hypotheses are eminently testable in the case of Sendero, as we shall see, and indeed have served as a springboard for research. But poverty and inequality are the norms in much of the Third World, and revolutionary movements such as Sendero Luminoso are by no means common. Thus, the hypothesis might be amended to state that these are necessary-but-not-sufficient conditions for revolutionary movements to occur, which immediately calls for some delineation of factors that can short-circuit revolutionary tendencies as well as factors that can catalyze inequality so as to produce revolutionary violence.

Mason (see Chapter 3) and others have noted that sociopolitical and economic inequities can be held in equilibrium by a series of mechanisms such as clientelism and that these mechanisms can produce a durable equilibrium. But social and economic dislocation and disruption can shake such equilibria and produce large numbers of people who become desperate for economic security or who might seek revenge for their difficulties. The circumstances under which Sendero Luminoso emerged in Peru will allow at least a partial testing of these and related ideas.

Finally, the role of ideology in any revolutionary movement has long been considered a critical issue (see, e.g., Leites and Wolf, 1970; Cordes, Jenkins, and Kellen, 1985). Virtually all revolutionary movements stress ideology in one form or another, but just how ideology can act as a binder for the group remains unsettled. A rigid and doctrinaire belief system can, for example, help to create feelings of closeness and solidarity but can simultaneously act as impediment for outsiders who may neither understand, nor be attracted to, what might be obscure or incomprehensible. Sendero Luminoso's ideology is a key component for the movement; but as will be pointed out, its rigidity and innate foreignness has apparently acted to dissuade large numbers from joining the group.

Other propositions and hypotheses will emerge as the essay unfolds, and they will be noted and explored in the conclusion. Before proceeding, one further word needs to be stressed. Anyone who sets out to discuss Sendero Luminoso will be hamstrung by a lack of new or original information. Sendero Luminoso is among the world's most closed movements: it publishes virtually nothing of its own, it grants no interviews, it seldom claims credit for its activities, and its members and adherents are sworn to secrecy. Much of what has been written therefore becomes repetitious, since new data about the movement and its operations are not forthcoming. I therefore distill a good deal of what exists in a summary fashion and, rather than repeating what is available elsewhere, try to provide bibliographic information as I concern myself more with the questions outlined above.

HISTORY OF SENDERO LUMINOSO

The history of Sendero has been recited many times, and there is no reason to go into it in great detail (e.g., Palmer, 1985; McClintock, 1983; Bennett, 1984; Degregori, 1987; Sanders, 1984; Harding, 1987; Mercado 1985; Favre, 1984; Anderson, 1983). Briefly stated, Sendero first appeared as a revolutionary movement in 1980. Its appearance coincided with the restoration of democracy in Peru, which had been under military rule since 1968. Presidential elections in 1980 put Fernando Belaúnde Terry in power, the man who had been ousted by the military in 1968. Sendero adherents burned ballot boxes in the peasant market town of Chuschi in the department (state) of Ayacucho and at the same time hanged dogs from lampposts in Lima and in the city of Ayacucho. These obscure acts, however, were simply the first public manifestations of a group that had been formed almost ten years earlier and that had been maturing and biding its time.

Sendero was founded under the leadership of Abimaél Guzmán, who was born in 1934 into a middle-class family in Arequipa. Guzmán earned two degrees in philosophy and in law, traveled to the People's Republic of China during the Great Cultural Revolution (Sanders, 1984), and in 1961 came to the National University of Saint Christopher of Huamanga in Ayacucho (reopened in 1959 after its closure in 1886), where he had been appointed as an instructor in philosophy. Despite his young age, reports indicate that he determined early on that he would initiate a radical movement in the area through the university. In 1964 a Maoist faction in Peru split from the Peruvian Communist party and formed a group called Bandera Roja (Red Flag), which was headed in Ayacucho by Guzmán. In 1970 Guzmán became disillusioned with what he saw as purely rhetorical obedience to the need for a people's revolutionary army and an armed struggle. Guzmán's Ayacucho group moved away from Bandera Roja and, taking a line from José Carlos Mariátegui (Peru's leading Marxist thinker of the 1920s), published a magazine with the subtitle *By the Shining Path of Comrade José Carlos Mariátegui*, whence the name Sendero Luminoso ("Shining Path"—the name the group gives itself today is, however, still the "Peruvian Communist party.") The group controlled student and faculty organizations at the University of Huamanga by the early 1970s; and in 1974 Guzmán, who by that time called himself Comrado Gonzalo, went underground and has not been seen since (Sanders, 1984; Pareja Pflucker, 1980).

The initial bizarre appearance of Sendero in 1980 gave way quickly to more serious and systematic activities, as the group began to bomb public buildings and assassinate local leaders (peasant as well as civil) in and around

Ayacucho. A large-scale and spectacularly successful jailbreak in 1982 in Ayacucho was coupled with a significant escalation of violence in the rural areas of Ayacucho as well as in Lima. By January of 1983 a state of emergency had been declared in five provinces in Ayacucho, and the military had moved in to try to put down the insurgence forcibly. And while the military was able to claim that it slowly regained control over regions that had been dominated by Sendero, it did so only at extreme cost, much bloodshed, and under much international scrutiny and criticism, especially from human rights groups such as Amnesty International and America's Watch. When in 1985 presidential elections were held and Alan García of the Popular American Revolutionary Alliance (APRA), Peru's 1930s radical party, won a landslide victory, some observers thought that Sendero Luminoso might either scale down or halt its activities for a trial honeymoon. However, no such break occurred; Sendero made it immediately clear that it would play no favorites and that it had as little use for García as it had had for Belaúnde (González, 1986: 36). Although García began his term by naming a peace commission,[2] violence and bloodshed continued unabated, and both civilian and military leaders showed their continuing frustration in a number of ways. The most spectacular was the February 1986 armed uprising in three prisons led by incarcerated Sendero suspects and guerrillas. The military was called in, and at least two hundred prisoners were killed. As Harding (1987) noted, "That a civilian regime committed to opening a dialogue with the insurgents when it took office in July 1985 should resort to such a drastic final solution after less than a year in office says much for the obstinacy of Sendero Luminoso, and underlies the overwhelming pressures under which President Alán García had been forced to operate" (p. 203).

By 1990 Sendero Luminoso and the Peruvian government seemed to have reached something of an impasse. Sendero was, from virtually all accounts, never going to be able to succeed in its ultimate goal of destroying the social, economic and political fabric of Peru; at the same time, military responses by and of themselves were not going to uproot Sendero. The movement could still carry off sizable operations both in the rural areas and in Lima, thereby saying a good deal about its military abilities, as well as the degree of at least passive acceptance among certain elements of Peru's populace (Harding, 1987). The movement had also been able to establish itself in different parts of Peru, especially Puno, La Libertad, Cerro de Pasco, and Junin, and to continue with its bombings, citywide blackouts, and assassinations in Lima. Yet it could not mount (or at least avoided trying to mount) large-scale operations against the Peruvian military, and there were signs that it had been unable to maintain what it once had claimed as "liberated zones" in the rural Ayacucho and Apurimac areas.

Insofar as voting is concerned, Ayacucho residents showed in 1983 that a "substantial reservoir of support (or fear) remains in the core areas of

Sendero's historic activity" (Palmer, 1985: 71). For example, in 1983 municipal elections could not be held in four rural Ayacucho provinces (Cangallo, Victor Fajardo, La Mar, and Huanta). In both 1985 and 1986, however, elections were held throughout all provinces of Ayacucho. In the 1983 municipal elections 56 percent of the votes cast in the province of Huamanga were blank or nonvalid, and over 50 percent of the population abstained. In fairly strong contrast, however, in the 1985 presidential contest in Huamanga, 28 percent of the votes were either blank or spoiled, and 89 percent of the registered voters cast a vote (91 percent voted nationally). In 1986's municipal election, 36 percent of the Huamanga votes were blank or spoiled and 31 percent of the voters abstained (20 percent abstained nationally) (Tuesta, 1987). Finally, in the 1989 municipal elections, unofficial reports claimed that the abstention rate in the city of Ayacucho approached 60 percent, as Sendero made a major effort throughout the Sierra region of Peru to delegitimize the electoral process through intimidation. Nationally, this effort appeared to have failed, as voters turned out in large numbers; but threats took their toll in specific regions and cities where Sendero's power has become clearly viable. Voters in Peru are thus still willing to vote despite considerable pressure form Sendero, which has repeatedly stated that voting is a bourgeois meaningless game and has urged the populace not to participate in elections.

THE SOCIOECONOMIC CONTEXT
OF SENDERO LUMINOSO

Much attention has bee paid to the fact that Ayacucho was the birthplace of Sendero Luminoso (McClintock, 1984; Palmer, 1985; Taylor, 1983; Degregori, 1987); and numerous observers have correlated the extreme poverty of Ayacucho with the emergence of Sendero Luminoso. The facts concerning Ayacucho do not admit argument; its rural areas comprise one of the poorest and most backward subregions of Latin America by virtually all indicators that deal with the physical quality of life (R. González, 1982: 61, 70–71). Despite its beginnings in the colonial period (founded in 1540) as a major trading and administrative center, Ayacucho (meaning "the corner of the dead" in Quechua) has been for centuries part of the core of the peasant Indian highland region that embraces Ayacucho, Apurimac, Cuzco, Huancavelica, and Puno. Degregori (1987) also points out that historically Ayacucho was at the center of cultural clashes and intricate, ethnic, intraregional conflicts during Incan and postconquest times (pp. 18–19). Yet its isolation from the dominant coastal and mestizo culture of Lima left Ayacucho marginalized over the years until by the beginning of the twentieth century it had become one of the poorest regions in Peru and indeed in the Western Hemisphere. Even by the early 1960s Ayacucho was almost entirely rural (90 percent) and almost completely Quechua-speaking. It suffered under conditions that are usually reserved for describing Fourth World nations (McClintock, 1984; Palmer, 1985; Degregori, 1987, esp. 9–18); and its populace had been either ignored, cheated, or neglected over the years. Reform schemes formulated by various administrations in Lima had seldom brought major beneficial consequences for the region (see Díaz Martínez, 1969 for a highly personal account of Ayacucho in the 1960s; also, e.g., Harding, 1987).

Palmer (1985) and others have noted that Ayacucho and its surrounding rural areas, along with Peru in general, underwent profound changes during the decades of the 1960s and 1970s, including infrastructural improvements throughout Ayacucho, the appearance of many outside developmental experts, and (perhaps most importantly) the reopening of the National University of Huamanga. The university had been closed for almost a century. When it reopened in 1959, it was with the deliberate intention of bringing about change in and for the region (see Romero Pintado, 1961; Millones, 1983). As Harding (1987: 182) describes it, "The allotted role of the university was to act as a powerhouse and laboratory of controlled social change and economic development. [The university's] academic programmes had a markedly vocational bias . . . [in] subjects relevant to a poor rural area which had become the focus of a series of government-sponsored, foreign-funded projects."

Yet such assistance and investment appear, ironically, to have been a major catalyst to Sendero's thinking. Díaz Martínez' 1969 book *Ayacucho: Hambre y esperanza* (Ayacucho: Hunger and hope) is, as Harding (1987) notes, a "sustained critique of the developmentalist approach to the region's problems" (p. 183). Díaz Martínez argues that the pilot projects and schemes never benefited the peasant population of Ayacucho. On the contrary, their technological and financial requirements "completed the integration of the region into the urban-dominated, dependent capitalist economy of Peru, . . . destroying what remained of the self-sufficiency ways of life of the traditional communities, leaving them at the mercy of market forces" (Harding, 1987: 183). According to Díaz Martínez, peasants should have had land from the large and decaying haciendas given to them and then should have been left to solve their own problems in their own ways. Anything that would interfere with this rather vague notion of a peasant utopia would have to be opposed, with force if necessary.

Ayacucho itself is historically the site of millenarian and chiliastic movements of various descriptions. While it is impossible to say how much such a tradition has played in the ability of Sendero Luminoso to integrate itself with the peasantry (i.e., to separate such a tradition from the fear that Sendero is clearly able to instill among the populace), such a historical context must at least be noted (see, e.g., Millones, 1988).

That Ayacucho as a city and region has had legitimate grievances against decades and centuries of neglect thus goes without saying, and it should not come as a surprise that Sendero violence has seldom been focused at a specific regime or incumbent. Sendero plays no favorites and views the world in almost totally black and white terms: "If you are not for me, you must therefore be against me, and I shall act accordingly." It makes no difference whether Belaúnde or García is in office; whether elections are held; or whether the "enemy" might be an uncooperative peasant, a mestizo local leader, a policeman or soldier or military leader, or a bourgeois capitalist. The enemy is anyone who objects to or opposes Sendero, directly or indirectly—a difficult position, since anyone who does not support the movement is deemed to oppose it. Of the eight thousand or more people killed since 1980 in Sendero-related activities, the majority have been peasants who have either been singled out by Sendero or by the Peruvian military as suspicious or who (more commonly) have simply been caught in the crossfire or have been in the wrong place at the wrong time.

To talk about a decline in the legitimacy of a particular regime is therefore obviously irrelevant for a revolutionary movement such as Sendero, since it sees all political parties, leaders, and all social and economic structures except its own as illegitimate. Grievances are so deeply held and so profoundly rooted that changes in leadership through elections contested by political parties are dismissed as not only irrelevant but a "parliamentary cretinism" and as "worn-out and reactionary institutions" (*A World to Win*, 1985b: 55).

THE IDEOLOGY OF SENDERO LUMINOSO

These last remarks are clearly relevant to the ideology of Sendero Luminoso, a topic that has received much attention (see, e.g., R. González, 1982, 1986; Centro de Altos Estudios Militares [henceforth CAEM], 1986; Granados, 1984; Mercado, 1985). Generally described as a mix of Gang of Four–Cultural Revolution Maoism, Cambodia's Pol Pot, some ideas freely adopted from José Carlos Mariátegui, and Incan mysticism and nationalism, it is an ideology that depends heavily on hard-line radical Marxism and on Abimaél Guzmán's interpretation of that line of thought. The ideology of Sendero is based upon a virulent antireformism and the imperative to create a revolutionary situation. Guzmán's writings and ideas are, to his followers, the "fourth sword" of world revolution (the first three being Marx, Lenin, and Mao). These writings build with doctrinal care on their predecessors, but they are quick and merciless in pointing out what they consider to be errors. For instance, Guzmán holds firmly to two basic tenets of Maoism—that the struggle will be a prolonged and difficult one and that it will move from rural toward urban areas—but he holds as well that Mao erred in creating a broad front that included the rural petty bourgeoisie (R.

González, 1986: 36). Sendero sees as one of its tasks the need to correct such an error.

Sendero Luminoso has laid out its long-term plans in some detail; they are composed of five stages. The first consisted of agitation and armed propaganda to convert backward areas into a solid foundation for larger activities in the future (May 1980 to the end of 1981). The second involved attacks on the bourgeois state through systematic sabotage and initial regular guerrilla actions (all of 1982). The third stage included more generalized guerrilla warfare and violence and necessarily involved confrontations with the armed forces of the country (all of 1983). The fourth stage is a complex step that has a number of substages; it includes conquering a permanent support base, setting up a power structure through a chain of people's committees, strengthening the people's militias, and expanding guerrilla activities into more areas to disperse enemy forces. Toward the end, stage 4 will probably involve large-scale troop movements in something resembling a war. The fifth stage finally swells to full-scale civil war that will lay siege to the cities and bring on the final collapse of the state (R. González, 1986: 36; Palmer, 1985: 70; CAEM, 1986: 9–17; McClintock, 1983: 20). Throughout all of these stages, Sendero has spelled out not only its military tactics and strategies but has also given considerable attention to the psychological aspects of their struggle (CAEM, 1986: 14–17). By 1985 and the election of García, Sendero Luminoso had perhaps (debatably) entered into the early phases of stage 4: "Its actions aimed to destabilize the political system, polarize the country and create the necessary conditions in the countryside for the revolt of the Maoist support bases" (R.González, 1986: 36).

Sendero Luminoso has always stated that it is a rural-based insurgency and that it depends upon Mao's theories of guerrilla warfare to operate and to achieve its success; that is, Sendero members must develop the ability to "swim in the sea of the peasantry" and to derive their sustenance and support from the peasants. Yet there have been numerous incidents where Sendero threatened, beat, and killed peasant (leaders and otherwise) who were considered to be counterrevolutionary in any way (R. González 1986) and destroyed peasant-owned goods (tractors, feed, seed, livestock) when it considered that such goods were being used in a counterrevolutionary fashion. Harding (1987: 192) notes that "some of the poorest of the poor [in Ayacucho] have provided the armed forces with their most enthusiastic allies and the guerrillas with their most implacable enemies. It seems that Sendero has found great difficulty in penetrating the uniformly poor upland communities, finding a readier welcome in valley towns and villages where there is more social differentiation."

Sendero behavior would seemingly alienate precisely those people who should be the target of persuasion and blandishments, but such is the ideology of Sendero that it will attack anyone perceived as even possibly capitalist, bourgeois, or otherwise unreliable.

These rigid and doctrinaire perspectives can be seen in documents that paint Sendero's utter contempt for the status quo and its absolute certainty that violence is necessary both as a means to an end as well as an end in itself. These documents are rather widely available (see various issues of *A World to Win*, esp. 1985a and 1985b; Mercado, 1985: 85ff.) and have been discussed and dissected by sympathizers as well as opponents, both of whom agree that Sendero Luminoso demands that its members accept its positions and its policies unquestioningly. Sendero has no patience for other revolutionary movements elsewhere in Peru, Latin America, and the Third World. Guzmán was at the University of Huamanga in 1965 when a group called the Revolutionary Leftist Movement (MIR) attempted to ignite an armed revolt in the Ayacucho area. Guzmán has publicly dismissed the group as misguided and premature; he made no effort to join them in any fashion in the 1960s. More recently, Sendero has taken special pains to dismiss Peru's "electoral Left," a loose coalition of several parties and movements that have joined together to form the United Left (IU), a front that has had some considerable electoral success (Dietz, 1985; Tuesta, 1985). The United Left's leader, Alfonso Barrantes has come in for particular contempt, being described as "slimy," "obliging," and "phoney" (*A World to Win*, 1985b: 55). It should be noted that all members of IU have in their turn made it clear that they do not support Sendero Luminoso insofar as their ideology or (especially) their violent tactics are concerned, although much soul-searching went on among the Left when Sendero first appeared on the scene in 1980.

Sendero has consistently excoriated all current ruling Communist parties in the Soviet Union, Cuba, and the People's Republic of China and has described Castro, the Sandinistas in Nicaragua, the insurgents in Honduras, and the M-19 in Colombia as "petty bourgeois reformists" (Harding, 1987: 185). Sendero is therefore more in the line of the Khmer Rouge in Cambodia; and if one is to take its writings seriously, Peru would suffer the same scale of destruction as did Cambodia under Pol Pot if Sendero ever achieved power.

It is difficult to determine whether or how ideology has been a major factor in Sendero's ability to take root in the Ayacucho area. Sendero's ideology is probably vital as a belief system to those who hold to it, but it is just as probably either irrelevant or incomprehensible (to those who do not understand it) or repugnant (to those who understand but reject it). Virtually all members of IU reject not only Sendero's tactics but its view of Peru's society as feudal and static, incorrect, and indeed ludicrous (J. González 1983). Given the fanatical commitment of Sendero followers to the worldview proposed by Guzmán, however, what role has and does ideology play in the movement's success? Perhaps Favre (1984: 18) is correct when he notes that "Sendero is a classic example of the irrelevance of a political movement's formal ideology when trying to account for its success" (Harding, 1987: 187).

LEADERSHIP IN SENDERO LUMINOSO

As has been implied throughout, Sendero Luminoso's founding can be traced directly to Abimaél Guzmán; and it is assumed that he remains today as its ideological and secular leader although he has not been seen in Peru since 1974, thus sparking innumerable reports of his death or of his residence overseas (Bonner, 1988: 37). Dead or alive, Guzmán continues to be the symbol of the movement, and it is clear that his ideas and his enunciations of plans and goals are the prime motivating factor behind Sendero. In July 1988 *El Diario* in Lima, a paper with overt Sendero Luminoso sympathies, published what it claimed was a first-hand interview with Guzmán. This lengthy account has been the subject of much speculation, and whether it was actually conducted with Guzmán may be less important than its value as a prolonged sounding board of Sendero thoughts, viewpoints, and ideological opinions.

Many of the party's followers and most important disciples come either from Ayacucho itself and were former students of Guzmán at the University or are of a more urban, mestizo origin, coming either from Lima or Arequipa or other provincial cities and towns. Obviously many of these leaders and ideologues are not known; only occasionally have lists been made public (e.g., Mercado, 1985: 289; Harding, 1987: 188; see also *A World to Win*, 1985a: 34), and these are at best incomplete. The police and military have many times made sweeps through rural cities and Lima, sometimes arresting thousands of people (the great majority being innocent bystanders who happened to be in the way) and later releasing them. One sweep was carried out in Lima in February 1987, when some four thousand policemen raided three of Lima's major universities, arresting almost eight hundred students and seizing large quantities of Sendero and associated printed materials along with some weapons. Such raids and other assorted intelligence activities have led to the capture of many putative Sendero leaders, some hundreds of whom were jailed together and who in turn virtually took over certain prison cell blocks. In the February 1986 prison massacres in Lima, many of these suspects were killed when the military moved in to quell uprisings; but the impact of these losses on Sendero as a movement remains unclear (Harding, 1987: 205).

Leadership in Sendero Luminoso is therefore not diffused; it depends on Abimaél Guzmán (or his myth) and his interpretation of Marx and the situation in Peru. To debate whether the leadership of Sendero is "issue-oriented" or not is to miss the point that its principal leader and his ideological goals are inseparable from one another, and that power and decisionmaking apparently flow very much from the top down, despite all rhetorical protestations of a "people's war." Sendero is thus very much cut from the classic cloth of the Marxist or (better said) Leninist vanguard party.

ORGANIZATION OF SENDERO LUMINOSO

The organization of Sendero Luminoso (or what is known of it) presents few surprises. It is (as far as can be determined) structured much like other Leninist-Maoist movements, along rigid, close-knit, and secretive lines. Small groups of five to nine activists are led by a single cadre leader. Each group's members probably know one another and no one else in the movement, making it almost impossible for a traitor to inform on large numbers of members, as well as making infiltration both difficult and extremely limited in its usefulness. Dircote, Peru's military counterinsurgency operation, has sketched in five levels of organization on which Sendero Luminoso operates in metropolitan Lima (*Caretas*, 23 March 1987: 14–16). From the bottom up, these include (1) sympathizers—individuals who provide funds, food and medicine and act as messengers; (2) activists—individuals who hang posters, paint slogans, and carry out so-called armed propaganda; (3) militants—individuals who participate directly in violent actions and are what Sendero Luminoso calls the "militia" and form the nucleus of the hypothetical Popular Revolutionary Army; (4) the *cuadros* (roughly, "commanders")—individuals who manage regions and zones; and (5) the *cupola* of top-level organizers, which includes Guzmán and the central committee. The organization of Sendero in the countryside is analogous.

To come up with accurate numbers for any or all of these levels is, not surprisingly, to indulge in guesswork and little more. Sympathizers and activists are considered to be the rank and file, and there is no way even to estimate their numbers. The passage from activist to militant separates the rank and file from the organized apparatus, and anyone who wishes to make such a passage apparently does so only after an extremely thorough background security check and a demonstrated willingness to obey orders without question. *Caretas* (23 March 1987: 15) estimates (on what basis it is not clear) that in Lima militants total in the hundreds, while members of the *cuadros* probably number only in the dozens.

Recruitment strategies can only be guessed at; likewise the personality type of those attracted to the movement. Most reports from Ayacucho indicate that many individuals attracted to Sendero during the 1960s were students at the National University of Huamanga who were the sons and daughters of peasant families in the area and who were initially recruited into the movement under the tutelage of Guzmán and others. Favre (1984) describes support for Sendero Luminoso as deriving from younger individuals who are the first nonpeasant generation. Such people cannot and do not wish to grow food in the fields, nor can they find work in the cities. Degregori (1986) describes the backgrounds and certain traits of Sendero prisoners under arrest in 1985 and notes high levels of internal discipline (see also *Caretas*, 1982: 22ff.; González, 1986; *El Comercio*, 4 April 1985: A8). In another vein, numerous and conflicting reports tell of peasants being forced to join

Sendero or at least to support it in various ways. Sendero's attempts to hold "liberated zones" or even villages for anything more than a relatively short time have often been frustrated, not only by the Peruvian military but also by intervillage and zonal clashes. González (1985) and Degregori (1986) describe a series of clashes and disputes among different types of peasant villages in rural Ayacucho. Both also note that by 1983 or so Sendero activists began to move toward building peasant support bases in a serious and permanent fashion. Such moves required that Sendero assure itself that these bases were secure, thereby leading to clashes between Sendero and community leaders, occasionally to the assassination of recalcitrant peasant opposition, and sometimes to widespread peasant alienation. Degregori (1987) and Harding (1987) both argue that Sendero has been successful in recruiting young, middle-class provincials to the movement, largely because many such individuals see themselves restricted in Ayacucho and discriminated against in Lima (see Harding, 1987: 198). Within Lima it is clear that Sendero Luminoso has made serious attempts to infiltrate into the large shantytown population; and while it has doubtless had some success, a variety of surveys among the city's populace indicate that terrorism is seen as among the most serious problems facing Peru and that democracy is far and away the most preferred form of government for the country (*Caretas*, 13 December 1982 and 20 February 1984).

While estimates vary widely, most place total Sendero strength (militants and above) at something like five thousand, which in a country of twenty million is an infinitesimal proportion. Thus, it would appear that Sendero Luminoso's organization is one of its major strengths, since the movement clearly does not depend on vast numbers of recruits to cause so much damage and concern.

EXTERNAL SUPPORT FOR SENDERO LUMINOSO

By every account available, Sendero Luminoso receives virtually nothing from outside sources (ideological inspiration aside, or course). Moreover, this absence of material support is by intent. Sendero's ideological rigidity and its unwillingness to abide by anything but its own *weltanschauung* logically might lead to such a result, but it is still surprising to find a group that adheres to its own doctrine so thoroughly. Sendero has depended primarily on raids on police posts for its weapons and on dynamite stolen from mining camps, a tactic that allows the movement to be largely self-sustaining and free from dependence on outside or foreign sources for assistance and from potential interference in its affairs and plans.

Within Peru reports have from time to time speculated (perhaps accurately, perhaps not) that Sendero receives logistical and financial support from a series of front organizations (*Caretas* 4 May 1987: 16). These include various radical labor organizations, rural peasant and urban shantytown associations, and some other radical women's and intellectual groups. These groups apparently work to gain sympathy and sympathizers and to raise funds for Sendero. No one, however, has any idea if such reports are accurate or (if so) what the magnitude of such activities might be. Sendero has undoubtedly used money taken during bank robberies and bombings, but again no one knows how much this might have amounted to over the years.

Ever since 1980, nevertheless, rumors have circulated throughout Lima that Sendero is tied into some vague but threatening international terrorist ring and that money, advice, and assistance have flowed into Peru from London, New York, and elsewhere. It is apparently true that Sendero did become associated with an ill-defined international group known as the Revolutionary Internationalist Movement (RIM) (see *A World to Win*, 1985a: 30–31; 1985b: 60). Sendero and RIM exchanged messages of mutual support in 1985, but whether the exchange went beyond comradely greetings and involved money or weapons is unknown. But to take such scanty evidence and blow it up into international conspiracy theories (as some government spokesmen and Lima newspapers have done) is to engage in purest fantasy (Harding, 1987: 185–186 and 201, n. 20; Bonner, 1988: 37).

Global actors have thus had only no or minimal influence on Sendero aside from rhetorical ideological statements of support; and the reverse is true as well: Sendero has not had, nor has it sought to have, influence on other revolutionary movements. Secure in the correctness of its actions and completely engrossed in those activities, Sendero apparently has neither time nor desire to expand its influence or to associate itself with any other organization.

GOVERNMENTAL RESPONSE TO SENDERO LUMINOSO

From all of the above, it should be immediately clear that Sendero has been able to generate an extraordinary amount of serious difficulty for the government of Peru, its military, and the populace in general. While no complete figures were available (and while those figures that do exist frequently disagree with one another), the number of terrorists acts (variously defined; see McClintock 1986: 10) committed by Sendero since 1980 has, by some counts, risen from around thirty in Lima and Ica and fifty in Ayacucho and Huancavelica in 1980 to seven hundred and four hundred in 1986 (*Caretas*, 29 December 1986 and 27 March 1987). About fifteen thousand people have died since 1980, including Sendero operatives, military, police, peasants, and others. The governments of Fernando Belaúnde and Alán García have been forced to spend their time and energies and money (all scarce resources) combating Sendero. Finally, of course, Peru as a nation and its populace have had to live with the fear and the day-to-day violence that naturally accompanies such civil conflict.[3] Any nation-state confronted with an intransigent, radical movement like Sendero must devise a response that can (ideally) eliminate the military threat and at the same time reduce the potential for future outbreaks by coping with the structural and socioeconomic conditions that serve as its breeding ground in the first place. But these two goals are by no means separable and indeed may easily grow at odds with one another. Any number of governments (including the United States) has discovered to its dismay that determined military efforts to take on an indigenously entrenched movement may produce bloodshed, innocent deaths, disruption, and fairly rapid widespread alienation among the peasants whose support and confidence are vital if the government is to survive.

The military and civilian leaders of Peru have found themselves facing precisely this situation. The outbreak of violence in 1980 was at first ignored and then treated as a minor disturbance undertaken by some misguided radicals. The level and bloodiness of attacks soon escalated, however, and Belaúnde was forced to take things more seriously (as he had been forced to do in 1965 when the MIR launched its ill-fated rebellion). While legislative members of leftist opposition parties (who all rather hurriedly disassociated themselves from Sendero violence) urged Belaúnde to accompany his military pacification with some effort at social and economic development, it was clear that Belaúnde was not interested in long-term preventive measures. In late 1981 increasing numbers of Sinchi troops were moved into the Ayacucho areas. The Sinchis are a specially trained counterinsurgency group with the Guardia Civil that was formed in 1965 after the MIR uprising. Their methods proved to be brutal and mixed in their effectiveness. While some areas under Sendero control were recaptured, there were widespread reports of Sinchi-inflicted abuses, beatings, and deaths. As a result there was relief if and when the Sinchi were defeated and outmaneuvered by the guerrillas (Harding, 1987: 190). But Sendero continued its activities and even stepped up the base of attacks, so that in 1983 Belaúnde named army general Clemente Noel as regional military commander. Noel began a two-phase operation consisting of (1) sweeps through the mountainous area to clean up the area of active Sendero operatives and (2) enlistment of local peasant support in a civil defense effort against Sendero to "drain the sea of the peasantry so as to expose the fish of Sendero" (Barton, 1983: 39). Noel used extremely heavy handed and brutal methods to attain the first goal; and the inherent difficulties involved in what amounted to starting a controlled civil war to attain the second created even more bloodshed and allowed indigenous ethnic, communal, and personal animosities to become involved. Noel's successor, General Adrián Huamán, tried to persuade the Belaúnde government to invest more resources in both military and developmental efforts; and when his complaints became too loud and frequent, he was relieved of his duties as well. Despite all vicissitudes, the military's considerable firepower created severe losses for the guerrillas in the Ayacucho area. Yet in 1984 Sendero Luminoso stunned military and civilian leaders by opening up new theaters of operation in Peru's northern departments of Cerro de Pasco, Huánuco, and La Libertad, moving as well in 1985 into Puno, the country's southernmost highland area that borders Lake Titicaca and Bolivia, and carrying on its campaign of violence and bombings in Lima. Indeed, within Lima the García administration faced the unpopular and embarrassing situation of having to declare a curfew several months after its assumption of power in 1985 (it was lifted in mid-1987).

As noted earlier, Sendero Luminoso made no distinction between the Belaúnde and García administrations. That García took office with an overwhelmingly popular mandate carried no weight with Sendero, which continued with its guerrilla violence unabated. García's attempt to establish a Colombian-style peace commission failed, principally because neither Sendero nor the Peruvian military showed any interest in a cease-fire. By mid-1988, García (whose frustration was doubtless extreme because of the failures associated with his peace commission, the massacres at the prisons in 1986, and the country's overall climate of violence and its manifest social problems) had more or less given the matter over to the military to handle as it saw fit. The García administration made some moves to assist Peru's low-income groups; those included efforts at targeting the jobless and employers (this latter by encouraging job creation), and outreach programs by the Ministry of Education. García also tried to combat the inefficiencies and corruption that ran rife throughout Peruvian bureaucracies and public life. But convincing the public that it will be promptly and equitably treated will be a long and arduous process whose complete or ultimate success remains in doubt.

Government response to Sendero Luminoso has since 1980 frequently answered violence with violence. Such a policy has had its successes, but the military's brutal and repressive tactics have also produced extreme resentment, alienation, and distrust among the peasantry. Over the past two or three years another effect of the guerrilla war has become increasingly clear: the highland regions in which Sendero and the military have been operating are becoming depopulated. Whole villages have been deserted, with houses, outbuildings, and even livestock abandoned (R. González 1988: 47–52). Just where the peasant refugees have gone is open to some question: some have undoubtedly gone to neighboring villages or sierra towns, while others have moved to provincial cities and to Lima. The ecological and agricultural effects of such desertion can only be guessed at for the present. But a set of problems such as these would take years to heal under the best of conditions (i.e., even if Sendero were to disappear, which it is not going to do); and given Peru's current economic crisis, the probabilities of sustained, long-term, and sensitively administered economic assistance to Ayacucho are low indeed. The predictable outcome, therefore, is a bleak picture of sustained, low-intensity conflict in various parts of Peru for the foreseeable future.

SENDERO'S SUCCESSES AND ITS FUTURE

Sendero has from time to time suffered losses in manpower and in its ability to hold liberated areas and has been forced in recent months to rethink some of its basic strategies. Yet it has been able to extend its sway over an increasingly large part of Peru, if measured by populations living in so-called emergency zones. In 1981, 2.2 percent of Peru's population lived in such zones; by the beginning of 1989, that figure had increased to 43 percent ([DESCO] 1989: 352). At the same time, Sendero has not been able to mobilize the peasantry on a large scale into people's armies, nor has it been able to win over the "hearts and minds" of the peasantry on a long-term basis (R. González, 1988: 54). Sendero has also found itself exacerbating, and entangled in, internecine peasant ethnic differences that went against Sendero's plans and goals. As noted earlier, the movement has shown extraordinary resilience in its ability to emerge in one part of Peru when it appears to be vanquished in another. Yet its losses have apparently caused the movement recently to reconsider some of what appeared to be its most rigid and set ideological positions.

Sendero held a first plenary session (following its Fourth National Conference in mid-1986) in May or June of 1987. That both meetings were held but that the authorities do not know where or even precisely when argues that Sendero still has a remarkable security system. In this session (according to sketchy reports largely found in R. González, 1988: 53–55), Sendero leaders undertook a major self-criticism during which they found not only errors committed by themselves but also a social reality that might force them to rethink their major strategy of "approaching the cities from the countryside" and make the cities a necessary, instead of complementary, target and theater of operations (what follows here draws almost exclusively on González's 1988 discussion). To this end and to understand better the problems the movement will face in a major urban phase, Sendero discussed the advisability of a congress of the party to be held later in 1988 in a series of documents entitled *Bases de discusión* (Bases for Discussion). These documents set forth four major points: (1) that the old bourgeois state had to be destroyed and the New Democratic Popular Republic created in its place; (2) that the struggle for these objectives would be long; (3) that certain social classes (such as the middle-class bourgeoisie) previously seen as enemies of the struggle might have to been incorporated into the movement; and (4) that revolutionary violence still constituted "the universal law for taking power and is the core by which one social class can be substituted for another" (Gonzales, 1988: 58). These four points illuminate Sendero's two major problems still to be resolved: the incapacity of the movement to organize the masses and to incorporate them into the new order of "popular committees" designed by the movement and the simultaneous opportunity and challenge of the city as the largest and most logical source of just such masses, who (from Sendero's point of view) are still largely unconvinced, distrusting, and unmobilized. One of the major difficulties confronting Sendero if it does indeed decide to concentrate on the urban areas lies in the numerous political groups in competition for support from precisely these same masses. Perhaps the most important is the United Left, which has had some considerable success in Lima and elsewhere, especially in local and municipal elections (Dietz, 1985; Tuesta, 1983, 1985). Other leftist groups of a more radical (at least in rhetoric if not in armed activity) nature also exist in Lima and elsewhere, as does the Tupac Amaro Revolutionary Movement (MRTA), an armed movement that is most active in Lima as well as in several rural areas, most notably the Upper Huallaga Valley, where in March of 1987 Sendero and the MRTA shot it out with one another, with a reported forty to sixty MRTA guerrillas killed. The animosities between Sendero and the MRTA revolve around profound ideological, political, and methodological differences (R. González, 1988: 60–62); and from all appearances it is likely that Peru will see more of such armed confrontations between its two most radical and militant revolutionary movements.

Sendero has made it clear that it intends to continue to focus on disrupting the electoral process. An account in the Lima newspaper *La republica* (1989) showed that from 1984 to 1989 some ninety-three mayors were assassinated, more than half of these (forty-eight) in 1989 alone (see also DESCO, 1989). Sendero Luminoso obviously intends to persuade through any and all means that running for, or serving in, public office in Peru must be viewed as a life-threatening undertaking. It just as obviously hopes to persuade individual citizens that voting can be as dangerous. Sendero has made some use of what it calls the *paro armado* (armed strike), by which it announces to a community that on a given day all activities are to stop. Such a tactic has worked in a number of highland villages and even cities (most notably Huancayo), but an effort to shut down Lima for a day the week prior to the 1989 municipal elections resulted in a shoot-out in downtown Lima while business in the city went on much as usual.

CONCLUSIONS

It is tempting to conclude that Sendero Luminoso is simply unique, and that its historical trajectory, aims, means, and ideology are, as Palmer concludes, sui generis (Palmer, 1985: 67, 87–88). In many ways such a characterization is correct. But there are some generalizable features of the movement and of its interactions with the government and military of Peru that exemplify the problems any revolutionary movement encounters as it attempts to become operational and the problems any government encounters as it attempts to confront this operationalization. These features can be put as either propositions or (occasionally) hypotheses.

As a first hypothesis, the greater the disparities between elites and masses (in terms of wealth, income, landownership, power), the more potential for a revolutionary movement to take root, especially if and when such disparities are intensified by ethnic or racial divisions. In the Ayacucho instance, all observers agree that Ayacucho is among the poorest regions of Peru; all also agree that Ayacucho has been stricken by such poverty for decades and even centuries. Yet to apply this hypothesis in the Third World is to utter one of those famous statements that explains everything and therefore nothing. Poverty and inequity are givens and constants in much of the Third World, and in and by themselves are necessary (perhaps) but certainly insufficient to produce revolutionary predilections among large numbers of people. Indeed, with certain kinds of social arrangements, such as clientelism, in place, inequities can provide the basis for a durable equilibrium.

As Mason (see Chapter 3) notes, however, a social and economic equilibrium (inequitable or otherwise) can be intruded on, and shaken, by economic disruption and dislocation, which in turn can produce large numbers of people desperate for economic security and perhaps for revenge against perceived enemies and rivals (if possible without excessive risk). In such circumstances, a revolutionary movement with a solid and well-established base of operations may be able to take advantage. It was precisely this that Sendero Luminoso was able to do after having established its base in the University of Huamanga in the city of Ayacucho. Over an extended period of time Sendero identified (and came to identify with) first-time university students from peasant backgrounds whose education exceeded the opportunities their local, and indeed national, societies could make available to them.

Insofar as the role of ideology is concerned, Sendero's belief system may be an essential factor to those who participate in the movement; but to outsiders it may well be opaque, irrelevant, and threatening. An inherently paradoxical hypothesis may thus exist: the more rigid and doctrinaire a movement's ideology, the more it may succeed in binding the group together and the less it may succeed in being widely and readily attractive to the uncommitted. To broaden the ideology's appeal may thus risk alienating older members who were initially attracted to the rigid nature of the original movement.

In many revolutionary movements, ideology and leadership are inextricably entwined, and Sendero is no exception. Guzmán's role as the unchallenged leader springs in large part from his ideological writings, which in turn are read and digested with such fervor as to keep him in a position of leadership. The absolute secrecy surrounding Guzmán's whereabouts or even his state of health since 1974 lends a certain quasi-mythological haze to his status within the organization. As far as is known today, Guzmán remains in complete charge of the movement. Leadership that is so completely focused on one individual has costs, of course; jealousy and disagreements within the ranks are always possible, as is the capture or death of the leader, any of which can produce intraorganizational power struggles.

Sendero's decision to reject outside assistance (in any meaningful amount) from any group within or outside of Peru likewise has costs and benefits. Advantages include the necessity of developing strategies for living off the land, for a self-reliance that can be of enormous value for a prolonged, low-profile conflict, and for claiming nationalism as an integral part of the movement's attractiveness, thereby linking the whole matter of outside assistance to the movement's ideology. Costs are fairly obvious and are frequently the opposite face of the advantages: a strategy of complete autonomy has its limitations, whether events go favorably for the movement (thereby creating the need for additional supplies and manpower) or unfavorably (thereby creating the need for some sort of assistance in the face of extinction). In addition, if the group has competition on the Left (as Sendero has), a rigid autonomy and disdain for other radical groups may lead to confrontations that are distracting, and perhaps even threatening, to the group itself and to the Left overall.

As far as governmental response is concerned, Peru's reactions to, and strategies toward, Sendero Luminoso have little to offer nations (Third World or otherwise) that might face a similar problem. The pattern in Peru has unfortunately been predictable: first to dismiss the problem and then to react to it by handing it to the military, which in turn employs tactics that are often as brutal as those of the movement it faces. The results are also predictable: alienation, dislocation, widespread fear, and escalating violence on both sides. Such tactics occur for a number of reasons: civilian leaders may be forced by the military into accepting purely military options, or civilians may not have any other ideas except military options. But both civilian and military leaders may have a profound lack of understanding of the peasant world in which the fighting is going on. It is clear from all accounts in Peru that the military or civilian leader who had (or has) any real sensitivity of peasant life in Ayacucho is not only a rare individual indeed but is seldom listened to or heard. As a result, the military proceeds with fairly predictable counterinsurgency tactics; the revolutionary movement proceeds with its own terrorist and insurgency tactics; and the peasant, caught (as usual) in the crossfire, must decide either to stay in his native territory and be forced to take a side in the conflict or to leave his land and attempt to start again in a setting and a world he never made and does not know. It is perhaps these choices that are most predictable; after all, they have been forced on the poor wherever revolutionary violence has arisen, and there seems to be no way to avoid them.

NOTES

1. I would like to express my thanks to a variety of people whose work I have used, especially Scott Palmer, Cynthia McClintock, and Fernando Tuesta. I would also like to thank the University Research Institute at the University of Texas for research funds and Steve Brennen and Joe Schafer for their bibliographic assistance and the enthusiasm they brought to the task.

2. Fernando Cabieses was named by Alán García to head the peace commission. In October 1987, after the commission had been disbanded, Cabieses was in Miami and related how he made contact with Sendero and met with a spokesman. Worried about the overall rising level of violence in Peru brought on not only by guerrilla activities but also by economic crisis, Cabieses asked the Senderista spokesman to put aside all partisan political thoughts and simply to tell him what he—as a citizen of Peru—could do that would be most useful. According to Cabieses, the Sendero spokesman replied, "Dr. Cabieses, so far as we're concerned, the best thing you can do is drop dead"—hardly a promising start for a peace commission.

3. This chapter purposely does not address the macrolevel social and economic changes that have taken place in Peru since World War II and that have had manifold and complex effects on the country and its populace. Instead, it concentrates on microfactors that have directly influenced Sendero Luminoso and the context in which it operates. Mason (see Chapter 3) discusses in general terms factors indigenous to Third World nations that may give rise to revolutionary movements.

REFERENCES

Anderson, James (1983). *Peru's Maoist Guerrillas*. London: Control Risks.

Barton, Carol (1983). "'Dirty War' in Ayacucho." *NACLA Report on the Americas*, May–June, pp. 36–38.

Bennett, Philip (1984). "Peru: Corner of the Dead." *Atlantic*, May, pp. 28–33.

Bonner, Raymond (1988). "Letter from Peru." *New Yorker*, 4 January, pp. 31–58.

Borja, Luis Arce, and Janet Talavera (1988). "Habla el Presidente Gonzalo," in *El Diario*. Lima: 2–47.

Caretas, various issues since 1980.

Centro de Altos Estudios Militares (1986). *Visión resumida de la situación subversiva en el Perú*. Chorrillos: CAEM.

El comercio, various issues since 1980.

Cordes, Bonnie, Brian Jenkins, and Konrad Kellen (1985). *A Conceptual Framework for Analyzing Terrorist Groups*. Report R–3151. Santa Monica: Rand Corporation.

Degregori, Carlos Iván (1987a). *Sendero Luminoso*, 5th ed. *Documento de Trabajo* nos. 4, 6. Lima: Instituto de Estudios Peruanos.

(DESCO) (1989). *Violencia política en el Peru, 1980–1989*. Vols. 1–2. Lima: DESCO.

Díaz Martínez, Antonio (1969). *Ayacucho: hambre y esperanza.* Ayacucho: Ediciones Waman Poma.

Dietz, Henry (1985). "Political Participation in the Barriadas: A Reexamination and Extension." *Comparative Political Studies* 18, no. 4 (October): 323–355.

Favre, Henri (1984). "Peroú: Sentier lumineux et horizons obscurs." *Problèmes d'Amérique latine* no. 72 (2d trimester): 3–27.

González, José (1987). "¿Se despunta Sendero?" *Debate*, November, pp. 33–39.

González, Raúl (1982). "Ayacucho; por los caminos de Sendero." *Quehacer*, September–October, pp. 35–37.

——— (1985). "Gonzalo's Thought, Belaúnde's Answer." *NACLA Report on the Americas*, May–June, pp. 34–36.

——— (1988). "Sendero: Los problemas del campo y a ciudad . . . y además el MRTA." *Quehacer*, January–February, pp. 46–62.

Grandos, Manuel Jesús (1984). "El PCP Sendero Luminoso: aproximaciones a su ideología." *Socialismo y participación* no. 37: 15–30.

Harding, Colin (1987). "The Rise of Sendero Luminoso." In Roy Miller, ed., *Region and Class in Modern Peruvian History.* Institute of Latin American Studies Monograph no. 14. Liverpool: University of Liverpool.

Leites, Nathan, and Charles Wolf (1970). *Rebellion and Authority: An Analytic Essay on Insurgent Conflicts.* Chicago: Markham.

McClintock, Cynthia (1983). "Sendero Luminoso: Peru's Maoist Guerrillas." *Problems of Communism* 32 (September–October): 19–34.

——— (1984). "Why Peasants Rebel, The Case of Peru's Sendero Luminoso." *World Politics* 37, no. 1 (October): 48–84.

——— (1986). "Why Alán García Is a Man on the Move." *LASA Forum* 16, no. 4 (Winter): 9–12.

Mercado, Rogger (1985). *El partido comunista del Perú: Sendero Luminoso.* Lima: Ediciones Latinoamericanas.

Midlarsky, Manus (1988). "Rulers and the Ruled: Patterned Inequality and the Onset of Mass Political Violence." *American Political Science Review* 82:491–509.

——— (1989). "Rejoinder." *American Political Science Review* 83:587–595.

Millones, Luis (1983). "Informe sobre Uchuraccay." In *Informe de la comisión de los sucesos de Uchuraccay.* Lima: Editora Peru.

——— (1988). *Historia y poder en los Andes centrales.* Madrid: Alianza Editorial.

Muller, Edward, Mitchell Seligson, and Hung-der Fu (1989). "Land Inequality and Political Violence." *American Political Science Review* 83:577–586.

Palmer, David Scott (1985). "The Sendero Luminoso Rebellion in Rural Peru." In Georges Fauriol, ed., *Latin American Insurgencies.* Washington, DC: Georgetown University and National Defense University.

Pareja Pflucker, Piedad (1980). *Orígenes de Sendero Luminoso y sindicalismo en el Perú.* Lima: Mosca Azul.

Romero Pintado, Fernando (1961). "New Design for an Old University: San Cristóbal de Huamanga." *Américas*, December, n.p.

Sanders, Thomas (1984). "Peru between Democracy and the Sendero

Luminoso." *University Field Staff Reports* no. 21/South America TGS-4-84].

Taylor, Lewis (1983). "Maoism in the Andes: Sendero Luminoso and the Contemporary Guerrilla Movement in Peru." Center for Latin American Studies Working Paper no. 2. Liverpool: University of Liverpool.

Tuesta, Fernando (1983). *Elecciones municipales: cifras y escenario político.* Lima: DESCO.

―――― (1985). *El neuvo rostro electoral: las municipales del 83,* Lima: DESCO.

―――― (1987). *Perú político en cifras: elite política y elecciones.* Lima: Fundación Ebert.

A World to Win (London) (1985a), no. 1. "Peru," pp. 24–43.

CHAPTER SEVEN

Regime Illegitimacy
and Revolutionary Movements

It can be argued that regimes characterized by external economic dependency, internal economic inequality and land deprivation, and perceived vital strategic importance to the superpowers are becoming the most predominant context for revolutionary activity. The cases of the Central American states and the Philippines, although geographically disparate, reflect classic studies of regimes that have, through the failure to implement and redress policies that establish democratic legitimacy, created an environment conducive to continuing popular resistance and a search for the redistribution of land and resources. Each of these cases demonstrates internal popular perceptions of external economic exploitation and regime-military collaboration, as alluded to by Mason in his theoretical overview of indigenous factors (see Chapter 3).

*Both the Philippine and Central American cases also demonstrate the complex interrelationships of external factors, an exploitative regime, and revolutionary models and aspirations. Three critical external aspects are highlighted in these essays. First, as Foltz suggests, the emulation of the Cuban model was a far more significant factor in the evolution of the Central American revolutionary movements than has been any Soviet or Eastern bloc instigation. However, there is some evidence to suggest the impact of contagion from one contiguous country to the other in the Central American region. Second, the capacity of an interested external power to influence significantly a dynamic revolutionary situation seems severely limited. Thus, as both Rosenberg and LeoGrande suggest, the role of external actors in the Philippines and Central America has been secondary to the more critical internal configuration. Indeed, the third and most curious effect of external involvement on these cases is to exacerbate the revolutionary tendencies building up against the regime itself.—*The Editors

Central America

WILLIAM M. LEOGRANDE

Central America was one of the major foreign policy issues facing the United States in the 1980s. Three of the nations in the region, Nicaragua, El Salvador, and Guatemala, were torn by civil war. The other two, Costa Rica and Honduras, were gradually drawn into the conflicts of their neighbors, thereby endangering their own stability and raising the risk of international confrontation and conflict. The violence led to severe economic contraction throughout the region, and together these produced an unprecedented exodus of people seeking both physical safety and economic survival.

A REGION IN CRISIS

The roots of contemporary Central American society lie in the Spanish colonial period (when the system of large landed estates originated) and in the coffee and banana booms of the late nineteenth century (when the predominant economic and political power of Central America's landed oligarchies was consolidated). Despite gross inequalities between rich and poor and an agricultural system that was little better than slavery, the traditional societies of Central America survived more or less intact into the latter half of the twentieth century.[1]

The governments of the region emerged from World War II with a determination to modernize and industrialize. In 1960 they joined together in the Central American Common Market to create a free trade area in the region and to erect tariff barriers to protect developing industry. After 1961 the efforts of the Common Market were boosted by assistance from the United States under the Alliance for Progress.

The success of the Central American Common Market at promoting economic growth and industrialization stands as a model for regional cooperation. Yet the very success of this strategy proved destabilizing. As export agriculture expanded in order to earn foreign exchange to pay the costs of imports for new industries, peasants were forced off the land. The living conditions of the poor deteriorated not just in relative terms but absolutely. The expansion of transportation and communication, the creation of an urban working class, and the expansion of the middle class all combined to produce an unprecedented level of social change and political awareness.

At the same time, the role of the Catholic Church was changing dramatically. Historically, the church has been one of the pillars of the established order, pacifying the peasantry with promises of paradise in the afterlife for those who stoically accepted misery on earth. But after the Conference of Latin American bishops in Medellin, Colombia in 1968, at which the church charted the applicability of the Second Vatican Council to Latin America, the role of the church began to change.

The clergy accepted a new responsibility to minister to the region's poor, and that ministry soon evolved beyond the spiritual to engage social issues. By organizing peasants into local religious communities (Christian Base Communities), the church touched a sensitive political nerve. Organized peasants with a growing sense of their own self-worth inevitably began to make economic demands on their landlords. Most often, the response from established authority was one of political violence. Leaders in many base communities in El Salvador and Guatemala became targets of the death squads. In response some Christians—and even some clergy—moved beyond the social gospel of Medellin to the theology of liberation, calling for armed struggle and social revolution.[2]

But the initial political response to the social and economic changes unleashed after World War II was not revolutionary. Reformist political movements, led most often by Christian and Social Democratic parties, arose to challenge the political monopoly so long enjoyed by the tiny landed oligarchy. These movements found the road of peaceful political change closed, however. Everywhere but in Costa Rica they were met by violence from dictatorial regimes that did little more than safeguard the interests of the rich. The suppression of the reformist challenge set in motion a spiral of polarization and political violence that produced major insurgencies in Guatemala, Nicaragua, and El Salvador, thereby fulfilling President John F. Kennedy's prophecy, "Those who make peaceful revolution impossible will make violent revolution inevitable."

CHARACTERISTICS OF CENTRAL AMERICA'S REVOLUTIONS

The revolutionary movements that developed in the 1970s were indigenous reactions to deep socioeconomic inequalities enforced by undemocratic political elites who were willing to use force to stifle even moderate efforts at change. Even those that began initially with just a handful of cadres who received training in Cuba did not become a serious threat to their governments until they had managed to tap a deep wellspring of popular alienation and frustration with the established order.

In Nicaragua the Sandinistas were founded in the 1960s but did not grow beyond a few dozen members until over a decade later when the Somoza regime's excesses alienated virtually every sector of Nicaraguan society. In El Salvador most of the guerrilla movements that today comprise the Farabundo

Marti National Liberation Front (FMLN) were founded in the early 1970s. But the impetus for their rapid expansion at the end of the decade was the military's theft of the 1972 and 1977 elections from the moderate reformist political parties and the subsequent repression of their supporters. Moreover, the consolidation of the Revolutionary Democratic Front (FDR), a coalition of unarmed opposition politicians that entered into alliance with the guerrillas in 1980, came about when a broad range of political parties and associations concluded that nonviolent change was no longer possible.[3]

In Guatemala the persistence of significant guerrilla activity for almost three decades despite a military highly skilled in counterinsurgency war and willing to go to virtually any lengths to eradicate the guerrillas was due to the government's unwillingness to address the economic and political demands of the nation's poor majority, especially the Indian population.[4]

By way of contrast, democratic Costa Rica, whose politics were marked by a high degree of participation and legitimacy, had no insurgency to contend with despite occasional acts of terrorism. Even Honduras, where the government exhibited only limited flexibility and responsiveness, did not develop any significant insurgency. There were efforts to create one; but popular grievances simply had not been severe enough, and the use of repressive force by the government was too limited to produce the political base of support necessary to sustain a significant revolutionary movement.

Revolutionary movements are, by definition, radical in the sense that they reject the legitimacy of existing political and social institutions. They come into being as significant movements only when socioeconomic inequalities are serious and persistent and when legal means for seeking reform do not exist. To the extent that such movements are motivated by socioeconomic grievances, they tend to have at least some ideological affinity with Marxism. Certainly, that was true in Central America. As in most Third World revolutions, nationalism was another important component of their ideological makeup. Because of the dominant role the United States has played historically in Central America, the nationalism of revolutionary movements there tended to be directed against the United States.[5]

Since Leninism offers an effective form of political organization under repressive conditions most revolutionary movements have some Leninist element. Of course, it is not always easy to predict what the "Leninism" of a revolutionary movement portends for the revolution in power, especially since the basic tenets of what has been known as the Leninist model since 1917 are under radical revision in the original Leninist state. Moreover, in Central America, the Leninism of revolutionary movements was tempered by a strong dose of radical Christianity introduced into the movement by leaders whose initial political formation came within the church in the 1970s.

For revolutionary movements to be effective, they must also incorporate broad sectors of the population into a united front coalition against the existing regime. The successful accomplishment of this task generally requires a considerable degree of ideological flexibility, adapting the revolutionary creed to the political culture of the nation and accommodating a certain ideological heterodoxy within the movement.

Which elements of a revolutionary coalition will ultimately predominate is therefore not easy to predict. It depends on a whole range of actors for example, the breadth of the revolutionary coalition, the degree of political polarization, the relative degree of organization among different elements of the revolutionary coalition, who holds the arms, and whether the conflict is ultimately resolved by force of arms or by some political negotiation.

NICARAGUA

In Nicaragua the original founders of the Sandinista National Liberation Front (FSLN) were disaffected members of the Nicaraguan Communist party who felt that the party was too timid in its opposition to Somoza and too wedded to electoral methods of struggle. Inspired by the Cuban Revolution, they founded the FSLN in 1961 to begin armed struggle against the Somoza dynasty. The movement was avowedly Marxist-Leninist, while at the same time intensely nationalist (hence the name Sandinista, after Augusto Sandino, the military leader who fought a guerrilla war against the U.S. Marines in the 1930s) and more oriented toward Cuba than toward the Soviet Union. In the 1970s, the second generation of recruits to the FSLN came largely out of Catholic high schools and out of a political background of radical Christianity, adding another element to the FSLN's ideological mix.[6]

The FSLN had scant success during its first decade, being routed by the national guard in its only two serious military ventures. Its one major success came on 27 December 1974, when a squad of FSLN guerrillas invaded a Managua Christmas party, capturing a dozen of Nicaragua's most prominent business and political leaders. The guerrillas exchanged their hostages for fourteen political prisoners, one million dollars in ransom, and safe passage to Cuba. The boldness of the Christmas operation brought the Sandinistas national recognition.

Somoza's embarrassment over the Christmas raid led him to embark on a war of extermination against the FSLN. He declared a state of siege and unleashed the national guard to conduct a reign of terror in the northern departments of Matagalpa, Jinotega, Esteli, Zelaya, and Nueva Segovia, where the FSLN had been most active.

The guerrillas were badly hurt; and after the death in combat of FSLN founder Carlos Fonseca, the movement split into three factions over the proper strategy for overthrowing the Somoza regime. The Prolonged Popular War Tendency (GPP) favored gradual political and military organization among poor peasants. The Proletarian Tendency (TP) favored concentrating political work among the urban poor. The Insurrectional Tendency, popularly known as the Third Tendency (Tercerista), argued that the entire population hated Somoza; all that was needed was a spark to ignite a mass uprising. They favored cooperation with the "progressive bourgeoisie," that is, those who were willing to join the national effort to oust Somoza.

The Terceristas had begun building bridges to the moderate upper-class opposition to Somoza when the dynasty suddenly came unhinged. On 10 January 1978 Pedro Joaquin Chamorro, leader of the moderate opposition and editor of the newspaper *La prensa* was assassinated in Managua. The nation erupted in a paroxysm of outrage and spontaneous violence. For the next six months, Nicaragua was rocked by sporadic violence—strikes, demonstrations, and street fighting—most of it uncoordinated and organized by a widely disparate array of opposition groups. During this crucial period, the political initiative slipped inexorably from the moderates to the FSLN. The Sandinistas spent those months gathering their forces, stockpiling arms, and organizing the urban and rural poor. Paralyzed by their inability to bring Somoza down by themselves and their fear of the Sandinistas' radicalism, the moderates spent the time waiting for the United States to push Somoza out of power for them.

In August 1978 the FSLN seized the National Palace while the Congress was in session, taking fifteen hundred hostages. The Sandinistas' audacity captured the popular imagination and with it the leadership of the anti-Somoza struggle. As the attackers and fifty-nine newly freed political prisoners drove to the airport for a flight to Panama, thousands of Nicaraguans lined the streets to cheer their triumph.

The palace assault was followed swiftly by a general strike and small-scale attacks on the national guard in several cities. To almost everyone's surprise, the guerrilla actions sparked mass insurrections in the cities of Matagalpa, Masaya, Leon, Esteli, and Chinandega. To save the cities from the rebels the national guard was forced to destroy them from the air. It took nearly two weeks and over three thousand dead before the guard prevailed. When the Sandinistas withdrew, taking thousands of new recruits with them, the guard "mopped up" with hundreds of summary executions. After the September insurrection, no political compromise that would retain Somoza in power was possible.

When the FSLN's three factions reunited on the eve of the final offensive, the Terceristas emerged as the first among equals. Their analysis of the political situation had proven most astute, and their cadres had born the brunt of the fighting.

The Sandinistas launched their "final offensive" against the Somoza dynasty in June 1979. Any illusions concerning the viability of the Somoza regime quickly melted away. Within weeks the FSLN controlled the nation's major cities, virtually all the countryside, and half of Managua. Unable to enlist Washington's aid to continue the fighting, Somoza fled; and on 19 July 1979 a provisional government appointed by the FSLN took power.

EL SALVADOR

Historically, El Salvador was burdened with one of the most rigid class structures and worst income inequalities in all of Latin America. For over a century the social and economic life of the nation was dominated by a small landed elite known popularly as "the fourteen families" (*los catorce*), though their actual number was well over fourteen. The family clans comprising the oligarchy include only a few thousand people in a nation of nearly five million; but until recently they owned 60 percent of the farmland, the entire banking system, and most of the nation's industry. Among them, they received 50 percent of national income.

The dominance of the oligarchy and the persistence of rural poverty produced an immense potential for class conflict. For decades, the oligarchy's primary political objective was to prevent this latent conflict from erupting into class war. Despite its economic preeminence, the Salvadorean oligarchy exercised political hegemony indirectly. The military ruled El Salvador from 1932 until the 1980s, serving as the guardian of the oligarchy and suppressing by force of arms any challenge to the established order. The history of governing El Salvador has been largely a history of the twists and turns in the political alliance between oligarchs and officers.

This alliance was forged in 1932 when the armed forces took control of the government to suppress a massive peasant uprising. The insurrection, endorsed but by no means controlled by the Salvadoran Communist party, was crushed at a cost of some thirty thousand dead. The psychic scars left by this abortive revolution and its suppression disfigured the nation's political culture in ways that are still visible. For the oligarchy, the growth of even moderate opposition has always raised the specter of 1932.

Political polarization accelerated in 1972 when the Christian Democrats (PDC) led by Jose Napolean Duarte and the Social Democrats (MNR) led by Guillermo Ungo won the presidential election but were cheated out of victory by the military's fraudulent counting of the ballots. In the wake of this electoral fiasco, the armed forces unleashed a wave of repression against the moderate parties, driving most of their leaders into exile. Despairing of the prospects for peaceful change, many rank-and-file Christian Democrats and Social Democrats looked to the radical Left as the only viable opposition.

El Salvador's first guerrilla group, the Popular Liberation Forces (FPL) was founded by the former head of the Salvadoran Communist party, Cayetano Carpio, in 1970. Carpio was disgusted with the Party's refusal to engage in armed struggle after the model of Cuba. Instead, the party insisted on following Moscow's general recommendation that Latin American communists engage in peaceful political organizing.

For many years the FPL was the largest of the Salvadoran guerrilla organizations, operating in the north-central department of Chaletenango. The ideology of the FPL remained fairly orthodox Marxist-Leninist, reflecting

Carpio's influence. Up until Carpio's death in 1983, the FPL adhered to a politicomilitary strategy of prolonged people's war, putting heavy emphasis on political work in the countryside (see Montgomery, 1982: 119–158).

The People's Revolutionary Army (ERP) was founded in 1972 by disaffected youths from the Communist and Christian Democratic parties. Initially, the ERP had a Maoist ideological orientation, denouncing both Cuba and the Soviet Union for insufficient revolutionary zeal. Gradually, it seemed to outgrow this orientation and become more eclectically leftist. Its strategy for seizing power, however, remained based on Mao's dictum that political power grows out of the barrel of a gun. Among all the guerrilla groups in El Salvador, the ERP put the highest premium on military action over political work. Geographically, its activity was concentrated in the northeastern department of Morazan.

The third major guerrilla group in El Salvador was the Armed Forces of National Resistance (FARN), which split from the ERP in the mid-1970s. The FARN always had a more social democratic ideological tinge than the other guerrilla organizations and was the most willing to compromise and build alliance with more moderate elements of the opposition and even with reformist sectors of the armed forces. The FARN was reminiscent of the FSLN's Terceristas in this regard. Militarily, the FARN was active in a number of departments but usually in collaboration with either the ERP or FPL.

Although political conflict grew rapidly during the late 1970s, the full-scale civil war that engulfed El Salvador in the 1980s was triggered by the failure of one final effort at reform. On 15 October 1979 reformist young officers overthrew the military government and pledged a thorough overhaul of the nation's antiquated social and political system. The new government quickly incorporated civilian leaders from the centrist opposition parties and even suggested its willingness to reach an accord with the radical Left.

Unfortunately, the October government was unable to carry out its promises. Resistance from conservatives who retained powerful posts in the armed forces paralyzed the regime, and after just a few short months the civilian members resigned in frustration. The Christian Democratic party rejoined the government at Washington's urging and remained in coalition with the military for the next several years; but every other opposition group from the center to the far Left—including a dissident wing of the PDC itself—joined in a broad opposition coalition called the Revolutionary Democratic Front (FDR).

Five armed groups on the radical Left—the FPL, ERP, FARN, and two smaller organizations (the Communist party of El Salvador, and the Central American Revolutionary Workers party)—began pursuing a coordinated military strategy in 1980 under the auspices of the Farabundo Marti Front for National Liberation (FMLN), though they retained their independent structures. Shortly thereafter, the Revolutionary Democratic Front (FDR) and the FMLN agreed to ally with one another in one, grand opposition front. The political platform of the FDR–FMLN called for extensive social and economic reform to benefit the poor, a mixed economy, and a nonaligned foreign policy. Unlike earlier programs of the armed groups, it did not call for the establishment of socialism (see Montgomery, 1982: 119–158).

During the early 1980s, bloody repression directed by the armed forces took the lives of some forty thousand noncombatant civilians who were suspected of leftist sympathies. This modern *matanza* destroyed virtually all the nonclandestine urban-based opposition organizations that had arisen during the 1970s, leaving the FMLN as the only effective challenger to the regime on the Left. During eight years of civil war the ERP emerged as the dominant member of the FMLN, although its military strategy gradually moved into closer accord with the prolonged-war approach of the FPL. The ERP's commander, Joaquin Villalobos, was named overall military commander of the FMLN in 1984.

The regime also underwent considerable evolution during the decade of fighting. Legislative and presidential elections were held in 1982, 1984, 1985, 1988, and 1989. The FDR–FMLN boycotted all but the last of these contests on the grounds that repression by the government made a fair contest impossible. In 1989, however, the FDR broke with the FMLN and decided to participate in the electoral process, thereby giving the existing regime new legitimacy. The FDR fared poorly, winning less than 5 percent of the vote.

Direct talks between the FDR–FMLN and the government were opened in 1984 and held sporadically throughout the remainder of the decade in order to find a negotiated solution to the conflict. No real progress was made toward ending the war, however, because neither side was willing to make fundamental compromises in its negotiating position. In the meantime, the war remained stalemated, with neither side able to deal the other a decisive blow.

GUATEMALA

The Guatemalan guerrilla movement has a long history, dating back to the early 1960s. The movement was rooted in the disappointed expectations aroused by the Guatemalan revolution of 1944 and dashed ten years later by the CIA-sponsored coup against the government of Jacobo Arbenz. Intense counterinsurgency efforts during the late 1960s, during which tens of thousands of noncombatants were killed by the armed forces, nearly eradicated the guerrillas.

By the mid-1970s, however, the guerrilla movement had begun to revive stronger than ever as a result of successful organizing among the majority Indian population in the countryside. There were four armed groups: the Guatemalan Labor party (PGT), an orthodox Communist party drawing its support mainly from urban workers; the Rebel Armed Forces (FAR), which was formed in the early 1960s by dissident army officers who pursued a guerrilla *foco* strategy and then turned its attention to urban organizing in the 1970s; the Guerrilla Army of the Poor (EGP), organized in the early 1970s among the Ixil Indians in Quiche; and the Organization of the People in Arms (ORPA), also organized during the 1970s in the Sierra Madre. The EGP was the largest of the groups and the most active (see Black, 1984: 61–112).

The most significant difference between the guerrilla movement in the 1960s and that of the 1970s and 1980s was that the base of support of the former was almost entirely Ladino, whereas the latter had considerable success organizing the Indian population. By the early 1980s the combined forces of the four groups were four thousand to six thousand, almost ten times the size of the guerrilla forces that fought in the 1960s.

The Guatemalan guerrilla movement grew most rapidly in the late 1970s, during the reign of General Romeo Lucas Garcia, who took office after a fraudulent election in 1978. Lucas Garcia was faced with both a rising tide of urban political activity by center-left political parties and pressure from the Carter administration to improve Guatemala's human rights performance. Lucas Garcia reacted to these challenges with a wave of repression as bad as any Guatemala had seen. In the first three months of 1979 the two most popular leaders of the moderate opposition, Alberto Fuentes Mohr and Manuel Colom Argueta, were assassinated by death squads. In the cities thousands of political activists, trade unionists, and students were murdered over the next few years as Lucas Garcia sought to eliminate all vestiges of opposition. In the countryside, massacres of Indians by government troops became so common and indiscriminant that previously apolitical villages were drawn to the guerrillas as a matter of self-defense.

"Secret detentions and summary executions are part of a clearly defined program of the government," Amnesty International charged in a particularly harsh assessment in 1981. Control of the death squads, it continued, was "under the direct control of the president of the republic."[7]

The effect of these murders and the scores more that followed was reminiscent of the effect similar violence had in Nicaragua and El Salvador. The moderate opposition was left demoralized and leaderless, the guerrilla armies of the Left gained new adherents, and the prospects for evolutionary change faded even further.

In 1982, following the example of the Nicaraguan and Salvadoran revolutionary movements, the four Guatemala guerrilla organizations formed an alliance, the Guatemalan National Revolutionary Unity (URNG), and adopted a common program. The program did not call for socialism but rather for a "revolutionary, patriotic, popular, and democratic government" dedicated to ending state repression, providing equality for Indians, carrying out social reform (especially agrarian reform), and providing for basic human needs.[8]

Also in 1982, Lucas Garcia was overthrown by his fellow officers after trying to install his handpicked successor in another election fraud. He was succeeded by General Efrain Rios Montt, who had become an evangelical protestant preacher after retiring from the armed forces in the mid-1970s. At first, Rios Montt seemed intent on restoring some semblance of civility to Guatemalan politics. Death squads operations ceased in the cities; but before long the government had devised a new counterinsurgency plan for the rural areas that was more efficient than Lucas Garcia's but no less brutal.

The armed forces classified Indian villages as either progovernment, proguerrilla, or contested. Proguerrilla villages were then systematically eliminated by a combination of bombing and scorched earth infantry sweeps. Thousands were massacred, and tens of thousands were driven from their homes into refugee camps in Mexico or in government-controlled zones. In contested areas, the population was herded together into new fortified "model villages," reminiscent of the strategic hamlet program in Vietnam. In this way the logistical support system the Guatemalan guerrillas depended on was eliminated and the number of insurgents was reduced by between 50 percent and 75 percent (see Trudeau and Schoultz, 1986: 23–49; Christian, 1982).

Rios Montt's eccentric behavior and his effort to raise property taxes to make the wealthy pay for the war led to his ouster in 1983 by General Humberto Mejia Victores. The new government continued Rios Montt's counterinsurgency program but at the same time undertook to fashion a transition to electoral democracy in hopes of ending Guatemala's economically debilitating status as an international pariah.

Elections were held in 1985 and Vinicio Cerezo, candidate of the centrist Christian Democratic party, won a landslide victory. Cerezo took office acknowledging that he would at best be sharing power with the armed forces, but he resolved to end human rights abuses and begin the process of building democratic institutions. As the end of Cerezo's term approached in 1990, he had survived two major attempted coups; but he had not been able to put an end to death squad violence or undertaken any major social reforms.

The weakened guerrilla movement was seeking a negotiated peace with Cerezo's government, but his initial efforts to open a dialogue with the insurgents met with intense opposition in the armed forces and were not continued.

CUBAN AND SOVIET ASSISTANCE
TO CENTRAL AMERICAN REVOLUTIONS

Almost every revolutionary movement attracts the support and opposition of outside powers who have a stake in the outcome of the internal contest between the rebels and the government. Whenever governments or opposition movements seek and receive outside support, the donor powers gain some degree of leverage over the recipients. The more dependent recipients become on such aid, the more leverage outsiders will have. This holds true whether the donor is the Soviet Union or the United States. Nevertheless, it would be a mistake to believe that economic or military assistance automatically purchases obedience. Washington's difficulties in compelling El Salvador to improve its human rights record and actively to implement agrarian reform during the 1980s are a case in point.

The National Bipartisan Commission on Central America (the Kissinger Commission) concluded that indigenous revolutionary movements in Central America do not, in themselves, pose any threat to the interests of the United States. But because Central America is so close, and because of the long history of our involvement there, the United States has been especially concerned about the ties between the region's indigenous revolutionary movements and the Soviet bloc, especially Cuba. From the viewpoint of the United States, those links introduced an East-West dimension to the Central American conflict. Washington's response to the crisis could not focus solely on the regional situation but had to consider its implications for the global balance between the United States and the Soviet Union.

Historically, the Soviet Union has seen Latin America as marginal to its global interests. Having little faith in the prospects for revolution in the region, the Soviets have preferred to develop diplomatic and trade relations with existing regimes. Moscow-oriented Communist parties in Latin America have generally reflected Soviet priorities by advocating peaceful, electoral opposition rather than armed revolution. In fact, Soviet attitudes caused considerable friction with Cuba in the 1960s. The Cubans accused the Soviets of abandoning their revolutionary duty (see Blasier, 1986: 256–270).

Soviet policy toward Central America during the 1980s was one of cautious optimism about the prospects for revolution, but at the same time a reluctance to invest many resources in a region so remote from core Soviet interests. Thus, when the Salvador guerrillas approached the Soviets for arms assistance in 1980, they were disappointed at how little they received. Similarly, in Nicaragua the Soviets were willing to provide significant amounts of military aid, especially as the war between the Sandinistas and the Contras expanded in the mid-1980s, but Soviet economic aid did not keep pace. The Soviets were quite explicit about their unwillingness to finance another socialist economic experiment like Cuba's in the Western Hemisphere (see Blasier, 1986: 256–270).

Moscow's reticence in Central America grew even stronger as a result of Mikhail Gorbachev's "new thinking" in foreign policy. Gorbachev moved to disengage the Soviet Union from regional conflicts in the Third World generally, concentrating instead on the domestic demands of *perestroika* and *glasnost*. Central American was no exception. The Soviets called for "stability" in the region and an end to regional conflicts on terms specified by the Central American presidents—terms that were not fortuitous to guerrilla movements.

Cuban interests were more directly engaged in Central America than were Soviet interests, and the Cubans had been more actively involved than the Soviets even in the pre-Gorbachev era. The ideology of the Cuban revolution has always had a strong internationalist dimension, and its leaders have felt a special affinity for national liberation struggles. Even before Cuba adopted a socialist path of development, the new government offered the island as a haven for revolutionaries from around the hemisphere and in some instances supported their conspiratorial activities.

Throughout the 1960s the FSLN received arms and training from Cuba, though the amount of Cuban assistance was circumscribed by the FSLN's small size—fewer than fifty members—and its inability to establish a guerrilla *foco* against the well-trained and well-equipped Nicaraguan National Guard (see Millet, 1977: 258). When Cuba reduced its support for Latin American guerrillas in the 1970s, arms aid to the FSLN was halted and the training of cadres was greatly reduced. Cuba's sympathy for the Sandinistas was never in doubt, but it was not until the insurrection against Somoza was far advanced that Cuba again offered the FSLN more than moral support.

Until the last few weeks of the Nicaraguan insurrection, the Cuban role was relatively minor. After September 1978, the Cubans increased the training of FSLN combatants, provided some arms shipments, and helped the Sandinistas establish contact with other international arms sources. The Cubans also encouraged Central American Communist parties to provide whatever assistance they could to the Nicaraguan Revolution. Perhaps the most important Cuban contribution was its mediation of the differences between the FSLN's three factions. As a result of this effort the FSLN concluded a pact in March 1979 that reunified the movement and set the stage for the final offensive against the dynasty. Most of the arms for the final phase of the war were provided by Venezuela and Panama, which transshipped them to Nicaragua through Costa Rica. Cuban arms shipments did not become significant until the last few weeks of the war when military aid to the FSLN from Venezuela declined after the electoral victory of the Venezuelan Christian Democrats.

Cuba greeted the victory of the FSLN on 19 July 1979 with great fanfare and immediately pledged to help in the massive task of rebuilding Nicaragua's war-torn economy. Castro (1979) even challenged the United States to a peaceful competition to see which nation would give more to Nicaragua; Cuba, he promised, would begin sending food, teachers, and medical personnel immediately.

Some Cuban advisors also worked with the armed forces and security ministries, although their exact number was unclear. The Cuban military presence expanded with the escalation of the Contra's war. By 1985

Washington was claiming that there were twenty-five hundred to three thousand Cuban military advisors in Nicaragua; the Nicaraguans acknowledged the presence of only 786 (see *Newsweek*, May 1985).

Moreover, Fidel Castro became a key advisor to the Sandinista leadership. Ironically, his advice tended toward pragmatism rather than militancy. He warned the Sandinistas not to follow the Cuban model of a rapid transition to socialism, which had led to the exodus of the middle class, profound economic dislocation, dependency on the Soviet Union, and enduring hostility from the United States. Instead, he advised them to maintain a mixed economy with a role for the middle class so that its economic and managerial talents would not be lost. He advised against a break with the United States, lest Nicaragua be forced to devote vast resources to defense and throw itself upon the Soviet Union for both economic and military security—a burden that the Soviet Union might not be willing to shoulder and a dependency that the Nicaraguans should avoid in any case.[9]

In short, Castro warned the Sandinistas to avoid becoming the focal point of the new cold war, entangling themselves in the same dilemmas of international politics that Cuba had been struggling with for two decades.

The degree of Soviet bloc assistance to the Salvadoran guerrillas has been a matter of great controversy. There was general agreement that Cuba and Nicaragua did not provide significant aid to the Salvadoran guerrillas prior to the fall of 1980.[10] Intelligence reports revealed an increasing flow of arms leading up to the guerrillas' January 1980 offensive, much of this material flowing through Nicaragua.

Since that time, the extent of Cuban and Nicaraguan aid to the Salvadoran insurgents has been a matter of controversy. The Reagan administration insisted that the arms flow resumed in May 1981, eventually reaching a volume equivalent to the flow just prior to the final offensive. But little evidence was provided to support the claim. Administration officials argued that to release evidence would jeopardize sensitive sources and methods of intelligence collection; skeptics doubted that it had any convincing evidence to release.

On the other side of the ledger, the House Permanent Select Committee on Intelligence (1983: 2) concluded in 1983 that the Nicaraguans and Cubans were involved in smuggling arms to El Salvador, although the report was silent on the quantities involved, thereby papering over differences within the committee on that key issue. The administration also produced several defectors form Nicaragua and the Salvadoran guerrilla movement to testify about Cuban and Nicaraguan arms smuggling.[11] Reports of Nicaraguan assistance to the FMLN continued throughout the Reagan and into the Bush administration.

The Cuban role in Guatemala was surprisingly limited. As in Nicaragua and El Salvador, Cuba helped forge a unified front among the four Guatemalan guerrilla groups. The Guatemalans, however, seemed less amenable to Cuba's good offices; for the most part, the four groups continued to operate independently. Whether because the Guatemalans were unable to build a truly unified movement or because they were never near enough to victory, Cuba provided them with few arms.[12]

THE GLOBAL BALANCE

During the 1980s the role of the United States in Central America's conflicts expanded enormously. The Reagan administration regarded the region as vital for U.S. security and therefore gave it high priority. As described by various administration spokesmen, the security threat in Central America had several dimensions: (1) that revolutionary regimes such as Nicaragua's would act as "platforms" for exporting subversion to their neighbors; (2) that revolutionary regimes would align themselves with the Soviet Union and undertake a military buildup threatening the security of neighboring states and possibly even that of the United States itself; and (3) that the credibility of U.S. security guarantees elsewhere in the world would be undermined by the inability or unwillingness of the United States to prevent the establishment of hostile regimes in its recognized sphere of influence—"its own backyard."[13]

The Reagan administration's new domino theory held that revolutionary regimes in Central America would "export revolution" to their neighbors. Some officials went so far as to argue that external subversion was the "source" of internal turmoil, that if it were not for the subversive activities of Moscow, Cuba, and Nicaragua, there would be no political instability in Central America. But few specialists took this view seriously. Central America's long history of socioeconomic inequality and political dictatorship provided more than sufficient cause for insurgency. Moreover, there was general agreement that the guerrilla movements in Nicaragua, El Salvador, and Guatemala did not receive any significant assistance from abroad during the mid-1970s when they were growing most rapidly.

But a more sophisticated version of the domino theory was more credible. Acknowledging that political instability in Central America was indeed caused by internal grievances, its proponents held that the success of a revolutionary movement in one nation still tended to increase the risk for others. Even indigenous rebellions required outside assistance to succeed. In El Salvador, for example, the army would be able to contain and eventually defeat the insurgency if it were not for Nicaraguan and Cuban aid to the rebels.

Collapsing dominoes in Central America were seen as threatening the United States by eventually toppling governments in Panama and Mexico. The Kissinger Report provided a comprehensive rationale for the Reagan administration's Central America policy and focused on the danger to Mexico.

One of the key geostrategic advantages enjoyed by the United States over other nations in the world, the report argued, has been the security of its borders. If the Mexican government were replaced by one hostile to the United States, this geostrategic advantage would be lost and the entire global position of the United States would be endangered. The withdrawal of U.S. military forces from around the globe and the advent of a "fortress America" mentality would quickly follow (see U.S. Department of State, 1984).

Critics of the administration, especially among congressional Democrats, argued that outside assistance was of minimal importance to the conflicts in Central America. Moreover, they disputed the idea that falling dominoes would destabilize the vitally important countries of Panama and Mexico. Though both had serious political and economic problems, they were fundamentally different than the problems found in Central America. Moreover, neither Panama nor Mexico faced any armed insurgency. Ironically, General Manuel Noriega's government in Panama proved to be much more resilient than Washington anticipated when, in 1988, the Reagan administration initiated its own effort to unseat the Panamanian strongman.

Historically, Mexico had the most durable political institutions in Latin America. Challenges to the ruling Institutional Party of the Revolution (PRI) in the late 1980s, combined with Mexico's severe economic difficulties, inaugurated a period of unprecedented change and potential instability. But Mexico's problems were not imported from Central America, and the outcome of Central America's conflicts were unlikely to have great impact on how well Mexico handled its internal difficulties.

The Reagan administration's concern about the buildup of hostile conventional military forces in Central America focused on Nicaragua. Two dangers were generally cited: that the Sandinistas might launch an attack on one of their neighbors or that they might use their conventional forces to interdict the sea lanes of the Caribbean. Regularly mentioned as potential targets of conventional attack were Venezuelan and Mexican oil fields and the Panama Canal.

Yet even within the administration, intelligence analysts doubted the likelihood of such action, since it would involve Nicaragua in a military confrontation with the United States. An attack on a neighboring country would give the United States justification under the Rio Treaty of Reciprocal Security Assistance for retaliating against Nicaragua. A brief interruption of the sea lanes, which is all that Nicaragua would be able to manage, could only have strategic significance in a scenario of major conventional war in Europe or the Middle East between NATO and the Warsaw Pact. Assuming that such a conflict did not cross the nuclear threshold, the ability of the United States to move reinforcements and resupply quickly across the Atlantic by ship would be strategically important. If a country in the

Caribbean Basin used its conventional forces to interdict U.S. shipping even for a few days, the interruption could prove critical.

Yet this, too, seemed an unlikely contingency. An attack on U.S. shipping in international waters would be an act of war calling forth a response certain quickly to destroy the aggressor's ability to launch subsequent attacks. Would Nicaragua be prepared to suffer devastating U.S. retaliation in order to give the Soviet Union a marginal and fleeting advantage in a global conventional conflict? On the contrary, Nicaragua had provided no military bases to the Soviets and had offered to ban both foreign troops and advisers under the auspices of a regional Contadora peace agreement.

In the end, the damage done to U.S. credibility by the crisis in Central America was largely self-inflicted. Credibility is at risk in direct proportion to how much of it is wagered. With its inflated rhetoric, the Reagan administration itself raised the stakes in the region, turning it into a test of U.S. resolve. That much of this rhetoric was designed to convince a reluctant Congress to persevere with Reagan's policy did not lessen its escalatory effect.

In the Congress, many Democrats disputed the Reagan administration's claims that developments in Central America posed a threat to vital U.S. interests. As a consequence, they were reluctant to support the administration's massive military buildup in El Salvador and Honduras and its financing of a proxy war against the Sandinista regime in Nicaragua. Both policies became the subject of intense domestic debate.

In the case of El Salvador, the administration prevailed. The election of Jose Napoleon Duarte as president in 1984 allowed Reagan to establish a bipartisan consensus in favor of aid to El Salvador and cleared the way for a combined economic and military aid program totalling over three billion dollars. The economic aid kept the Salvadoran economy afloat, and the military aid blunted the advances of the FMLN; but as Ronald Reagan left office, the war in El Salvador seemed no closer to resolution than it had when he was inaugurated.

The administration lost the domestic debate on Nicaragua. In 1984 Congress temporarily cut off aid to the Nicaraguan Contras, but after his landslide reelection, Reagan was able to reassemble a slender majority for resuming the war. That majority evaporated, however, when it was revealed that the administration had secretly continued supplying aid to the Contras during the period when Congress had prohibited it. The Iran-Contra scandal demolished the administration's policy of trying to overthrow the Sandinista government militarily, and Reagan never developed a new one.

One of the most telling lessons of the Reagan administration's experience in Central America was that even a determined government in Washington with huge resources at its disposal could not easily resolve the conflicts in Central America to its satisfaction.

CONCLUSION

At times the Washington policy debate over Central America was posed in terms of whether the region's revolutionary movements were "indigenous" or "externally supported." They were both, of course, but noting that did not help a great deal in clarifying the debate. Too often, Washington fell back on a disease model of revolution in which social inequality and political oppression serve to weaken the immune system of the body politic, making it vulnerable to infection by the outside bacteria of alien ideologies.

Such a model rules out the possibility that people suffering under an unjust government might take armed action against it of their own accord, without prompting from Moscow or Havana. The disease model also carries implicit policy prescriptions: a strong dose of antibiotic military aid to kill the bacteria and a regimen of reform to make the patient less vulnerable in the future.

The reason that policy choices in Central America were so controversial and difficult was that the region's revolutionary movements were indigenous, authentic, and therefore legitimate responses to horrific conditions that contravened basic U.S. values. Yet at the same time, they were also generally hostile toward the United States and were receiving assistance from our global adversaries.

NOTES

1. On the history of Central America, see Woodward (1976) and Anderson (1982).

2. On the role of the church in the Nicaraguan and Salvadoran revolutions, see Dodson and Montgomery (1982) and Montgomery (1982).

3. On the origins and growth of the FSLN see Booth (1982), Walker (1986), and Gilbert (1986). On the origins and growth of the revolutionary movement in El Salvador see Montgomery (1982), Baloyra (1982), and Diskin and Sharpe (1986).

4. On the origins and growth of the guerrilla movement in Guatemala, see Schlesinger and Kinzer (1982), Black (1984), and Trudeau and Schoultz (1986).

5. In the Nicaraguan case, for example, the U.S. occupation of the 1920s and 1930s, followed by Washington's close association with the Somoza dynasty made Nicaraguan nationalists anti-U.S. For a good history of these events, see Millet (1977).

6. For a history of the ideological development of the FSLN, see Gilbert (n.d.).

7. Amnesty International report quoted in U.S. House Committee on Foreign Affairs (1981: 8).

8. The text of the agreement is in Black (1984: 183–186).

9. See *Washington Post*, 2 and 9 November 1980; *New York Times*, 6

July 1981. Castro has also publicly praised the Sandinistas for their moderation and argued that the preservation of pluralism and the private sector were correct policies for Nicaragua's circumstances; see his speech in Managua on the first anniversary of the Sandinista triumph and his speech on 26 July 1980 (Castro 1981).

10. The U.S. State Department's February 1980 White Paper on El Salvador acknowledged, "Before September 1980 . . . the insurgents acquired weapons predominantly through purchases on the international market and from dealers who participated in the supply of arms to the Sandinistas in Nicaragua" (U.S. Department of State, 1981a: 2).

11. See, e.g., *New York Times* (1984).

12. The paucity of evidence for any Cuban role outside of El Salvador is demonstrated by how little the Reagan administration was able to find to put in its various white papers designed to demonstrate Cuba's aggressiveness. See, for instance, U.S. Department of State (1981b) and U.S. Departments of State and Defense (1985, 1983).

13. These security issues are discussed in detail in Schoultz (1987).

REFERENCES

Anderson, Thomas P. (1982). *Politics in Central America*. New York: Praeger.

Baloyra, Enrique (1982). *El Salvador in Transition*. Chapel Hill: University of North Carolina Press.

Black, George (1984). *Garrison Guatemala*. New York: Monthly Review.

Blasier, Cole (1986). "The Soviet Union." In Morris Blachman, William LeoGrande, and Kenneth Sharpe, eds. *Confronting Revolution*. New York: Pantheon.

Booth, John A. (1982). *The End and the Beginning: The Nicaraguan Revolution*. Boulder: Westview.

Castro, Fidel (1979). *Gramma Weekly Review* (Havana), 5 August 1979.

——— (1981). In *Fidel Castro Speeches: Cuba's Internationalist Policies*. New York: Pathfinder.

Diskin, Martin, and Kenneth E. Sharpe (1986). "El Salvador." In Morris Blachman, William LeoGrande, and Kenneth Sharpe, eds., *Confronting Revolution*. New York: Pantheon.

Dodson, Michael, and Tommie Sue Montgomery (1982). "The Churches in the Nicaraguan Revolution." In Thomas W. Walker, ed., *Nicaragua in Revolution*. New York: Praeger.

Gilbert, Dennis (1986). "Nicaragua." In Morris Blachman, William LeoGrande, and Kenneth Sharpe, eds., *Confronting Revolution*. New York: Pantheon.

——— (n.d.). *The Sandinistas and the Nicaraguan Revolution*. New York: Basil and Blackwell. Forthcoming.

Millet, Richard (1977). *Guardians of the Dynasty*. New York: Orbis.

Montgomery, Tommie Sue (1982). *Revolution in El Salvador: Origins and Evolution*. Boulder: Westview.

Newsweek (1985). May.

New York Times (1981). 6 July.

New York Times (1984). 11 June.

Schlesinger, Stephen, and Stephen Kinzer (1982). *Bitter Fruit.* New York: Doubleday.

Schoultz, Lars (1987). *National Security and United States Policy Toward Latin America.* Princeton: Princeton University Press.

Trudeau, Robert, and Lars Schoultz (1986). "Guatemala." In Morris Blachman, William LeoGrande, and Kenneth Sharpe, eds., *Confronting Revolution.* New York: Pantheon.

U.S. Department of State (1981a) *Communist Interference in El Salvador.* Washington, DC: GPO.

———— (1981b) *Cuba's Renewed Support for Violence in Latin America.* Special Report no. 90. Washington, DC: GPO, 14 December.

———— (1984). *Report of the U.S. National Bipartisan Commission on Central America.* Washington, DC: GPO.

U.S. Departments of State and Defense (1983). *Background Paper: Central America.* Washington, DC: GPO, 27 May.

———— (1985). *The Soviet-Cuban Connection in Central America and the Caribbean.* Washington, DC: GPO, March.

U.S. House. Committee on Foreign Affairs. Subcommittees on Human Rights and International Organization and on Inter-American Affairs (1981). *Hearings on Human Rights in Guatemala.* 97th Cong., 1st sess.

U.S. House. Committee on Intelligence (1983). *Amendment to the Intelligence Authorization Act for Fiscal Year 1983.* 98th Cong., 1st sess., H. Rept. 98–122, pt. 1.

Woodward, Ralph Lee (1976). *Central America: A Nation Divided.* New York: Oxford University Press.

The Philippines

David Rosenberg

After the ouster of Ferdinand Marcos in February 1986, it was widely expected that the revolutionary movement in the Philippines would fade away. However, after a brief cease-fire, the Communist party of the Philippines (CPP) and its military force, the New People's Army (NPA) have once again taken up arms to overthrow what is now widely accepted to be the legitimate authority of the government of President Corazon Aquino. Why did thousands of Filipino rebels return to armed struggle? How long will they persist in this increasingly costly warfare? What are the dynamics of revolutionary change in the Philippines?

These are important and timely questions to consider for at least two reasons. First, there have been several major recent changes in the strategy and tactics of insurgency and counterinsurgency in the Philippines. Second, there is now a lot more information about the nature of the insurgency from the cease-fire period and from a number of important recent studies.[1] In this study of revolutionary change, four major factors are viewed as essential to analyze the rise and fall and the success or failure of a revolutionary movement:

Massive poverty. The first factor deals with the most deeply rooted and long-term phenomenon at the bottom of many insurgencies, namely, massive poverty and deteriorating economic conditions. Peasants become rebellious when the actions (or inactions) of their local elites threaten their minimal subsistence needs—when they raise land rents, increase the charges on farm inputs, refuse customary credits, or take some land from their tenants. Then peasants become desperate, outraged, and rebellious.

Injustice due to authoritarian rule and military abuse. Poverty alone does not lead to rebellion. Only when poor people perceive themselves to be exploited beyond sufferance will they become rebellious. In the Philippines, rebellions have resulted from exploitation by colonial government, social oligarchy, and capitalist markets; all harmed peasants by destroying the social systems that had previously provided them with a minimum of adequate security. These rebellions were often reactions—unfocused outbursts of rage—against the insecurity that the modern world had brought.

During the Marcos years there was a lot of poverty, injustice, and rebellion in the Philippines. However, most rebellions did not develop into revolutionary movements. Most rebellions remained local and ephemeral. Peasants were often guided more by rage at current conditions than by any careful calculation of a strategy of how to improve their positions. In the past two decades, however, rebellion has led to a sustained revolutionary movement throughout the country. Why? This leads us to the third factor—an effective strategy for revolutionary change.

Strategy for revolutionary change with effective leadership and durable organization. If it is to succeed, a revolutionary movement needs leadership to formulate a strategy that will actually improve the condition of the poor, that will relieve the oppression or restrain the exploitation. Organization is needed to channel the rebels' blind, hopeless rage into a large, strong, and durable basis of support. The revolutionary movement will be successful to the extent that it can provide immediately useful services and concrete benefits; for example, lower rents, lower interest rates, or protection from abusive authorities.

Transformation of legitimacy from established government authority to the revolutionary movement. If a revolutionary movement is to achieve power, what is finally needed is a triggering event that punctures the myths and symbols of established authority and provides legitimacy to the revolutionary bid for power. A dramatic catalyst is needed to arouse and polarize public opinion, to disrupt the customary obedience to authority, and to spark a genuine popular insurgency against the government. In the absence of normalizing electoral or constitutional methods of regime change, the existing government will crumble due to massive disaffection, civil disobedience, and popular insurgency, acting in concert with, or under the direction of, the fully mobilized, national, radical insurgency.

Each of these four factors are discussed below with regard to the revolutionary movement in the Philippines. The prospects for revolutionary change are then evaluated in the final section.

MASSIVE POVERTY AND
DETERIORATING ECONOMIC CONDITIONS

Most Filipinos live and work in the rural agricultural sector where the capitalist transformation of traditional subsistence agriculture has occurred under conditions of high population pressure, costly and rapid technological change, and polarizing rural, social class relations. As a result, Philippine rural society has been undergoing a profound structural transformation that has created a new rural, social class system and a new land tenure pattern.

A very few subsistence farmers have become modern, commercially oriented, profit-maximizing agribusinessmen. Some have become modestly prosperous, small-scale farmers. A few have found industrial jobs to earn an adequate living through wage labor. On the other hand, the plurality of traditional farm households have been reduced to the status of landless laborers. They own few or no assets or tools and, in particular, little or no land. Typically, the immediate cause of their poverty is land alienation due to distress sales, debt foreclosures, evictions, and the fragmentation of smallholdings, especially of insecure farm owners and tenants. Then the rural poor have no way to earn a living except through their own manual labor efforts as wage laborers in agriculture, plantation workers, migrant workers, or petty traders, gatherers, craft workers, or any combination of the above. They are almost always underemployed, but they cannot afford to be unemployed. After twenty years of declining real wages, many Filipino workers were frequent victims of intimidation, extortion, and repression by rural elites and their private armies of security guards and other paramilitary groups. These lumpen proletariat became cannon fodder for both sides in the civil war.

The domestic economy is highly vulnerable to external shocks from the world economy. Import costs increased significantly during the 1970s and 1980s, especially oil prices. A major recession in the industrial countries and a decline in world trade also decreased demand for Philippine exports. The result was a steady increase in the balance-of-payments deficit. Rising interest rates and new protectionist policies in industrial countries exacerbated the problem into a major debt crisis.

In order to qualify for foreign credit to finance the growing Philippine debt, the Marcos government had to negotiate a standby agreement with the International Monetary Fund detailing the fiscal and monetary policies to be implemented to reduce the growing debt and to restore the country's creditworthiness. As negotiated with the IMF, these austerity measures included a devaluation of the peso, budget cutbacks, and deferrals of development programs considered less essential, a wage freeze on public sector employment, and a variety of other monitoring and reporting controls. As a result, consumer prices increased, especially for food, causing a decline in living standards for many.

The task of managing the balance-of-payments deficit under conditions of stagnant economic growth would have been difficult for any well-intentioned, reasonably competent government. However, financial scandals cast grave doubts on the intentions and competence of the Marcos government.[2] These revelations were followed by charges of financial mismanagement and corruption against the business friends of President Marcos.

By the 1980s the scarcity of material benefits had reached the middle class and upper class as well. This was evident in declining savings rates, bank deposit withdrawals, capital flight, and the high number of bankruptcies and mergers. Many Filipinos, in particular skilled workers and professionals, left the country to seek better opportunities abroad.

President Marcos began to lose the support of a large part of the domestic and international business community. Many Filipino business groups took up active opposition to the Marcos government. The chief cause of the current economic crisis, they said, was not the sagging internal market for Philippine exports. Rather, it was the incompetence of the Marcos administration. The best way to cure the problem, they said, was to remove the Marcos administration not by armed struggle but by international financial pressure against the system of "crony capitalism" (see Campbell, 1983: D1, 38; Sesit, 1983: 30). Marcos was finding it increasingly difficult to continue his well-practiced techniques of payoff politics. Under conditions of economic austerity, there just weren't enough material benefits to go around.

Economic austerity had long been the case among the majority of the population. It was evident in the persistence of high unemployment, declining real wages, widespread malnutrition, and high infant mortality rates. All in all, the Philippines had one of the least equal distributions of national income in Asia. It has been estimated that the top 10 percent of the population had more than fifteen times the income of the poorest 10 percent. The Philippines' income distribution appears particularly unequal when compared with some other developing countries in the region, such as South Korea and Taiwan. According to the 1985 Family Income and Expenditures Survey, nearly thirty million people out of a population of fifty-six million were living in absolute poverty in the sense of having an income that did not enable them to satisfy basic needs. Poverty is concentrated in the rural areas, among small-scale, subsistence farmers and agricultural laborers. For example, during the early 1980s on the island of Negros, starvation was widespread among the children of unemployed sugarcane workers. It is a tragic irony that while the average Filipino consumes only about 89 percent of the calories needed for adequate nutrition, the country exports about 800 calories per person per day in the form of coconut oil alone.

The severity of the economic crisis was summarized by one international management firm, indicating that "the Philippines is entering an era of widespread instability, characterized by a worsening economic situation, growing political unrest, and rampant corruption." It also noted that the economic crisis would further undermine an already-faltering regime, wracked by corruption and cronyism. It advised its foreign business clients not to make any new investments in the Philippines.[3]

INJUSTICE: AUTHORITARIAN RULE AND MILITARY ABUSE

Hunger and poverty in the Philippines are vastly out of proportion to the natural wealth of the country. The Philippines has fertile volcanic soils, abundant rainfall, extensive fishing grounds, mineral deposits, including gold and iron ores, and a relatively well educated population. Other countries with much less natural wealth have achieved much more prosperity. Why is there so much poverty amid all this wealth of natural resources? The difference can largely be explained by the government's development priorities and performance.

The historical pattern of economic growth in the Philippines was neither inevitable nor natural. It has been influenced at many points by government policies. Past government policies have exacerbated high population growth rates, declining real wages, an unequal distribution of wealth and income, and the stratification of social classes. These trends have occurred not despite economic growth but because of it. Given the high population growth rate and the highly unequal distribution of income, a higher economic growth rate *of the same style* could create more poverty rather than alleviate it.

What has the Philippine government done to reduce massive poverty? Historically, through generations of bitter experience, Filipinos have learned that the state cannot provide most services that the citizens of other nations expect from their governments. In this century the state has collapsed, partially or wholly, at least four times in the midst of war and revolution—during the Philippine Revolution (1896–1902), the Japanese occupation (1941–1945), the postwar Huk communist revolt (1947–1955), and the "people's power revolution" (February 1986). After independence in 1946, moreover, the Philippine central government effectively lost control over much of the country to powerful regional warlords. With their economic power and monopoly of local political office, backed by well-armed private armies, the warlords terrorized the peasantry and extracted a de facto regional autonomy as the price for delivering votes to Manila politicians (see McCoy, 1988).

Poor rural Filipinos became rebellious, like most subsistence farmers, when their landlords or patrons or local officials (who often might be the same person) withdrew their patronage or protection and threatened the minimal subsistence needs of their tenants. Under the rapidly deteriorating circumstances of the early 1980s poor people became even poorer, their basic subsistence needs were threatened, and they became desperate and outraged. As in the past, their protests were ignored, suppressed, or deflected with promises of reform.

Land Reform

The problem of rural poverty has long been known in the Philippines; so has the solution: land reform. There are many compelling reasons for the government to pursue agrarian reform: it can ameliorate a significant amount of rural poverty, it can give the government a large (although poor) base of support in the countryside, it can increase productivity, it can give the government an opportunity to restructure the declining sugar industry, and it can increase investment in industry by compensated landowners. Historically, land redistribution has been a prerequisite to sustained development in postwar Japan, South Korea, Taiwan, India, Malaysia, and other developing countries. Land reform can also reduce one of the major causes of the communist insurgency.

The government estimates that 90 percent of the country's agricultural land is in the hands of just 10 percent of the population. Two-thirds of all poor farmers are full or partial tenants. In addition, there is a growing body of landless agricultural workers who lack access to land. The problem is particularly acute in sugar land areas, where large estates are operated with landless wage labor.

Leaders of the communist insurgency have said repeatedly that land imbalances are at the heart of their movement. They advocate a "land-to-the-tiller" policy in which they have seized idle or abandoned holdings without compensation. Their message is addressed to the great majority of farm workers who work on land they do not own as low-paid laborers or as sharecroppers who give their landlords as much as half their crop.

Ferdinand Marcos realized the need to defuse the potential for rural rebellion when he declared martial law in 1972. One of his first decrees was "the emancipation of the tiller from his bondage to the soil." Marcos did seize political control from the traditional landed elite; but rather than implement genuine land reform, he transferred control over most of the land to a few of his "crony capitalists." As agricultural wages steadily declined, poverty increased and protest increased correspondingly.

The Aquino government has found it difficult to generate the political will or administrative capacity to achieve its stated goals for land reform. The government's high-level Agricultural Policy and Strategy Team pointed out in its 1986 Agenda for Action for the Philippine Rural Sector that "the minimum requirements for a successful land reform are: (1) the dismantling of private armed groups (which have been used by landlords to intimidate the peasantry), (2) a democratically-based and non-economically based selection of local officials, whose loyalties would be more to the masses of their constituents than to the economic powers of their areas, and (3) the effective administrative separation of the function of promoting agricultural and natural resource productivity from the function of promoting land justice." So far, none of these "minimum requirements" has been achieved. A land reform bill has been passed by the legislature, but its funding and implementation remain uncertain. With a seven-hectare retention limit for each individual owner, the land reform bill will not change the status quo, given the large size of Filipino families. The current government land reform proposal appears to be just as vulnerable as were past attempts to procedural delays, legal loopholes, and obstructionist tactics by landlords and other rural elites.

Military Abuse

Injustice in the form of military abuse also contributes to the prospects for revolutionary change. During the Marcos years, despite the overall increase in government forces and despite the increase in anti-New People's Army (NPA) combat battalions and the transfer of military units from Muslim rebellion areas to NPA areas, there was a dramatic communist resurgence. Some argued that it was precisely the increase in government forces that led to an increase in communist activity. Bishop Francisco Claver blamed the military directly: "The biggest factor that makes the communists viable are your abuses, the way the military steals from people, robs them, kills them, tortures them. There are social injustices but the main problem is your men" (see Browning, 1983: 3).

In some areas, the NPA are regarded as liberators, according to Mayor Aquilino Pimentel of Cagayan de Oro. The NPA "has grown tremendously as a result of the repressive policies of the Marcos Government as well as corruption and economic exploitation attributed to some of the President's associates," said Samuel Occena, a prominent Davao lawyer (Trumbull, 1983: A16).

Abuses of military authority were widely noted and condemned by national and international human rights groups. One of the most influential of these was the Philippine Bishops' Conference, which circulated a pastoral letter in February 1983 denouncing "the torture and murder of citizens simply because they are of a different political persuasion from that of present or would-be power-holders" (see *Honolulu Star Bulletin*, 1983: A4). While a few military offenders were disciplined or dismissed, the problems of military abuses continued. "It isn't because people like the [communist] ideology," said the Reverend Oscar Millar, rector of Xavier University in Mindanao. "They're the only opposition really" (see *Honolulu Star Bulletin*, 1983: A4).

After the assassination of Benigno Aquino, Jr. in August 1983, Marcos increasingly relied on his military and paramilitary forces to suppress growing dissent. However, abuses by some corrupt officers and undisciplined personnel undermined popular respect for the military and the police. These problems were magnified for the Civil Home Defense Force (CHDF), the government-sponsored local militia with forty thousand members. The poorly trained CHDF was also a source of many abuses of the civilian population. The *Asia 1986 Yearbook* contrasted the "exceptionally disciplined NPA" with government armed forces "involved in kidnappings, torture, 'salvaging' (or summary execution), intimidation of the rural population and frequent drunken binges at night with indiscriminate firing."

Many Filipinos questioned the Marcos government's ability to protect them from lawless elements and to dispense justice equitably. Murder, kidnappings, torture, and lesser abuses were commonplace occurrences in the last Marcos years. The combined crises of declining political authority, increasing political violence, and deteriorating economic performance raised fundamental doubts about the political system and its leader of the previous nineteen years. The "New Society" of Ferdinand Marcos had not produced its promised benefits of political order or economic prosperity for many Filipinos. Many people were increasingly frustrated with it, alienated from it, and rebelling against it. Increasingly, they were looking for, and demanding, alternatives. As a result, radical opposition groups had a greater opportunity to acquire support for more militant challenges to state authority.

REVOLUTIONARY STRATEGY

The most important postwar development in the theory and practice of revolutionary change in the Philippines has been the decline of the old, Communist party, the Partido Komunista ng Pilipinas, or the PKP, and the rise of the new Communist Party of the Philippines. The CPP was formally founded on 26 December 1968 by eleven young revolutionaries who convened a "congress of reestablishment" to reestablish the party "guided by Marxism-Leninism-Mao-Zedong thought." Their first public statement on May Day hailed the Cultural Revolution, condemned Liu Shaoqi and the Soviet Union, and depicted the older generation of PKP leadership as "the bearers of modern revisionism in the Philippines." Head of the new CPP was Jose Maria Sison, also known as Amado Guerrero, a poet and former English professor at the University of the Philippines.

One of the most important documents prepared and passed at the founding meeting was a detailed critique of PKP policy entitled "Rectify Errors and Rebuild the Party."[4] Beginning with the Maoist principle that power grows out of the barrel of a gun and the party holds the gun, it advocated armed struggle as the correct strategy for a truly revolutionary party. It criticized the "putschist line" of a quick seizure of power such as PKP leaders had attempted in 1950. Because they were ignorant of Mao's military writings and the principles of guerrilla warfare, the rebel commander relied on U.S. Army field manuals and more or less conventional tactics to try to defeat the government forces by primarily military means.

The old PKP leadership "overstrained the limited revolutionary forces, made them leap over unstable areas instead of advancing wave after wave, and impelled the imposition of bourgeois rules of war and sectarian punishments on the overstrained cadres, soldiers, and masses." They did not construe the armed struggle as a "protracted people's war in which the revolutionary forces would gradually strangle the enemy-controlled cities from stable bases in the countryside."

The document "Rectify Errors and Rebuild the Party" also criticized the PKP leadership for concentrating its efforts in Manila and the surrounding areas of Central and Southern Luzon, thereby ignoring the rural mass base and also exposing forces to nearby government troops. "Rectify Errors and Rebuild the Party" marks a dividing line between two traditions in Philippine communism. It explained the failures of the Huk rebellion, questioned the legitimacy of the PKP, and provided the basis of analysis and action for a new generation of revolutionaries.

The new generation soon put their revolutionary zeal into practice with demonstrations in downtown Manila in 1970 to protest what they viewed as broken campaign promises of the recently reelected President Marcos. Fighting spread throughout the area, resulting in one fatality, several injuries, and hundreds of arrests. A few days later several thousand demonstrators—including CPP members, Christian Left militants, workers, and students—stormed Malacanang Palace. The "First Quarter Storm" of street demonstrations in 1970 was a period of exuberant leftism, in which the guerrilla mystique was reflected in acts of increasingly violent protest against the government.

The CPP was relatively well prepared for the imposition of martial law in September 1972. Hundreds of Marcos critics and opposition leaders were detained at the outset of martial law; however, almost all CPP cadres in Manila managed to escape.

The first major policy statement made by the CPP Central Committee after martial law, in October 1972, viewed "the present situation far more favorable to the revolutionary movement than ever before. . . . The entire country has been made far more fertile than before for revolutionary seeding and growth" (Communist Party of the Philippines, 1972: 10). While some CPP members and supporters remained in cities and towns to work in trade unions and universities, others who could no longer safely remain in the Manila region were sent to work with NPA units in the rural areas. The party also had an opportunity to recruit and train many more cadres and send them to new regions to organize popular support.

The CPP began to organize protest actions against the new martial law government in a cautious way, for example, by urging people to wear black ribbons to symbolize the "death of democracy." Within a short time, however, there were many issues available for organizing more militant protest actions. The wage freeze and strike ban in the midst of inflation, the construction of energy projects in places sacred to the mountain tribes, the slum clearance programs, the luxury hotel projects all provided a wealth of ammunition for the CPP to increase the scope and intensity of antigovernment agitation. Deprived of a representative government, freedom of speech, and other civil liberties for expressing their views, many Filipinos turned to the CPP and other underground organizations to protest their grievances. In the years after martial law was declared, the CPP benefited considerably from its creative and resourceful ability to provide Filipinos an opportunity to register their dissent from the policies of the martial law government.

It is particularly notable that the CPP developed with very little assistance from any foreign supporter. With the possible exception of a brief period in the early 1970s when the People's Republic of China provided some outside ideological and material support, the CPP relied primarily on indigenous support. When the Philippine government established diplomatic relations with the PRC in June 1975, the PRC and the CPP broke all ties. The two are now opposed on a number of issues. For example, the PRC supports the continuation of U.S. bases in the Philippines "as a necessary counterweight to Soviet 'expansionism,'" while the CPP works for their removal (quoted in Staas, 1984: 267).

The Soviet Union also provided no support for the CPP. On the contrary, it pursued stronger Soviet-Philippine government relations and the expansion of trade and cultural ties (see *Metro Manila Times*, 1983: 4). Perhaps the most important foreign support for the CPP during its early years came from expatriate Filipino community groups who were opposed to the Marcos government.

The New People's Army (NPA)

When the small band of radical activists met in December 1968 to establish the new Communist party of the Philippines, they faced a basic problem: they advocated a peasant-based revolutionary strategy, but they had no peasant base. They were themselves students and young professionals drawn from the ranks of the urban intelligentsia. Although they were well schooled in Maoist theory, they had no practice in mass struggle. Within a few weeks, however, they were able to attract the support of a group of peasant guerrillas under the leadership of Bernabe Buscayno, also known as Commander Dante, son of a poor farm family and a veteran of the Huk rebellion. Their fusion established the New People's Army on 29 March 1969.

The New People's Army (1969) was clearly inspired by the Maoist model of a People's Liberation Army:

> It is only by having stable base areas that the New People's Army can wage a protracted people's war. From these stable base areas, it can advance wave upon wave against the enemy. By building stable base areas to encircle the city, the biggest graveyard of the enemy forces is created. It is here in the countryside that the enemy is compelled to spread out thinly and (is) destroyed piece by piece over a long period of time. It is here in the countryside that the enemy becomes exhausted and defeated before the main forces of the New People's Army march in on the cities to seize power, with the help of the workers in general strike or in general uprising together with the urban petty bourgeoisie.

The CPP and NPA initially attempted to establish base areas in the remote provinces of Isabela and Quezon. Their efforts were halted in mid-1972, however, when government forces discovered a fishing vessel, the *M/V Karagatan*, grounded off the northern coast of Quezon Province and fully loaded with arms and ammunition. The boat allegedly came from China and was intended for the NPA. This led to a major government counterinsurgency operation in the region that took a heavy toll on NPA forces.

The *Karagatan* affair and the imposition of martial law forced the CPP to reexamine the relevance of the Maoist revolutionary model to the Philippine case. "We have to fight within narrow fronts," argued Amado Guerrero (1979: 9). "In a small, fragmented country like the Philippines," he continued, "it would be foolhardy for the central leadership to esconce itself in one limited area, concentrate all the limited party personnel and all efforts there and consequently invite the enemy to concentrate his own forces there." The party should strive to create guerrilla fronts in "a few major islands first, then the other islands later."

A guerrilla front would encompass several adjacent towns and villages and would consist of a party organ, an NPA unit, and a network of mass organizations. Given the highly fragmented terrain and highly diverse ethnolinguistic groups, each guerrilla front was to be as self-sufficient as possible. Given the difficulties of transportation and communication, it would be extremely difficult for the party to direct activities from a central base area.

The implications for party leadership were clear. The best cadres were often sent to the regional committees and guerrilla fronts rather than concentrated at party headquarters. They were given a great measure of autonomy and were urged to rely on their own initiative in applying party policy to local circumstances. The central committee of the Party, in turn, limited its role to the formulation of general policies and guidelines. Guerrero summed up this new "Filipinized" strategy in the slogan *Centralized leadership and decentralized operations.*

The advantages of the new principles of party strategy were numerous. The party could exercise a high degree of tactical flexibility, which was necessary, given the high degree of cultural diversity in the country. Small, integrated units were better adapted to strike roots in local cultures such as the Kalinga and Bontoc in isolated Mountain Province. They had the autonomy and initiative to experiment with various tactics to implement general party policies.

NPA recruits are organized into local militias, guerrilla bands, and regular mobile forces. Young activists from urban areas, despite their "bourgeois education," gain acceptance from local villagers by helping to provide simple irrigation facilities, crop rotation methods, public health techniques, and other useful services. Gradually, the NPA units become accepted by villagers not only as soldiers but also as social workers, teachers, and development advisors who are "more effective than the police in clearing up carabao thieves, usurers, abusive overseers, and other hated elements." The NPA (in *Ang Bayan*, 1980) "attacks soldiers, policemen, suspected government informers and rural officials whom it considers corrupt, but usually does not harm ordinary villagers," reports the *New York Times*. Recruitment of local farm youth was also reported to be high, a good measure of the success of the new strategy.

As the new guidelines went into effect, NPA units set aside their weapons and began political work in the main areas designated by the party. The number of NPA clashes with government forces declined after 1975, giving the false impression that the communists had been rooted out by the Armed Forces of the Philippines (AFP). Government troops were reassigned to the southern Philippines to fight in the secessionist war being waged by the Moro National Liberation Front (MNLF). This gave the NPA several years of valuable time to pursue clandestine work and political activity to establish local guerrilla fronts and develop local support.

By 1980, on the occasion of the eleventh anniversary of the New People's Army, a statement was published in *Ang Bayan*, the NPA newspaper, declaring that conditions were right for the NPA to resume the military offensive. Daylight assassinations of police, military men, government officials and reputed informers by NPA liquidation squads became more common, especially on the island of Mindanao in the southern Philippines (see Branigin, 1983: A32). In one two-week period during November 1983, at least thirty-one killings were reported in the city of Davao (see Branigin, 1983: A32).

While the Philippine government groped for an effective way to deal with the communist resurgence, the NPA was very careful to avoid getting caught the way the HMB had been three decades earlier. They remained in the countryside in areas where they were sure of local support. They maintained high mobility with small, highly self-sufficient units. They avoided direct confrontations with government troops in positional combat. As a consequence, they could hardly claim any major military victory to date. However, they were successful in avoiding any crushing blow from the government. The no-win, no-lose situation was actually a gain for the movement as a whole. All that the NPA had to do was to survive and maintain its credibility as a fighting force by occasional ambushes to keep alive the flames of revolution while causing considerable harm to the public image of the martial law regime.

The NPA and CPP expanded rapidly in the poorest regions of the country; for example, in the sugar-producing regions of Negros and Panay islands and into northern Mindanao, where firefights and general strikes occurred with regularity and where shadow governments were formed in the hinterland villages. The NPA also began expanding outside the Mountain Province regions in northern Luzon to provinces such as Ilocos Sur on the western side and in Nueva Viscaya and Nueva Ecija to the east. It also now has some units in the Zambales Mountains close to the U.S. Subic Naval Base. Cebu, the bastion of traditional moderate political opposition factions, also became a target for expansion. Before the February 1986 "snap revolution," CPP spokesmen predicted a strategic stalemate on Negros Island by 1987. Members of the CPP and NPA were able to enter and leave the seaport capital of Bacolod under cover and freely roam sugarcane fields just outside city limits. Masses of unemployed peasants and workers are still ripe for the rebels.[5]

During the Marcos years, the military initiative clearly rested with the NPA. Its guerrillas were supplied almost entirely with weapons captured, and occasionally purchased, from the Philippine Armed Forces. The U.S. Senate Select Committee on Intelligence (1985) estimated that during the three years from 1983 to 1986, the NPA was growing at a rate of 20 percent a year, constrained by the shortage of arms and money, not recruits. Before the Aquino government, the NPA had planned to step up operations. Guerrilla units in the most advanced NPA areas—Mindinao, for example—had already been told to launch operations at least four times a week. By 1987, the NPA aimed to have sixty thousand fighters in all, and daily operations in their more advanced zones. They planned to attack and briefly hold major provincial towns (see Quinn-Judge, 1985).

During the last year of the Marcos government, NPA activity in the Manila area also increased. Armed City Partisans (ACP) launched successful operations on several towns and cities of metropolitan Manila, according to the National Democratic Front's (NDF's) biweekly newspaper, *Taliba ng bayan*. Guerrilla operations included arms seizures, liquidation of policemen and military agents, and the freeing of a political prisoner. The newspaper said that the ACP would be engaged in firearms seizures, liquidation of "enemies of the people," sabotage of military installations, counterespionage, raids on military "safe houses" and the freeing of jailed dissidents."[6] Although infiltration and operations increased in the metropolitan Manila area, they were few compared to some rural areas, such as Davao City, where the NPA clashed daily with government forces until the December 1986 cease-fire.

National Democratic Front (NDF)

The NDF is the political front created and led by the Communist party. It has developed support among some radical Christian groups, labor organizations, student groups, and others. The NDF was able to spread its anti-Marcos and anti-U.S. views among radical opposition groups and moderate opposition groups in rural and urban areas. For example, NDF influence was evident in Bayan ("Nation," from *Ba*gong Aly*an*sang Maka*bayan*, "New Nationalist Alliance"), a legal opposition coalition founded in April, 1985, which emerged after the Aquino killing. A conflict over leadership structure and the role of CPP supporters led to the departure of important supporters, including Agapito "Butz" Aquino, the brother of Benigno Aquino, and Jose Diokno, an elder statesman of Filipino nationalism.

An important component of the NDF is a radical church group founded in 1972 and known as Christians for National Liberation (CNL). Although the CNL was soon declared illegal by martial law authorities, the organization has expanded considerably. A recent report (McBeth, 1989) estimates that two thousand to four thousand priests are members, supporters, or sympathizers of CNL. This amounts to roughly 10 percent to 15 percent of the entire clergy in the Philippines. Its guiding ideology has been described as "a combination of Latin American liberation theology and secular Maoism." It attempts to provide several important services to the NDF, including assistance in communication and transportation of cadres and organizational work in new areas for recruitment. Substantial amounts of money had been channeled through church social action programs to the NDF until a crackdown by church authorities. The Catholic Bishops Conference issued a pastoral letter in 1987 forbidding priests to join or support organizations advocating class struggle or violent means of social change. Nevertheless, more and more church workers are attracted to the NDF. "Part of the attraction," said

Fely Carino, general secretary of the National Council of Churches, "is that it has a clear programme—on education, on the economy, on workers' wages. The government side is more vague" (McBeth, 1989).

In areas where guerrilla fronts have been established, the NDF functions as the provisional local government. It provides a regular exchange of material benefits for political support. It collects taxes, implements land reforms, organizes public works and schools, and administers "revolutionary justice." The NDF represented the armed insurgents in negotiations with the Aquino government. However, the country's austerity affected CPP finances. According to one party statement, "the leadership of the movement has to devise ways and means by which to raise funds, and among these are what we call revolutionary taxation. The basic idea is to impose some taxes on the big corporations, whether foreign or local, that are exploiting the natural resources and human resources of the country, like the mining areas, logging areas that are denuding the forest, or the huge plantations in Mindanao" (see *Far Eastern Economic Review*, 1986: 14).

But revolutionary taxation was an unpopular CPP policy and may have been a factor in leading the party into negotiations. The more the communists squeezed the incomes of wealthier peasants, the more they risked losing their support in the revolution. The CPP believes in the basic idea of class struggle, but it also realizes it needs to form class alliances. This is a "widespread dilemma" among party leaders (see C. Jones, 1986). How much should they compromise their ideals with the so-called middle forces in order to win power? How much should they compromise on land reform goals? So far, their land reform demands have been modest, usually limited to raising the share of the crop for tenant farmers or raising worker wages. Rarely is land confiscated outright. The party has dealt with large and small landlords rather gently. Confiscation is only used where persuasion, protest, and boycott fail. "We are not going to establish a communist society quite yet. That is still several generations away," said Jaime Lanoy, party secretary for southeast Mindanao. "In the meantime, we will allow even anticommunists to coexist with us" (C. Jones, 1986).

In many areas, this new generation of Filipino revolutionary leadership was able to provide more physical security and material benefits for landless workers than the Marcos government could or would. But they still face many years of building on these early and local gains before they might be in a position to attempt bigger objectives such as a national land reform program. The CPP has a built-in structural weakness: the decentralized organizational and operational structure that accounts for a lot of its success in mobilizing local support is also a difficult factor to overcome in responding quickly to changing circumstances and formulating a coherent nationwide policy. This weakness was evident in the CPP's response to the crisis created by the assassination of Benigno "Ninoy" Aquino, Jr. It will take many more years of, first, consolidating gains at the local level and second, demonstrating a viable alternative government at the national level before the rebels will ever be in a position to take power through armed struggle. This leads to the fourth factor, the transformation of legitimacy from established government authority to revolutionary authority.

TRANSFORMATION OF LEGITIMACY

More than any other single event, the assassination of Benigno Aquino, Jr. undermined the legitimacy and credibility of the Marcos government. The initial popular reactions of shock, grief, fear, and panic over the Aquino assassination were turned into political protest. Millions of Filipinos turned out to mourn Aquino's death and to demand Marcos's resignation. The Aquino assassination marked an important turning point in Filipino politics from generally passive compliance to active protest to government policy, especially on the part of the middle and upper classes. Many individuals, previously uninvolved in politics, took to the streets with their neighbors, coworkers, classmates, or other social or religious groups. The demonstrations quickly became more explicitly antigovernment over the next few weeks. By 21 September 1983, on the eleventh anniversary of the declaration of martial law, half a million Filipinos attended a rally in Manila to denounce the Marcos government. A radical "Manifesto of Freedom, Democracy, and Sovereignty" (1983) condemned both the Marcos government and the United States government for the political crisis. The Communist Party of the Philippines (1984) was quick to align itself with the popular outrage over the Aquino killing.

Aquino's assassination signified a major loss of hope for peaceful reform through constitutional or parliamentary means. Aquino had sought to create a "national reconciliation program" with President Marcos, an idea that had also been advocated by another moderate critic of President Marcos, Cardinal Jaime Sin. As the legitimacy and credibility of the Marcos government declined, organized mass protest became more radical. After years of relatively passive compliance, many Filipinos were taking active resistance to the Marcos government. The appeal of violent resistance increased and the prospects for revolutionary change improved significantly. "By murdering Aquino, Marcos has totally isolated himself," wrote one political analyst. "He has pushed the polarization of the country further than it has traveled in the last few years" (see Rocamora, 1983).

The CPP could and did argue persuasively that President Marcos would resort to any means, including assassination, to remain in power. The Aquino assassination offered dramatic proof that there was no hope for peaceful compromise with Marcos. It became widely agreed that Marcos would not share his power with any elite opposition group, not to mention any popular political organization. It was also widely agreed that Marcos would never resign willingly, that he would only be forced from office by physical incapacity or armed struggle.

Despite the popular insurgency in 1983 after the Aquino assassination, the CPP leadership decided that the revolutionary movement wasn't ready to seize power. Instead, they decided to boycott the 1984 national assembly elections and the February 1986 "snap" presidential elections. These elections caught the CPP unprepared. National Democratic Front party officials said the elections were "largely irrelevant" to the problems of the Philippines. The only way to remove Marcos, the rebels argued, was through armed struggle.

In retrospect, it seems clear the communists made a serious miscalculation in underestimating popular support for the bid for power by Benigno Aquino's wife, Corazon. Mrs. Aquino and the "people power" she generated formed a new coalition for political change with strong support from the church, the business community, and almost every socioeconomic group in the country. Her campaign rekindled the democratic spirit of the country and gave her a manifest electoral victory that could not be denied by widespread electoral graft, violence, and corruption by the Marcos forces. The Marcos government was immobilized by defections from within and noncooperation from without. Aquino won over important allies in the military, including secretary of national defense Juan Ponce Enrile, and deputy chief of the armed forces Fidel Ramos. On 26 February abandoned by all but his most faithful supporters, Marcos gave up power and left the country with a minimum of violence. He left with two of the most prominent targets of opposition criticism, Fabian Ver, chief of the armed forces, and Eduardo Cojuangco, the richest of the crony capitalists.

Despite Mrs. Aquino's enormously popular campaign for nonviolent civil disobedience, the Left was unable or unwilling to provide open support for her effort to oust Marcos. Traditional authority had been severely damaged by Marcos and his crony capitalists and crony militarists but not beyond repair by the church, by Cory Aquino, and the "People Power" movement. Hence, the 6 February 1986 "snap election" not only forced Marcos out of power, it also split the previously combined (moderate and radical) anti-Marcos opposition into two separate political forces, one in power and the other in disarray. Although the CPP eventually acknowledged the overwhelming popularity of the Aquino government, it still maintained its NPA forces. After the February 1986 change of government, the NPA was still fighting on many fronts around the country.

Counterinsurgency through Reconciliation or Confrontation?

In order to defuse the persistent insurgency, Mrs. Aquino began her government by fulfilling her campaign pledges of political reconciliation. Her first proclamation was to abolish the government's power to detain people without charge, a practice that Marcos had used widely in purported cases of subversion, sedition, and conspiracy.

Over five hundred political prisoners were ordered released by the Aquino government, despite some objections from top military officials. These included Jose Maria Sison, founder of the Communist party of the Philippines, and Bernabe Buscayno, reportedly the former head of the New People's Army. Both had been imprisoned for nearly ten years. Also released were Alexander Birondo, alleged chief of the Armed City Partisans in Manila, and Ruben Alegre, who had been captured in a shoot-out with police in Manila in June 1985. While the official CPP was still illegal, Sison, Buscayno, and other Filipinos organized a new legal leftist party, the Partido ng Bayan (People's party). It has the support of the May First Movement (KMU), a leftist labor federation that claims to have about half a million members, the largest in the country.

As part of her early military reform program, Mrs. Aquino dismissed many generals eligible for retirement, including nearly all senior commanders. She said she would cut the military intelligence budget and demobilize the CHDF. But these early moves made some military officers apprehensive, including Enrile, who publicly criticized Aquino's military reform proposals and her policy of reconciliation with the rebels.

A crisis soon developed between the Aquino government and the military over government counterinsurgency policy. On 5 August 1986 Aquino opened cease-fire talks with a proposal for a thirty-day truce. While this was under consideration, the NDF broke off negotiations after government forces arrested Communist party leader Rodolfo Salas. Cease-fire talks were resumed on 10 November when Aquino instructed her negotiators to reach an agreement by the end of the month. Two days later, Rolando Olalia, a prominent left-wing labor leader was assassinated. Again, NDF negotiators broke off talks and said they would not resume negotiations until his killer was found. On 23 November after two weeks of open conflict within the government; numerous rumors of a military coup; a farcical power grab attempt by Marcos's former vice president, Arturo Tolentino, involving several Marcos loyalists in the military; and some mysterious bombings around Manila, Aquino announced a major shake-up in her cabinet, including the resignation of defense minister Juan Ponce Enrile. In the same speech, Aquino set a deadline of 30 November for the communists to agree to a cease-fire and resume the talks. If they did not, she warned, she would step up military operations. The NDF soon came back to the negotiating table. On 10 December 1986 a sixty-day cease-fire began, ending over seventeen years of hostilities between government forces and communist guerrillas. Government and rebel representatives began negotiations over highly contentious issues, including the legalization and demilitarization of the CPP and NPA, amnesty for the rebels, power sharing by the CPP in the new Aquino government, redistribution of wealth and power concentrated during the Marcos years, and the status of U.S. bases in the Philippines.

While the military was blamed for brutality, Aquino's fledgling government received a vote of confidence 2 February 1987 when Filipino voters overwhelmingly approved a draft constitution for the new political system. Early returns indicated a majority upwards of 87 percent. Turnout among the twenty-five million registered voters was heavy, and proconstitution majorities were recorded in almost every region of the country, with the significant exception of voting areas around military bases. Of those among the 250-thousand-member armed forces who cast votes, only about 60 percent had backed the constitution. The air force was the only service to have registered a majority of *no* votes, but anticonstitution majorities had been recorded at such key facilities as Villamor Air Base and Camp Aguinaldo itself. Balloting passed peacefully, with little of the fraud or intimidation that Filipino voters had become used to before Aquino's eleven-month presidency. Communist rebels interfered in a few areas, but most appeared to sit out the occasion. Those against the charter included Bayan and the May First Movement on the Left, as well as Marcos supporters and former defense minister Juan Ponce Enrile (Fineman, 1987a; C. Jones, 1987a).

The cease-fire between the government and communist rebels ended 8 February after the communists ruled out an extension of the sixty-day truce. But discussion had never moved past wrangling over an agenda. Among the issues dividing the two sides were rebel demands for the government to "reform and reorient" the military, for political recognition of the NDF and for "meaningful" land reform. Both the government and the rebels accused each other of bad faith, a charge the NDF repeated, reiterating claims that the government had engineered the truce simply to weaken the rebel ranks with offers of amnesty. The government had not yet launched a planned full-scale rehabilitation program, but by one count some one thousand rebels had surrendered during the truce to accept government forgiveness and aid. For their part, conservative critics of the government said rebel leaders had seized on the truce merely to regroup forces and spread the communist message. A thorn in conservatives' sides was the free conduct passes issued fifty rebel officers, permits that gave communist leaders the unprecedented chance to make their case freely on television and in the press. The military and the Aquino government had been driven further apart as impatience with the cease-fire grew among officers and the ranks (C. Jones, 1987a).

In the weeks after the constitutional referendum and the end of the cease-fire talks, Aquino had pressed her campaign for individual cease-fires with regional groups within the Communist movement. She had also offered amnesty to the insurgents, announcing on 28 February that "full and complete" forgiveness would be extended to all rebels who surrendered within the next six months. In sketching the program's outlines, Aquino said she would set up "national reconciliation and development" centers that would give former insurgents the "means and training to resume productive roles in society." Officials added that rebels would be paid for the arms they surrendered and that those who feared reprisal would be relocated. But General Fidel Ramos, then army chief of staff, said that the Aquino government badly needed an aggressive and comprehensive antiinsurgency program. Not usually known as a critic of Aquino, Ramos had often acted as a broker between her government and elements in the military impatient for a harder line against the communists.

General Ramos also made public his order for the dismantling of "so-called fraternal organizations" within the armed forces. The order, which set a 16 March deadline, said the "proliferation" of the groups had caused "divisions." Chief among the organizations were the Guardian Brotherhood and the Reform the Armed Forces Movement (RAM). Members of each of the groups had taken a hand in coup attempts against Aquino. The brotherhood mainly drew on enlisted men, while RAM was made up of reform-minded young officers. Linked to former defense minister Juan Ponce Enrile, RAM had figured in the 1986 overthrow of Marcos and in negotiations to gain leniency for soldiers involved in a January 1987 coup attempt. The Reform the Armed Forces Movement had been founded to fight the cronyism fostered in the military under Marcos (Fineman, 1987b, 1987c).

On 16 March Aquino ordered the dissolution of "all private armies and other armed groups," but the next day the government issued a "clarification" saying "no immediate steps" were required to carry out the order. The country's new constitution bans private armed forces. Human rights advocates accused such groups of preying on innocent civilians. But many in the military welcomed the bands as allies in the fight against the stubborn communist insurgency. Aquino's personal military adviser, retired brigadier general Jose Magno, had made known his admiration for the CHDF, the only group specifically named in the president's 16 March order.

President Aquino's counterinsurgency policy began to change significantly after an apparently premature assassination attempt by disgruntled military elements in March 1987. Speaking at the Philippine Military Academy in Baguio four days later, Aquino asserted that the "answer to the terrorism of the left and the right is not social and economic reform but police and military action." Aquino said she had sought to settle matters peacefully: "God knows I have tried. But my offers of peace and reconciliation have been met with the most bloody and insolent rejections by the left and the right" (Fineman, 1987e; G. Jones, 1987b).

The Rise in Political Violence

The week of the blast was reported to be one of the bloodiest since the end of the communist peace talks and the cease-fire that had accompanied them.

Clashes between rebels and soldiers increased and a higher proportion of casualties were now soldiers (Fineman, 1987d). Killings in Manila increased, marking a departure from the guerrilla war that the communists had long waged in the countryside. In March President Aquino encouraged the activities of unarmed vigilante groups as a legitimate example of the "people power" that had helped propel her into office. By one count, there were 260 private armed bands in the Philippines (Mydans, 1987f; 1987g). These ranged from the private armies of warlords to the jungle religious sect commonly known as Tadtad ("Chopchop," in Tagalog). The first and most celebrated of these was Alsa Masa ("Arise, Masses" in Tagalog) founded in July 1986, a band that dominated Agdao, a slum district in Mindanao Island's Davao City. Residents were said to have welcomed the communists on their arrival in late 1982, but it was reported that by 1986 the slum's inhabitants had wearied of the tax collection, frequent executions, and unbending moral code said to accompany communist rule there.

Organized around a core of self-proclaimed NPA defectors, it made no secrets of mimicking the rebels' methods of propaganda, taxation, forced recruitment, and summary justice. Threats against suspected communists were broadcast daily over the radio. "Anybody who would not like to join Alsa Masa is a communist," said Colonel Franco M. Calida, the military commander of Davao. Calida acted as patron to the group and supplied it with firearms (C. Jones, 1987c; Fineman, 1987f).

Unidentified gunmen killed local government secretary Jaime Ferrer outside his home in the Manila suburb of Paranque on 2 August 1987. He was said to be the first cabinet official in Philippine history to be assassinated. The swift attack and escape by the handful of men resembled the killings mounted in Manila by the three-man "sparrow" units of the communist New People's Army. The group had publicly marked Ferrer for assassination. Once in the post, Ferrer had campaigned vigorously for creation of unarmed vigilante units to fight the communists. He had also ordered local officials to campaign for the government's candidates in the May 1987 congressional elections, which had reportedly fostered widespread vote fraud (see *New York Times*, August 1987).

The most serious attack against the Aquino government was launched by mutinous Philippine soldiers in Manila in the early hours of 28 August. Fifty-three people—twelve government troops, nineteen rebels, and twenty-two civilians—died in the fighting, according to government figures. Hundreds of others were wounded, including Mrs. Aquino's son. Nearly twelve hours of fighting took place before General Ramos announced that the Camp Aguinaldo military base (of which the rebels had taken control) had been totally secured and all mutineers had been captured. U.S. officials repeatedly expressed their support for the Aquino government and reportedly told mutiny leaders that all U.S. military aid would be cut off if the coup succeeded (Mydans, 1987h).

The uprising, at least the fifth against Aquino, was led by soldiers linked to the Reform the Armed Forces Movement, which had helped to topple Marcos. Aquino said that over 1,350 soldiers took part in the revolt and that 1,033 were in custody. Colonel Gregorio "Gringo" Honasan, the leader of the revolt, remained at large until his arrest in Manila in December. While the mutiny apparently found few sympathizers among civilians despite growing discontent with the Aquino government, the continued unease with the Aquino regime within the military posed an ongoing threat to the Philippine president. Army chief of staff General Fidel Ramos underscored that threat on 1 September when he said that the problem of factionalism in the armed forces "probably has become more serious than before." To help improve military morale, Ramos called for a 60-percent pay increase for enlisted men and a meeting of the National Security Council to review the government's fight against communist and Moslem insurgents (Mydans, 1987i).

Political instability surged again in late September when President Aquino reshuffled her cabinet and removed her closest adviser, executive secretary Joker Arroyo. The military had been pressing for the removal of Arroyo, as well as another adviser considered to be a leftist, special legal counsel Teodoro Locsin. Arroyo, considered by many Filipinos to be second in power only to President Aquino, had been increasingly condemned as a leftist by military and business leaders in the wake of the attempted coup. The military had accused Arroyo of interfering with its efforts to put down the revolt and of being too lenient toward the communist insurgents. At about the same time, Vice President Salvador H. Laurel left his cabinet post as foreign minister citing "basic, fundamental differences" with Aquino's policy toward the communist rebels. Laurel announced he would open an anticommunist publicity campaign nationwide. In late September, a top leftist leader was shot to death in Quezon City, near Manila. Leandro Alegnadro, secretary general of the left-wing Bayan coalition, was shot repeatedly in the head by gunmen firing from a passing vehicle. Alegnadro was the second Bayan leader slain during 1987.

To summarize, the Aquino government, after shrill and sometimes violent opposition and coup d'état attempts from right-wing groups, and after an increase in NPA attacks, reversed its early policy of reconciliation with the rebels, and started military and paramilitary actions against rebel groups and their suspected supporters. The United States increased its support for the new Aquino government counterinsurgency program with stepped up aid. The notorious CHDF of the Marcos era was to be replaced by so-called Citizens Voluntary Organizations (CVOs), defined as unarmed anticommunist groups, and Citizens Armed Forces Geographical Units (CAFGUs), their paramilitary counterpart. However, there were numerous indications of persistent massive poverty and abuses by military and paramilitary forces—the basic forces at the roots of the rebellion.

PROSPECTS

After twenty years of concentrating wealth and power, given the fragile government consensus and threats of political instability, will the Aquino administration be able or willing to pursue genuine reforms for national development? Will it be able to reduce massive poverty and military abuses—the basic forces at the root of the revolutionary movement? Or will the CPP finally succeed in formulating a nationwide strategy for revolutionary change?

In the short run, the Aquino government has considerable support for its political agenda: Mrs. Aquino still retains a lot of personal popularity; many of her early rivals for political leadership have been removed, in particular, Juan Ponce Enrile and Salvador Laurel; the Communist Party of the Philippines and the New People's Army have suffered several setbacks; Military coup attempts have ceased; and the government has strong support from the church, the business sector, and the international community., Long-term prospects, however, are not as clear.

Economic Development

Economic growth has been slowly increasing, based on the revival of consumer demand, construction, and manufacturing sales, especially in the metropolitan Manila region. The agricultural sector has stalled, however. Recent government figures show that output of most major crops were the same or even a little lower than the previous year (Richburg, 1988). The benefits of this growth need to be used to rebuild long-neglected transportation and communications systems, power supplies, and other components of the economic infrastructure. Electricity and telephone services were especially strained by the recent economic expansion. Power stoppages became so common that some factory owners put in standby generators. Continued growth will require a major upgrading of basic infrastructure (especially power supply, telephone and postal services, and transportation systems) and a speedup of government processing of business licenses and documents.

Economic growth has improved but not enough to provide adequate employment for a rapidly growing population. Estimates of population growth rates vary from 2.5 percent to 3.0 percent, among the highest in Asia. The high population growth rate and correspondingly high labor force growth rate have become problematic in relation to the poor record of economic growth and job creation. The combined result of these factors is that real wages have declined for over two decades. It can be expected that population growth rates will remain high where basic needs have not been met.

The outlook for the future is equally difficult. Every year about 750 thousand new entrants join a labor force that already contains about five million underemployed or unemployed workers. This labor force will be expanding even more rapidly in the future because of the compounding effect of high population growth rates. The new labor force for the rest of the century has already been born. It is estimated that about sixteen million new entrants will join the labor force in the next fifteen years. Without major changes in policies, it is not clear where these additional job seekers will be absorbed. Millions of new job seekers have not been absorbed by the formal labor market.

For the future, projections indicate that even a 6-percent growth rate of GDP will barely provide enough jobs to keep real wages from declining further. The World Bank Poverty Report on the Philippines forecasts that real wages will drop 3 percent between 1988 and the end of the century even if GDP rose by 6 percent a year. Substantial growth in real wages will be difficult to attain unless there is a significant drop in population and labor force growth rates. Hence, the Philippine economy needs a massive transfusion of investment funds, as well as a high priority on job creation in the allocation of capital in order to reduce current unemployment and provide jobs for new entrants to the labor force.

Domestic investment has increased significantly after the disinvestment years of 1983–1986; however, the hoped-for infusion of funds from the United States and Western Europe has failed to materialize. Japanese and Taiwanese investors, on the other hand, have lined up investment proposals totaling more than two hundred million dollars. The pace of new investment will remain slow due to apprehensions about political instability and frustrations about dealing with cumbersome regulations and bureaucracies. As a result, prospective investors have gone elsewhere. For example, in 1987 the Philippines received only 4 percent of all the investment going to Brunei, Indonesia, Malaysia, Singapore, Thailand, and the Philippines (Walsh, 1988).

The Philippine economy remains vulnerable to fluctuations in the world market. The recent surge in economic growth in the Philippines (8 percent in the first quarter of 1988) is mostly due to lower oil prices and higher gold and copra prices. Some export earnings have increased (e.g., copra), but the long-term prospects for most traditional exports are poor. It is uncertain how long the current commodity price rise will last. According to many reports, world market prospects are gloomy. What worked for South Korea and Taiwan during the boom years of the 1950s and 1960s may not work for the Philippines in the 1970s and 1980s because of changes in the world economic environment.

Political Reform

The reaction against martial law, the so-called "EDSA revolution," and the ascension of Corazon Aquino's government all raised hopes for the prospects of a more democratic political system in the post-Marcos era. Mrs. Aquino came to power in February 1986 with a revolutionary mandate for change and no significant debts to the old political families who had generally allied with Marcos's party. However, after initial attempts at reconciliation with the rebels proved futile, Mrs. Aquino made major concessions to the military and has gradually moved into an alliance with traditional regional elites to create a stronger base for her government.

Family oligarchies are reemerging through the newly created electoral apparatus. This was evident in the polls in May 1987 to elect a national legislature. The vote was generally held to be the country's freest and most honest since at least 1971, the last year elections had been held for the country's old two-chamber national legislature. Pro-Aquino candidates formed a loose coalition under the Laban party banner. The group had not bothered to issue a platform of common stands. The political party Laban had been founded in 1978 by Aquino's husband, the late Benigno Aquino, Jr. The name Laban ("Fight" in Tagalog) came from the group's full name: *La*kas ng *Bayan* ("People's Power Movement). Seventeen Senate candidates were fielded by the remnants of Marcos's New Society movement, and seven by the left-wing Alliance for New Politics (ANP). The Left had sat out the 1986 election that propelled Aquino to the presidency, as well as the February 1987 vote in which her constitution had been overwhelmingly approved. But members of the newly formed ANP coalition of groups said they wanted to see if they could bring their message peacefully to the public, as Aquino had promised. The Senate candidates included Bernabe Buscayno, who in 1969 had helped found the communist New People's Army and set it upon its ongoing guerrilla insurgency. The Grand Alliance for Democracy (GAD) candidates linked to Marcos and ANP candidates branded as communists both appeared to be taken to task in a pastoral letter issued 22 April by Cardinal Sin.

The results of the 11 May 1987 elections show that 130 out of 200 candidates elected to the House of Representatives belonged to traditional political families, while another 39 were relatives of these families. Only 31 elected representatives were "new political leaders," that is, not related to the traditionally dominant political families. Several of these ran as "antidynasty" candidates. On the other hand, of the 169 representatives from the traditional political clans, 102 were identified with the pre-1986 anti-Marcos forces, and 67 were identified with pro-Marcos clans. Of the 24 elected senators, the overwhelming majority were from traditional political clans who were prominent in the pre-martial law period (Mojares, 1988).

The persistence and the reemergence of the old dominant political families in the elections of 1987 and 1988 have dispelled hopes about the prospects for development and democracy in the Philippines. As elections restored provincial elites, Aquino restored expropriated corporations to the old oligarchy. For example, the Lopez family, which had been stripped of its wealth and driven into exile by Marcos, has returned to Manila and is rebuilding its national economic holdings and its provincial power base.

Elections are still held, but they don't have the same symbolic power as before. In the 1984 National Assembly elections and the 1986 presidential election, Filipino voters showed that they prefer ballots to bullets or boycotts, but voter withdrawal and resistance is increasing. Mojares (1988) notes that politicians have found that it is increasingly difficult to get the voters out.

At the same time, political mobilization outside the electoral arena is increasing. This is evident in the development of radical trade unions, Basic Christian Communities, various cause-oriented groups, the Moro National Liberation Front, the Muslim Independence Liberation Army, the Cordillera Peoples' Liberation Army, private paramilitary forces and vigilante groups, and especially the "New" Armed Forces of the Philippines and the New People's Army. All these groups want a larger say in national and local politics. They all oppose the traditional family oligarchy control over electoral politics. They are all willing to struggle for power in the "parliament of the streets," through "acoustical warfare," or in the underground.

Military Reform

Civilian control of the military may be more tenuous now than during the Marcos years. The Aquino government has been unable to reform or remove the remaining repressive instruments in the countryside. Reports of abuse of church workers by military and paramilitary forces persist and continue to swell rebel ranks, especially in Negros and Mindanao (Amnesty International, 1988; Clad, 1988; Heise, 1988).

The military has now achieved a major role in national politics. It has acquired a virtual veto power over cabinet personnel; it has a major voice in national policies and local affairs, especially with regard to a vague and broadly defined counterinsurgency policy. The military will have a major voice in the next presidential election. Indeed, they may even produce a candidate: Fidel Ramos, secretary of national defense, has been rumored to have presidential ambitions. Many military officers already believe they can govern better than civilians (for examples, see Miranda and Ciron, 1988). "There never has been a fully professionalized military in the Philippines," one scholar asserts (Kessler, 1989).

Along with factionalism, corruption has also reappeared in national politics. The Presidential Commission on Good Government (PCGG), created to try to regain the "illgotten wealth" of Marcos and his cronies, was itself accused of corruption by the solicitor general, Frank Chavez. In July 1988, Aquino replaced the PCGG chairman, Ramon Diaz. The commission has yet to prosecute a single crony. "Many are abused, but few are punished," writes one reporter (Walsh, 1988b). Mrs. Aquino herself is a victim of justice delayed, justice denied. The trial to determine who killed her husband has dragged on for years with no end in sight. Many courts are hopelessly overloaded with work. Cases may take years or even decades to be decided. Associate justice Antonio Sarmiento says he is just now sitting down to a tax case filed in 1938. Criminal justice is no better: the overwhelming proportion of murders go unsolved (Walsh, 1988).

Even prominent criminals in detention can find their way out. In November 1988, Romulo Kintanar, chief of the New People's Army, escaped from detention at national police headquarters in Camp Crame after being allowed to attend a birthday party of an officer he had befriended. Earlier in 1988, Gregorio Honasan, a former colonel who led the August 1987 coup attempt, escaped with several of his ostensible guards from a prison ship aboard a rubber raft that had been sent to augment security. And several years ago, Saturnino Ocampo, a former journalist and ranking leader of the rebels, escaped captivity through the back door of the Manila Press Club, where he had been allowed to go to vote in an election for club officers (Mydans, 1988).

Changing Strategy of the CPP

In the aftermath of the dramatic rise of the Aquino government in 1986, the CPP has had a major overhaul of leadership and strategy. There has been an intensive "rectification campaign" among leaders and rank and file of the CPP and NPA. The "rectificationists" challenged the hard-line neo-Maoist strategy of protracted people's war. New rebel factions advocated a "Nicaraguan model" with emphasis on forming strategic alliances with "bourgeois reformists" and liberal democrats in an "insurrectional strategy" to achieve power (Porter 1987, 1989). But the political strategies of the cease-fire period became militarized. The Aquino government was unable to consolidate its popular support into a durable power base to permit meaningful reforms that might have induced the rebel leaders to lay down their arms. Both sides took the occasion of the cease-fire to reorganize, resupply, and prepare to resume their armed struggles. The CPP and NPA changed tactics and leadership, signaling an escalation of violence—a "strategic counteroffensive"—in their twenty-year-old insurgency. According to a *Far Eastern Economic Review* (1987) cover story, "all indications are that [CPP] moderates have been replaced by hard-liners intent on regaining the momentum lost when former President Marcos was ousted by Corazon Aquino."

The NPA assassination of U.S. military aid official Colonel James "Nick" Rowe on 21 April 1989 was "a message to the American people." Rowe was selected as a target because he was chief of the army division of the Joint U.S. Military Assistance Group (JUSMAG); he was also a Green Beret who had spent five years in a Vietcong prisoner-of-war camp. "We want to let them know that their government is making the Philippines another Vietnam," one senior CPP cadre was told (Cohen, 1989).

Rebel forces also took the opportunity of the cease-fire to hold a party congress and to broaden their international contacts. The NDF maintains a fully open office in Utrecht, the Netherlands, where Luis Jalandoni, a former Roman Catholic priest, works with Sixto Carlos, a former political prisoner. The NDF has good informal ties with the Dutch Labor party and formal recognition from the governing Pasok party in Greece. As part of an NDF campaign to gain more international legitimacy for "international belligerency status," Jalandoni went to Harare, Zimbabwe during the nonaligned movement summit there in August 1986. The NDF is also reported to be preparing a petition to the UN Human Rights Commission in Geneva about alleged human rights violations.

The NDF also arranged "exposure visits" to Manila by various European and Australian parliamentarians, journalists, and trade unionists. Two Salvadoran rebels visited Manila and five NDF members visited Cuba during the cease-fire period. A Japanese United Red Army member was reported to be in the Philippines late in the year (Japan Economic Newswire, 1987). Moscow and Peking appear to have little influence on the Filipino rebels; however, fraternal relations with Communist parties in power have been pursued with the Soviet Union, North Korea, and Vietnam. "We are now in the process of seeking and establishing relations with the ruling parties in Eastern Europe and elsewhere," said a CPP bulletin (see *Ang Bayan*, 1987; Clad, 1987; Newmann, 1987).

In conclusion, most of the four factors of revolutionary change are still present in the Philippines. There is still enough poverty and injustice to provide fertile grounds for radical mobilization. As a result of the restoration of traditional family-based political dynasties, initial political reforms have not been complemented with essential economic and social reforms. The early momentum for economic and social reforms has been stalled in controversies over land reform and local autonomy. Opportunities created by the "People Power" movement, the establishment of the Aquino government, and its initial political reforms have diminished. Traditional family-based political dynasties have reemerged to resist proposed government reforms and to resume their domination of national and local politics. Democratic institutions have been revived, but they only provide democracy for the few. Mass poverty remains a massive obstacle to Philippine democracy.

The rebels will continue to attract recruits as long as the poor rural majority are victimized by land grabbing, tenancy and labor inequalities, and military abuses. After the demise of the Marcos government, the CPP lost popular support, but the remaining leadership is hard-core, hard-line, and adaptive to changing circumstances. It can still provide its own brand of revolutionary justice. It has intensified armed struggle to polarize the conflict between right-wing and left-wing forces. It expects that the legal Left and other moderate reform activists will be forced to choose sides and that many of them will choose to go underground and thereby expand the forces for revolutionary change in the Philippines. It is now seeking international support.

Finally, the transformation of legitimacy may yet be sparked by the national debate over the continued presence of U.S. military bases and increased U.S. aid for counterinsurgency. If the United States were to pursue its interests without basic economic and social reforms by the Philippine government, the United States and the Aquino administration would become obvious targets for radical nationalist movements.

NOTES

1. These include Kessler (1989), Chapman (1987), Porter (1987, 1989). A definitive history is available from Wurfel (1988). For a recent comprehensive bibliography see U.S. Department of Defense Army War College, 1988.

2. For example, IMF auditors discovered that the total foreign debt had been understated by over seven billion dollars for most of 1983 due to "accounting errors"; It was then revised and overestimated at twenty-five billion dollars. It was also revealed that the Philippine Central Bank had overstated its foreign exchange reserves by about six hundred million dollars. To make matters worse, it was also discovered that the money supply had been inexplicably expanded by about 30 percent during the last quarter of 1983, far in excess of past growth rates and IMF agreements. Some foreign bankers said that the increased money supply was part of an attempt by senior financial officers to bail out a number of ailing businesses and to transfer capital to safe deposits outside the country. For further details, see Galang (1984: 90–91), Sacerdito and Galang (1984: 42–43), Rowen (1984: G1, G18), and *Economist* (1984: 79).

3. See Business Environment Risk Analysis (1983: 1). Other equally gloomy independent risk assessments were Napier (1983) and International Business Government Counsellors (1983).

4. See Communist Party of the Philippines (1968).

5. For an account of the persistent causes of insurgency in poor areas like Negros, see Clad (1986).

6. See Foreign Broadcast Information Service (1985: 7); also Williams (1985).

REFERENCES

Amnesty International (1988). *Philippines: Unlawful Killings by Military and Paramilitary Forces.* New York: Amnesty International USA, March.
Ang Bayan (1987). "On the International Relations of the Communist Party of the Philippines," 7 July.

Branigan, William (1983). "Philippine Communist Rebels Press Ahead with Insurgency," *Washington Post*, 11 December, A32.

Browning, E. S. (1983). "Communist NAP Slowly Gains Influence in Philippines," *Asian Wall Street Journal*, 4 July, 3.

Business Environment Risk Analysis (1983). "FORCE '83 Report on the Philippines."

Campbell, Colin (1983). "Bankers Say Marcos Must Move," *New York Times*, 29 October, D1, 38.

Chapman, William (1987). *Inside the Philippine Revolution*. New York: Norton.

Clad, James (1988). "Targeting the Legal Left," *Far Eastern Economic Review*, 21 July.

―――― (1987). "Betting on Violence," *Far Eastern Economic Review*, 17 December.

Cohen, Margot (1989). "Lesson in Blood," *Far Eastern Economic Review*, 1 June.

Communist Party of the Philippines (1984). "Statement on the Assassination of Ninoy Aquino," 24 August.

―――― (1972). "Tasks of the Communist Party of the Philippines in the New Situation," 12 October.

―――― (1968). "Rectify Errors and Rebuild the Party," Mimeograph.

Economist (1984). "On the Back of a Manilla Envelop," 7 April.

Far Eastern Economic Review (1987). "Philippines' NPA: The Read Threat," 17 December, p. 11.

―――― (1986). "Back with the People," 2 January, p. 14.

Fineman, Mark (1987). "Acquino Triumph Dimmed by Lack of Unity, Stability," *Los Angeles Times*, 4 February.

―――― (1987a). "Ramos Battered in Role as Philippine Unifier," *Los Angeles Times*, 19 February.

―――― (1987b). "Philippine Military Under Fire," *Los Angeles Times*, 23 February.

―――― (1987c). "Aquino Ties Blast to Foes in Military," *Los Angeles Times*, 23 March.

―――― (1987d). "22 Soldiers Killed in Mine Bomb Attack," *Los Angeles Times*, 18 March.

―――― (1987e). "Cults Wage War on Philippines' Communists," *Los Angeles Times*, 3 April.

Foreign Broadcast Information Service (1985). 9 August, p. 7.

Galang, Jose (1984). "Things Fall Apart," *Far Eastern Economic Review*, 19 January, 90–91.

Guerrero, Amado (1979). "Specific Characteristics of People's War in the Philippines," Oakland, CA: International Association of Filipino Patriots.

Heise, Carol (1988). "Philippines: Squads," *Third World Week*, 29 July.

Honolulu Star Bulletin (1983). "Bishops Condemn Marcos," 21 February, A-4.

International Business Government Counsellors (1983). "The Philippines: A Country Risk Assessment," November.

Japan Economic Newswire (1987). "Red Army Man Eludes Police Manhunt," 5 December.

Jones, Clayton (1987a). "Acquino Grapples with Military Dissent on Charter," *Christian Science Monitor*, 5 February.

—————— (1987b). "Filipino 'Village Spies' Help Army," *Christian Science Monitor*, 23 March.

—————— (1986). "Filipino Rebels' Class Dilemma," *Christian Science Monitor*, 29 December.

Jones, Greg (1987). "Aquino Outlines Tough Policy," *Washington Post*, 23 March.

Kessler, Richard (1989). *The Politics of Repression in the Philippines*. New Haven: Yale University Press.

McBeth, John (1989). "Critical Solidarity," *Far Eastern Economic Review*, 1 June.

McCoy, Alfred W. (1988). "Oligarchy: Filipino Families and the Politics of Survival." Paper presented to the 40th Annual Meeting of the AAS, San Francisco, March.

Metro Manila Times (1983). "USSR-Philippines: Successful Rapprochement," 4 December, 4.

Mojares, Resil B. (1988). "The Dream Lives On and On." Paper presented to the 40th Annual Meeting of the AAS, San Francisco, March.

Miranda, Felipe B. and Ruben F. Ciron (1988). "Development and the Military Perceptions in a Time of Continuing Crisis." Singapore: Institute of Southeast Asian Studies, January.

Mydans, Seth (1981). "Philippine Mutiny Abets Communists, Top General Says."

—————— (1988). "Philippine Rebel Leader Escapes During Birthday Party for Captor," *New York Times*, 13 November.

—————— (1987a). "Troops in Manila Kill 12 in Crowd at Leftist Rally," *New York Times*, 23 January.

—————— (1987b). "Death in a Quiet Filipino Hamlet," *New York Times*, 17 February.

—————— (1987c). "Philippine Communists Say Fight Shifts to Cities," *New York Times*, 7 September.

—————— (1987d). "Manila Fights Rebels with Roundups," *New York Times*, 1 January.

—————— (1987e). "Aquino Demands Military Victory Over Insurgents," *New York Times*, 23 March.

—————— (1987f). "Right-Wing Vigilantes Spread in Philippines," *New York Times*, 4 April.

—————— (1987g). "For Aquino, a Growing Threat from Extremists," *New York Times*, 27 December.

—————— (1987h). "Aquino Demanding Arrest of Leaders in Military Revolt," *New York Times*, 30 August.

Napier, Ron (1983). "The Philippines: The Economics of 'No Choice,'" Data Resources Inc., May.

Neumann, A. Lin (1987). "Communists in Philippines Reportedly Near

Gaining Official Nod from Soviets," *San Francisco Examiner*, 29 November.

New People's Army (1980). "Statement on the Eleventh Annual Anniversary of the New People's Army" in *Ang Bayan*, 29 March, p. 1.

———— (1969). "Basic Document."

New York Times (1987). "Member of Aquino Cabinet Is Assassinated," 3 August, p. 1.

Philippine News (San Francisco) (1983). "Manifesto of Freedom, Democracy, and Sovereignty," Manila, 21 September; published in *Philippine News* (San Francisco, 5–11 October).

Porter, Gareth (1989). "Strategic Debates and Dilemmas in the Philippine Communist Movement," *Philipinas*, November.

———— (1987). "The Politics of Counterinsurgency in the Philippines: Military and Political Options," University of Hawaii, Center for Philippine Studies, Philippine Studies Occasional Paper No. 9, February.

Quinn-Judge, Paul (1985). "Insurgency in the Philippines Could Provoke Full-Scale War Unless Growth Is Checked," *Christian Science Monitor*, 15 October.

Richburg, Keith (1988). "New Philippine Prosperity: Are Figures Only an Illusion?" *Washington Post*, 18 August.

Rocamora, Joel (1983). "Is Marcos a Lame-Duck Dictator?" *Southeast Asia Chronicle*, Issue No. 92, December.

Rowen, Hobart (1984). "Philippine Debt Stunned Lenders," *Washington Post* 29 January, G1, G18.

Sacerdoti, Guy and Jose Galang (1984). "Manila Money Games," *Far Eastern Economic Review*, 26 January, 42–43.

Sesit, Michael (1983). "Bankers Delay Bailout Talks with Manila," *Wall Street Journal*, 12 December, 30.

Staas, Richard (1984). "Philippines" in *Yearbook on International Communist Affairs*, quotation of Ang Katipunan, Stanford, California: Hoover Institution.

Trumbull, Robert (1983). "Filipino Communist Rebels Press Attacks on Army and Corruption," *New York Times*, 30 November, A16.

US Army War College (1988). "The Communist Party of the Philippines (CPP) and the New People's Army (NPA): An Annotated Bibliography," Strategic Studies Institute, December.

United States Senate (1985). "The Situation in the Philippines," Select Committee on Intelligence, 1 November.

Walsh, Mary Williams (1988a). "Philippine Economy Mixes Hope, Hype," *Wall Street Journal*, May 9.

———— (1988b). "In the Philippines, Justice Delayed Is Still Justice Denied," *Wall Street Journal*, 24 October.

Williams, Nick (1985). "Philippine Insurgents Now Targeting Cities," *Los Angeles Times*, 5 September.

Wurfel, David (1988). *Filipino Politics: Development and Decay* Ithaca: Cornell University Press.

CHAPTER EIGHT

Anticolonial Revolutionary Nationalism

Revolutionary dynamism can be defined by the emergence of a nationalism directed against the narrow nationalist rule of a distinct immigrant, settler, or "fragment" regime. South Africa and Israel are two states with highly nationalist regimes that have evolved without including the political participation of the majority or near-majority indigenous population. The focus here is not regime illegitimacy but rather the existence of a legitimacy identified with the ethnically or racially defined ruling population stimulating an opposing legitimacy among the disenfranchised indigenous population. Emanating from this process is a confrontation between the entrenched legitimacy of the ruling oligarchy and the emerging nationalist legitimacy of a movement espousing full political participation and autonomy.

The cases of the African National Congress and the Palestine Liberation Organization illuminate a revolutionary contagion effect that is a variation of the concept introduced by Foltz in Chapter 3. However, in the cases of the ANC and PLO the "germ" of nationalism carried by the ruling regime is then "caught" or emulated by the indigenous population. In this sense, the link of these two nationalisms is closer to the colonial-anticolonial dynamic introduced by Chaliand in Chapter 2.

As in the classical case of Algeria, the revolutionary movement's challenge is political rather than ideological, that is, the movement ultimately emphasizes more a rearrangement of political power than the introduction of any new ideology. In both the PLO and ANC, ideology has been subordinated to the focus on the achievement of political power and to fractionalization of competing ideologies within the movements.

—THE EDITORS

South Africa: The ANC

STEPHEN M. DAVIS

The concept of revolution in South Africa has become the political equivalent of an apparition: some have seen it, others believe it can never be. President Ronald Reagan declared at a March 1988 press conference that in South Africa "we don't have an armed insurrection going on as we have in some other countries." South African State President P. W. Botha, on the other hand, charged that the outlawed African National Congress (ANC) was conspiring with the South African Communist party (SACP) to orchestrate a "total onslaught," including violence and terrorism against the state. Yet his minister of law and order, Adriaan Vlok, claimed in April 1988 that "the ANC and its communist masters had failed in inciting the masses to follow their line of thought." The ANC itself asserts that it has made progress using armed struggle together with nonviolent pressures to force an end to apartheid. Observers seeing twin images of carefree whites lounging around pools and blacks planting limpet bombs near government offices cannot determine with certainty whether a meaningful insurrection has been under way.

I argue that rebellion, if not revolution, has indeed been taking place in South Africa. Moreover, it can be shown to have achieved limited successes and to be contributing to the process of ending apartheid and ushering in majority rule. Yet South Africa's insurgency movement has never had the potential for bringing about complete collapse of the existing power structure, an action that would constitute fulfillment of the classic definition of a revolution.

FROM PETITION TO INSURGENCY

The ANC's weaknesses and strengths as an insurgency movement in the late 1980s can be traced to the early years of its existence. Founded in 1912 by a small, Christian-educated, middle-class elite, the Congress sought to expand rights for blacks in the new Union of South Africa by using constitutional instruments provided the country by Britain, the metropolitan power. They petitioned the crown and lobbied peacefully but achieved little. The government was preoccupied with the tensions of competing white nationalisms, English and Afrikaner, whose peoples had only recently clashed in a bitter civil war for primacy in South Africa. Having won at great cost, the English were seeking to build a stable accommodation with their white rivals. And one point on which nearly the entire white community agreed was that blacks should have no place in the governance of South Africa.

As the union's economy grew in the first decades of the century, and increasing numbers of blacks were conscripted into the mines and the manufacturing sector, black labor organizations initiated mass protests. But the ANC remained at its core a coalition of middle-class professionals and traditional chiefs with a national membership base of just one thousand. It sought change conservatively, using channels of negotiation marked out by the government. The Congress elite continued to trust in the possibility of a gentlemanly compromise that would grant blacks a say in ruling South Africa.

In a final act of faith in white governmental goodwill, the ANC endorsed Prime Minister Jan Smuts's entry into the international alliance against Nazi Germany, even as white Afrikaner members of the opposition National party lobbied for partnership with Hitler. Dr. Alfred Bitini Xuma and his Congress executive expected to be repaid at the war's end with abolition of the pass laws and a program of equal rights. In a shock to black leadership, however, Smuts soon abandoned his drive to lower racial barriers in order to fend off the surging National party.

The general reaffirmation of white supremacy in the 1943 general election brought the ANC to the first of three milestones that would determine its present character. The Congress executive declared the apparent futility of passive negotiation. Xuma struck out on a new path, converting his clubby organization into a national movement, complete with a new activist platform and a national political structure designed to challenge white rule assertively and insistently.

In the midst of this political foundation building, and in part in reaction to it, white voters swept the National party to power in the 1948 general election. The new government wasted no time in solidifying and formalizing the segregationist system it began to label "apartheid." Nor did it take long to manifest an implacable hostility toward the ANC and other groups opposed to white authority with arrests and bannings. The Communist party was outlawed completely in 1950. But the ANC, now controlled by a new generation of impatient activists including Nelson Mandela and Oliver Tambo, launched a series of nonviolent protest campaigns aimed at attracting a mass following in the black community. By 1952, it claimed a party membership of over one hundred thousand.

The ANC of the 1950s may have dramatically broadened its base and sharpened its opposition to minority rule, but it remained faithful to the notion that peaceful pressure could persuade the government to yield. To maximize its leverage, the Congress built alliances with organizations in the colored, Indian, and white communities and began working with underground members of the Communist party. Moreover, the ANC coordinated a multiracial, three-thousand-strong "Congress of the People," assembled in

Johannesburg's Kliptown Township in June of 1955, to adopt the manifesto of principles that came to be known as the Freedom Charter.

The document unequivocally endorsed multiracialism over black exclusivism and envisioned a postapartheid democracy with a mixed economy. In a South African context the charter was then, and remains today, a radical statement. Yet because it did not call for a complete overturning of the economic structure, Marxists and many labor leaders criticized the Freedom Charter as a liberal rather than revolutionary platform.

Those activists who saw the antiapartheid struggle as a blacks-only affair considered the charter an invitation to whites to dominate the liberation movement just as they controlled the government. In 1959, in a traumatic split with the ANC, these dissidents broke away and formed the rival Pan-Africanist Congress (PAC).

Ironically it was the PAC that brought the African National Congress to the second milestone in its development. Rushing to attract blacks impatient with the progress of the ANC, the PAC called a national demonstration against the pass laws for 21 March 1960. Police fired into a crowd at Sharpeville, killing sixty-seven blacks and sparking a worldwide storm of protest against apartheid. Within weeks, an unnerved Pretoria moved to outlaw both the upstart PAC and the ANC.

Suddenly the Congress had to face the failure of its forty-eight year policy of nonviolent pressure against white rule. A consensus developed within the leadership that the ANC would now have to resort to armed action, though moderates insisted that violence be tightly restricted to sabotage missions causing no casualties. Holding to the theory that Pretoria could still be brought to negotiations, they argued that a brief campaign of scattered bombings would provide the necessary shock. Instead, security forces crushed the amateur insurgency in 1963, and the National party reigned almost unchallenged for a decade. African National Congress officials who were not already incarcerated were forced into exile.

The third milestone determining the Congress's character was, like the first two, included by others. On 16 June 1976 twenty thousand black pupils marched through Soweto in another of many nonviolent, antiapartheid actions inspired by the five-year-old black consciousness movement (BCM). This time the police used lethal force to destroy the demonstration and in doing so triggered an eighteen-month period of black uprisings across South Africa.

The Soweto Rebellion introduced a new generation of blacks to the ANC. While the organization had had almost nothing to do with the uprisings, it had relocated its exile headquarters from Europe to southern Africa, revitalized its underground inside South Africa, and built the means to jump-start armed resistance. Therefore, when Pretoria banned key black consciousness groups in 1977 and when increasing numbers of blacks became convinced anew of the ineffectiveness of peaceful protest, the ANC was there to benefit. Suddenly its rear base training camps, schools, and administrative offices were overcrowded with recruits escaping South Africa for a chance to fight back.

The ANC's insurgency of the 1980's was to an unusual extent a product of these historical experiences. A political movement in a free society seeks to influence daily events and draws its agenda from uninhibited constituent debate. History for this type of body plays a relatively peripheral role in shaping platforms. But between 1960 and 1990 the ANC was frozen out of free debate in South Africa, its survival was under constant threat, and its principal objective was long-term. As a result, it developed its own all-embracing culture to justify sacrifices and sustain hope. Historical experience remains the cardinal ingredient of the ANC's portrait of its world.

The Congress, for example, instinctively cleaves to its social roots. The leadership remains a middle-class one, oriented toward liberal Western values and attentive to the church's influence even though there is a significant Communist party presence in the national executive. Black labor, which in the 1920s viewed the ANC as bourgeois, still privately suspects the movement of considering economic revolution of secondary importance. Moreover, the leadership reflects pragmatism in its persistent advocacy of nonracialism and its refusal to endorse unrestrained violence. Leaders of the ANC concede that the movement's openness to whites and its limit on casualties from Umkhonto we Sizwe operations produced frustration and dissension among militant activists in South Africa. But the national executive has revered ANC traditions in these areas and views them as endowing the organization with a moral superiority that could prove attractive to internal whites and external patrons.

Similarly, the ANC believes it learned lessons from 1943, 1960, and 1976. It sees the Smuts betrayal as teaching the importance of possessing political bargaining power that cannot be ignored. Consequently, the ANC stretches ideology to accommodate disparate viewpoints and factions, arguing that a broadened coalition maximizes power. It sees the Sharpeville bannings as proving that organizational survival depends on structures that can prevail against repression. As a result, the movement puts a premium on maintaining a secure network inside South Africa, even though the government decided in 1990 to unban the ANC and other insurgency groups. Finally, the Congress sees the Soweto Rebellion as showing the appeal of militancy. Therefore, it has emphasized armed resistance.

INFRASTRUCTURE OF RESISTANCE

Leadership

Although the name Nelson Mandela is intimately linked to the ANC, the Congress has never been a movement primarily dependent on particular leaders. This in part reflects the history of counterinsurgency tactics in South Africa; Pretoria did not wait long before detaining, banning, or otherwise immobilizing blacks who rose to command positions in resistance organizations. In addition, the ANC is a federation of interests rather than a Leninist party and as such must achieve intergroup consensus instead of depending on executive leadership to take action. Finally, the political culture of Congress constituents is one that demands a high degree of participation in decisionmaking. Blacks so long denied a say in how their lives are governed react by insisting on broad debate over ANC policy. As a result, ANC changes are often slow to emerge, and leaders have been important more for their symbolic position than for their individual power bases within the movement.

At the pinnacle of the ANC's organization is the thirty-member National Executive Committee (NEC). Expanded from twenty-two at the 1985 Consultative Conference, the NEC was reorganized as a kind of federal structure encompassing within its ranks representatives of major constituent units within the ANC, including the South African Communist party (SACP), the South African Congress of Trade Unions, Umkhonto we Sizwe, the women's section, and others.

Pretoria charges that over two-thirds of NEC members are communists, while experts such as Tom Karis say there are not more than three who are communists. The State Department in a January 1987 report estimated that "roughly half" of the NEC are Communist party members. The ANC itself has not released any numbers. But any measurement of communist influence within the ANC leadership must take into account the fact that within South Africa the SACP is thought to hold the allegiance of only a fraction of the black community. Many blacks are suspicious of the SACP's links to an outside power (the Soviet Union) and uncomfortable with its history as a party often controlled by whites. The current chairman, for example, is Joe Slovo, a white South African. As a result, the SACP is in a weak bargaining position within the national executive of the ANC, which remains dominated by black nationalists and moderates. The 1987 State Department report took the view that "the SACP appears to have little or no influence on political and labor groups inside South Africa" and that this lack of popular support gives noncommunist leaders of the ANC "considerable counterleverage against SACP efforts to dominate the group." In fact, in recent years the SACP has openly declared its subservience to African National Congress aims.

Ideology

The ANC is a nationalist movement that has paid only intermittent and cautious attention to ideology. In fact, the Congress leadership seems to regard ideology with a certain dread, recognizing its importance in motivating followers but fearful that it could divide the ranks rather than expand them. The last occasion on which the movement formally adopted any document close to an ideological statement was when the Congress of the People approved the Freedom Charter in 1955. Since then, the rare plenary meetings of ANC representatives have addressed operational matters almost exclusively. Even in 1988, when the ANC's Constitution Committee released its "Constitutional Guidelines" for a postapartheid South Africa, spokespersons reeled off a string of qualifiers. The eight-member drafting body emphasized that the document contained proposals for "discussion purposes" only, and could not be formally adopted as a constitutional model until elected representatives from South Africa could assemble to debate one.

Three important ideological clusters are evident within the Congress movement, though their relative strengths are difficult to measure. One is Marxism, which is propagated by the SACP. It attracts support among members with trade union experience and has grown in popularity among younger rank-and-file recruits, owing largely to the Soviet Union's high-profile assistance to the ANC. The Reagan administration's "constructive engagement" policy, which was regarded in ANC circles as a declaration of friendship for Pretoria, is often cited as another reason youths in recent years spurned the West and turned to communist thought. But the repudiation of Marxism-Leninism in Eastern Europe and parts of Africa (including neighboring Mozambique) has undercut this faction. Even the SACP has openly accepted the need for a mixed economy and multiparty system in postapartheid South Africa.

A second is black consciousness, the philosophy that brought the ANC's Soweto generation into antiapartheid activism. Some two-thirds of the estimated thirteen thousand Congress members in the exile community were schooled in BCM principles before escaping South Africa in search of an organization prepared to arm them. They entered the ANC suspicious of nonracialism, one of the canons of Congress practice, and of cooperation with the Communist party.

A third is what might be termed social democratic, and it encompasses the veteran leadership of the ANC. Adherents represent the traditional values of the ANC, the sort of ideological brew once associated with institutions such as the London School of Economics, which combines Christian teachings with Western liberal philosophy and enthusiasm for a restrained form of socialism.

To accommodate the often-contradictory ideological strains within the movement, the Congress leadership has sought constantly to persuade constituencies to defer pursuing their special ideological and programmatic agendas until after "liberation." It has argued with justification that intramovement differences have been exaggerated and exploited by the ANC's enemies, and it deploys a network of "commissars" to watch for signs of incipient divisions. As a result, the Congress ends up promoting a vaguely defined nationalist line that stresses the objective of substituting democracy for apartheid in a unitary South Africa. This lowest-common-denominator approach to ideology has been successful in securing unity if at the cost of some frustration, but it might well come under severe strain at the point at which the Congress negotiates with the National party and faces hard choices concerning South Africa's future.

Organization and Strategy

The ANC was forced to establish rear bases in host states far from the South African frontier when the organization relocated its operations to Africa from Britain in the early 1970s. One by one the majority-ruled nations on South Africa's border found themselves compelled through the force of Pretoria's economic and military might to bar permanent ANC camps on their soil. Consequently, the congress erected its facilities in a belt of states stretching from west Africa to east Africa. Camps assigned to the ANC's military wing, Umkhonto we Sizwe, were until 1990 located in northern and central Angola. Following the Angola-Namibia accord, troops were relocated to Uganda and Tanzania. The ANC's administrative offices were in Lusaka, Zambia, and the movement's educational facilities were near Morogoro, Tanzania. Some thirteen thousand exiles dwelled in these "sanctuary states." In contrast, Umkhonto normally used border countries only for rapid transit of guerrillas, couriers, and arms runners into and out of South Africa.

Inside the republic itself, before being unbanned, the ANC survived by virtue of its underground, which was laid out along lines first proposed by Nelson Mandela in the 1950s. The "M-Plan" network consisted of cells of as few as five members in rural areas and as many as twelve in urban townships. Their number throughout the country was unknown, but there were believed to be some ten to twelve regional commands.

The system was arrayed in such a way as to maximize security. Members used code names and covert communication techniques and were usually unaware of the identity of ANC members in other cells. On those occasions when government intelligence succeeded in exposing a cell, the damage to the Congress underground was therefore confined.

The underground, however, remained small relative to the ambitions of the ANC's leaders and the requirements of a full-blown rebellion. Most cells were located in urban areas, reflecting the Congress's traditional appeal to urban, politicized blacks more than rural dwellers. But even these township branches were too few to absorb or control all the activists seeking to participate in resistance.

The reason may be traced to the lateness of the ANC's conversion from what has been termed "armed propaganda" to a strategy of "people's war." Prior to 1985 the ANC depended largely upon guerrillas trained abroad infiltrating the country to carry out insurgent operations. Pretoria's improved border defenses, however, limited the number of those able to enter the country. Moreover, the insurgents who did get in concentrated more on executing actual missions than on recruiting large numbers of new members among the black population. But after the 1984 Nkomati Accord committed Mozambique to shut down ANC operations posts and after the ANC rank and file voted at the 1985 consultative conference to endorse intensified armed resistance, the Umkhonto command placed more emphasis on internal recruitment and home-based training. By its own assessment, there was incremental rather than rapid expansion of the ANC underground using these tactics. Security clampdowns, while unable to halt ANC operations, appeared nevertheless to have impeded them.

Beginning in 1985, when the ANC and the United Democratic Front (UDF) called on blacks to "make the townships ungovernable," the Congress sought to transplant the base of its insurgent campaign from external camps to internal sanctuaries. The new strategy called for sabotage missions launched from townships against targets identified with governmental power. In addition, the ANC sought to complement military operations with support for nonviolent labor and community organizations (Congress of South African Trade Unions [COSATU] and the UDF) aimed at placing increasing pressure on Pretoria. The objective was to attract a growing proportion of the public to the ANC and to undermine white confidence in the National party administration's capacity to determine the country's future or guarantee white security.

The Congress strategy was one fraught with risk because it suggested potentially contradictory tactics. On the one hand, satisfying impatient and angry young recruits was a policy that could have compelled Umkhonto to abandon the prohibitions against violence against civilians. Veteran ANC executives often fretted over the willingness of some young Congress members and supporters to engage in terror strikes against whites. On the other hand, the ANC leadership was eager to preserve and enhance the ANC's image as a responsible party, both to allay fears of whites inside South Africa and to attract more international sponsors. This tug of war between militancy and statesmanship grew more acute as black frustration mounted and the ANC continued to lag in its ability to extend effective command and control over its members inside the country. It is likely to remain a source of tension as the ANC negotiates with the National party while trying to avoid defections by radicals.

External Patrons

While barred from legal operations inside South Africa, the ANC depended on external patrons for resources, facilities and assistance. The Reagan administration, in its early hostility toward the ANC, often focused on the Congress's long-time relationship with the Soviet Union. But the reality was that ANC could have survived a break with Moscow with minimal difficulty, since most of the items the Soviets provided—arms, scholarships, equipment, and funds—were available from alternative sources. In contrast, a break with the three states that granted the movement sanctuary—Angola, Zambia, and Tanzania—could have been catastrophic, though not fatal. African National Congress facilities in these countries gave Umkhonto insurgents access to the nearby South African frontier; they were close enough to the border to allow relatively regular communication and contact. Expulsion from any one of the sanctuary states would have ruptured those links and resulted in a stressful regroupment to less convenient climes. This was precisely the impact of the 1989–1990 withdrawal from Angola. But expulsion from all three could have severely damaged morale and set the ANC back years.

For this reason, the ANC was constantly engaged in efforts to sustain the three host governments' commitment to assisting the movement. Such efforts involved regular contacts between Congress leaders and sanctuary state politicians. They also involved major ANC campaigns to generate continental or international diplomatic benefits to the three for supporting the Congress and costs for abandoning it. The more destabilization pain Pretoria inflicted on the three for hosting the ANC, the more the ANC worked in the region and around the world to guarantee that their frontline patrons held firm.

Dependence on Angola, Zambia, and Tanzania made the ANC leadership distinctly nervous. It was aware that the frontline states excercised enormous influence over Zimbabwe's Patriotic Front by virtue of the insurgent group's reliance on Mozambique and Zambia for bases. In fact, delegations from the two states, rather than the two constituent parties of the Patriotic Front, were the key negotiators with Britain at the Lancaster House talks that gave birth to Zimbabwe. Executives of the ANC worried that the sanctuary nations, under economic and military pressure from Pretoria, were capable of making policy demands of the ANC, ejecting the Congress altogether, or insisting on South African settlement terms far short of what the ANC would itself demand.

In this context, the ANC viewed Mozambique's ratification of the Nkomati Accord with Pretoria in 1984 as an ominous sign, even though the movement's facilities in the country were few in comparison with the three sanctuary states. Similarly, the Congress was set back when, as part of a package accord, Angola agreed to expel the ANC along with the Cubans as the price for a South African military withdrawal and independence for Namibia.

The Soviet Union—once an unquestioning ally—represents another source of anxiety for the ANC. Gorbachev's Africanists have signaled a change in course for Soviet policy in South Africa. Moscow's objective is now to find ways to avoid an extended war that could compel the Soviets to devote resources it cannot afford into a region in which it has little interest while risking a superpower confrontation it does not want. As a consequence, Soviet representatives have lobbied at the ANC to soften the terms Pretoria must meet for negotiations to occur. In addition, Soviet policymakers have pressed the ANC to consider a settlement formula that grants more minority guarantees to whites than the Congress has been prepared to concede. Moscow told its close ally, the South African Communist Party, that a mixed economy, rather than communism, is likely to prevail in South Africa and Soviet officials began quiet contacts with the South African government.

While the new Soviet policies unsettled the ANC, they suggested opportunities for joint superpower approaches to the crisis of apartheid. In addition, they opened a window for expanded U.S. contacts with the ANC, which was more eager than ever before to diversify its international patronage.

COUNTERING REBELLION

Pretoria's response to the ANC's insurgency was packaged under the label "total strategy." It assumed, correctly, that the government was facing a political conflict rather than a conventional military threat. It asserted that counterinsurgency plans would necessarily involve a political offensive using military tactics in concert with initiatives to resolve black grievances. On the military front the government constructed the continent's mightiest and most modern army. But implementing an effective political offensive depended most importantly on an accurate assessment of black motivations and aspirations, and in this the National party leadership miscalculated.

The Rabie Commission, whose diagnosis of black opposition became the basis for later counterinsurgency strategy, concluded in 1982 that "people in the black community who had pro-ANC feelings constituted a very small minority and that their influence should not be overestimated." The Botha government characterized the resistance movement as one controlled by communist agitators who held sway in the townships primarily on account of intimidation. The "broad middle" of the black community, in Pretoria's view, favored evolutionary, peaceful change. They could be persuaded to acquiesce to the government's timetable of "reform" and reject the militancy of the ANC.

An accurate assessment of an insurgent movement's base of support is critical to defense strategy because a guerrilla struggle is a contest for hearts and minds. To the extent that an insurgent group can mobilize public assistance, it has access to intelligence, sanctuary, food, protection, and additional manpower. Even when overwhelmingly outgunned, its soldiers can claim the advantage of surprise in carrying out missions. On the other hand, to the extent that the government has credibility among the populace, it can have ready access to intelligence information vital in defeating its foe. Deprived of that weapon, even the most modern hardware can only partially compensate commanders who do not know who their enemies are, where they are located, what they intend to hit, and when they intend to hit it.

The Botha "reform" package was fashioned with the objective of securing political support for the government among sufficient numbers of blacks to deprive the ANC of a critical mass of black assistance. Yet the measures, while meaningful in the eyes of many whites, fell radically short of minimum black demands. As a result, they proved incapable of significantly undercutting ANC support or attracting large numbers of blacks to the government promise of incremental, evolutionary changes in the distribution of power. In fact, Pretoria's 1983 drive to introduce a new constitution granting limited political rights to coloreds and Indians sparked a two-year, nationwide uprising and an intensified rebellion rather than greater confidence in National party authority. Ultimately, Pretoria imposed two states of emergency in 1985 and 1986, and in 1988 it banned the United Democratic Front, which had led the nonviolent, antiapartheid protests. National party strategists also launched drives to destablize the Congress camp by fostering black surrogate opponents and, as evidence now confirms, sponsoring assassination attacks on ANC supporters at home and abroad.

The ANC's insurgency benefited substantially from the government's failure to design a reform package capable of meeting minimum black political needs. Even as nonviolent protest withered under the pressure of detentions, bannings, and other security force actions, Umkhonto we Sizwe actually increased the number of guerrilla operations it carried out in 1987 to an average of at least five each week.

The rise in insurgent actions can be tracked over an eleven-year period to illustrate the trend in internal war. In 1976, authorities attributed an average of just four incidents to ANC guerrillas. In 1983 there were 56 Umkhonto strikes and in 1984 a dip to 44, reflecting the ANC's expulsion from Mozambique. But in 1985 the number tripled to a total of 136. The year 1986 saw a further dramatic rise, to 230. In 1987 attacks reached a new high of at least 247, in spite of the government's claim to have arrested 132 and killed 32 "trained terrorists," a record. More than half of those captured or killed, according to security forces, had been trained inside South Africa. Pretoria announced that it would no longer unveil the number of insurgent attacks, out of concern that opponents "will misuse the figures for political ends." Still, statistics based on what government reporting there was, showed a further climb in guerrilla attacks, to over 300, in 1988. The figure dropped to approximately 200 in 1989, the year in which the ANC Command oversaw a de facto year-end cease fire in response to positive moves by the new South African government.

A portion of Umkhonto attacks attracted national attention, while others affected only local communities. In most cases, they appeared to have accomplished one of their principal political objectives: rallying black support behind the ANC and boosting black morale. More surprisingly, Umkhonto achieved far more success in reaching its second objective—undermining the white community's sense of security and demoralizing supporters of apartheid—than is generally acknowledged.

After over a decade of expanding conflict, a variety of indicators suggested by the late 1980s that the white will to fight was weakening, not hardening, in response to the threat of rebellion. Draft evasion reached an estimated 25 to 40 percent of those called up for service in 1985, the last year for which the government released any figures on conscription results. More than one-third of the white-owned farms along the dangerous guerrilla infiltration belt in the northern Transvaal remained deserted despite more than a decade of generous government programs aimed at luring landowners to stay or return. Some 453 whites in the defense force attempted suicide in 1987, a 500-percent jump over the previous year. This evidence supported widespread reports of declining morale and discipline among draftees. The number of conscientious objector applications rose by 100 percent in 1986. Afrikanerdom split into two bitterly warring camps—the Conservative party and the National party—instead of uniting behind the legendary "laager." English speakers were leaving the country in increasing numbers. White business, religious, and academic delegations met with ANC delegations in Lusaka and returned home arguing that the Congress must be brought to negotiations rather than battled. These were symptoms of a white community confused and divided, not one convinced that current policies had to be defended.

CONCLUSION

By 1989, it was apparent that South Africa was trapped in a crisis growing inexorably more lethal and costly. The ANC leadership, caught between swelling militancy among the rank and file and conservative pressures emanating from the host states and international allies, remained committed to rebellion without revolution. The Botha government, incapable of crushing resistance and beset with constituent dissent, could see no alternative but repression for the purpose of survival. From an outside perspective, it seemed that the only hope for a solution lay in negotiations that included—at the least—the ANC and the National party. But it was equally clear that productive talks awaited the point when both sides would conclude that victory was unattainable.

As an awareness of deadlock began to dawn, positive signs abounded. The Congress leadership, though vulnerable, remained flexible and, true to its history, faithful still to the virtues of military restraint. The organization's external patrons, including the frontline states and the Soviet Union, were inclined toward compromise. Many whites reacted to domestic and international pressure with confusion and doubt behind a mask of bluster. For example, a 1989 public opinion survey conducted by the Investor Responsibility Research Center showed that fully 48 percent of South African whites believed it sensible to seek compromise with sanctions advocates, while only 9 percent said that the country should shun any compromise. Indeed, in the aftermath of the 1989 general elections, State President F. W. DeKlerk declared the combined NP and Democratic Party results a 70 percent mandate for reform and negotiation.

Pretoria's dramatic decisions to unban the ANC, PAC, and other organizations, and to release Nelson Mandela undermined the prediction among some analysts that antiapartheid tactics such as insurgency and sanctions would drive whites to the right. In fact, evidence suggests that the new opportunities for negotiation came about at least partly because increasing numbers of whites were sensing that violence, economic decline, and international isolation were bound to grow without a strategic course change. In this sense, the ANC's insurgency can best be understood as a bargaining chip in the prenegotiation process, rather than as a force with sufficient firepower to bring about revolution.

The Palestine Liberation Organization

As'ad Abu Khalil

The Palestinian popular uprising of 1987–1990 has served to underscore two fundamental aspects of the Palestinian problem, namely, that the Palestinian national movement and its institutional embodiment, the Palestine Liberation Organization (PLO), are the product of collective national consciousness and that Palestinian politics can not be explained in conspiratorial terms. The history of the Palestinian problem has been marred by the denial of the most obvious and pertinent facts by the major parties to the conflict. After all, it was an Israeli prime minister who said, "There is no such thing as a Palestinian."[1]

My objective is to investigate the legitimacy of the PLO as a self-proclaimed revolutionary movement through an analysis of the depth of its expression of Palestinian national consciousness. I will examine the general ideological and structural features of the Palestinian national movement. The analysis will draw on the experiences of the major PLO organizations, avoiding an exclusive focus on Fath, the largest PLO organization. I shall attempt to set claims made in the political literature of this or that PLO organization in the context of PLO political, military, and organizational practice.

The word *"revolutionary"* is used with caution and in a specific sense. The Palestinian national movement, which is headed and represented by the Palestine Liberation Organization, is "revolutionary" insofar as it aims at a radical and thorough change in the political—and only the political—structure of Palestinian territories. In other words, the very objective of establishing a Palestinian state is in itself "revolutionary." However, the reluctance on the part of the PLO, in its various organizations, to address social aspects of Palestinian existence critically is nonrevolutionary. The political objectives of the PLO were not coupled with a similar program regarding the nature of Palestinian society once a Palestinian state is established. Moreover, the PLO has promoted trends of conservatism and traditionalism (even in the realm of political leadership and representation) in Palestinian society. It could be argued that the PLO (in all of its factions) has adamantly resisted the "revolutionization" of Palestinian society in fear of jeopardizing its own interests and popular basis of support.

On the ideological-political spectrum, the PLO (more precisely, the Fath movement, which is its major component) could be situated to the right of center.[2] Since many of the founders of Fath were members of Islamic organizations, the PLO leadership has opted over the years to identify with a vague blend of Islam and Arab nationalism. Reflecting sometimes Arafat's flexible adjustments, sometimes political fluctuations, the PLO would on some occasions emphasize Arab nationalism and on others Islam, depending on the Palestinian public mood. Islam assumed more significance in the PLO's political literature in the aftermath of the Islamic revolution in Iran, which coincided with a decline in the appeal and popularity of Arab nationalism and leftism. Islam became such a favorite tenet of Fath's thought in the past decade that known Marxists in the movement, like Munir Shafiq (director of the PLO's Planning Center), a Palestinian Christian whose real name is George 'Asal, professed their allegiance to Islam as an ideological vehicle.[3]

The PLO is also led by forces that are staunchly anticommunist, either from Muslim, pan-Arab, or Ba'thist perspectives. Some of the key leaders of Fath came from professional jobs in the Arab Gulf countries, and believe in the value of the free enterprise system. The PLO leadership, including the leadership of the Popular Front for the Liberation of Palestine (PFLP) and the Democratic Front for the Liberation of Palestine (DFLP), as well as the other leftist groups, never address the class situation within the Palestinian community. Narrow Palestinian nationalism prevailed among the PLO organizations; and no attempt was made to categorize Palestinians on a class basis, not even by the Marxist-Leninist groups who referred to the

Palestinian bourgeoisie as "the patriotic bourgeoisie." The PLO perceived the Palestinian revolution as one that included all classes and forces in Palestinian society.[4]

The PLO did not attempt to change Palestinian society from within. To be sure, the creation of a Palestinian state, the ultimate objective of all PLO organizations, would affect the very structure of Palestinian society. Not only did the PLO organizations refuse to address certain problems within the Palestinian society, but they attributed all ills to Zionism. Thus, the oppression of Palestinian women by Palestinian men was viewed as a consequence of Israeli occupation of Palestinian lands. According to the PLO logic, all problems within the Palestinian community would disappear once the Palestinian state came into being.

The tendency of all official Palestinian institutions has been to focus on women's issues only insofar as they furthered the policies and public relations efforts of the male-dominated PLO. Thus, the main function of women's organizations in all guerrilla groups—from Fath to the minuscule Palestinian Popular Struggle Front—is to echo the political line of their sponsoring organization. The prevailing view within the political elite is to subordinate the struggle against the socioeconomic oppression of women to the war of liberation. Moreover, PLO organizations believe that the liberation of Palestine will inevitably result in the freedom of women in Palestinian society. The status of women in the Arab world gives no credence to such a belief.

The PLO organizations also serve as forces of conservatism and traditionalism. Products of strict patriarchal Arab societies, all PLO organizations emphasize male-related issues as symbols of the Palestinian revolution. Palestine Liberation Organization posters almost always portray the young Palestinian man with his rifle as a symbol of the Palestinian revolution. Many posters also portray the image of a pregnant woman in a traditional Palestinian dress. This image suggests the role of women as significant only insofar as they bear future male fighters. The emphasis on traditional female dress ignores the majority of modern, professional, nontraditional Palestinian women.

In the occupied territories, the PLO has not encouraged the emergence of a new leadership. Instead, it has made alliances with the traditional "prominent," historically wealthy families. The emergence of the Palestinian uprising, however, heralded a new generation of Palestinians led by a network of young people who do not necessarily descend from the landed families. These people have seized the initiative and relegated the traditional leaders of the Palestinian national movement in the occupied territories to the sidelines. The new leadership sprouted in the camps, the villages, and the poor neighborhoods in the cities.[5] That poorer Palestinians living under occupation would take the initiative and act spontaneously should have been expected. Occupation is felt more strongly by the poor than by the privileged Palestinians who have historically led the Palestinian national movement.

The Palestinian problem has been misrepresented—at best misunderstood—in the West, particularly in the United States, the staunchest supporter of Israel in the Western world. Popular culture and political discourse in the United States concerning Palestinians—and Arabs in general—have been affected by the prevalence of the "paradigm of terrorism," one through which much of the Arab world is viewed. The proliferation of books on the subject attests to the popularity of the paradigm in U.S. government circles as well as in the media. That these books on terrorism in the Middle East are completely discredited among Middle East academicians is apparently of no significance to policymakers. Whether the Palestinian national movement is "terrorist" or not is a political—not a scholarly—question. It is not disputed, however, that most organizations within the body of the PLO have engaged in acts of random violence against civilians.[6]

THE IDEOLOGY OF PALESTINIANISM AND PALESTINIAN IDEOLOGIES

The ideology—more accurately, ideologies—of the Palestinian political organizations have undergone major changes over the years.[7] The most important change has been the assertion of Palestinian national identity, what Shafiq al-Hut (1986) calls "the revitalization of the Palestinian national personality." The emergence of the Fath organization in the 1950s was the result of frustration in the ranks of Palestinian activists concerning the monopolization of Palestinian political representation by Arab regimes. In fact, the Palestinian question was used by the prerevolutionary and postrevolutionary regimes in the Levant as a source of legitimacy.

The Nasserite state, led by Jamal 'Abdul Nasser, the most popular Arab leader in contemporary history, was particularly uncomfortable with the rise of independent Palestinian political will. Nasser had made the commitment to the liberation of Palestine a criterion by which an Arab regime can be termed either "reactionary" or "progressive." Fearful of the implications of Palestinian radicalism, Egypt under Nasser, along with other Arab regimes, sought to create the PLO in order to contain the tide of Palestinian nationalism and to curtail Palestinian political and military activities so as to maintain the status quo with Israel. All these limitations heralded the emergence of Fath as a purely Palestinian organization. Fath (1970: 8) made it clear that "the Palestinian people are the vanguard of the battle of liberation." Arab regimes, whether "revolutionary" or "reactionary" were not permitted to speak for the Palestinians.

Fath's ability to appeal to Palestinians across class and ideological lines lies in its vague ideological expressions or in its lack of ideology. Fath introduced the "ideology of Palestinianism" as a vehicle to secure what Yasir Arafat calls "independent Palestinian decisionmaking."[8] The message of Fath was popular among Palestinians who were disillusioned with official Arab policies concerning the Palestinian question. The credibility that Nasser had in the eyes of some Palestinians as a champion of the Palestinian cause was undermined with the 1967 defeat by Israel—a "setback" (naksah) in Nasserite terminology. Nowhere was the loss of Nasserite credibility more evident than in the politics of the Movement of Arab Nationalists (MAN), which was until then supportive of Nasserite policies.

The very disintegration of the MAN and the transformation of its cells into new Marxist-Leninist organizations reflected the rise of "the ideology of Palestinianism" in Palestinian politics. New Palestinian organizations, originally comprising the Popular Front for the Liberation of Palestine, emerged with Palestinian names to underlie the break with Arab officialdom. Palestinian political control over the plight of the Palestinians was a new phenomenon in the history of the Palestinian problem. Fath went further than other groups by declaring its commitment, theoretically at least, to the slogan of "noninterference in Arab internal affairs." The slogan was intended to comfort Arab regimes who were fearful of the rise of new Palestinian radicalism.

This new version of Palestinian nationalism characterized the PLO presence in Jordan until 1970 and in Lebanon until 1982. The emphasis on Palestinian decisionmaking and indigenous institutions as the only means for the liberation of Palestine clashed with the agendas of most Arab regimes, particularly those who are directly involved with the repercussions of the Palestinian-Israeli conflict. Moreover, the PLO ignored those sections of the population who were sympathetic to the Palestinian cause in the respective host countries. The DFLP (1971: 26–27) later admitted that PLO misconduct and policies in Jordan consolidated narrow Jordanian nationalistic feelings among the "Jordanian masses." However, it was none other than Nayif Hawatmah, the leader of the DFLP, who raised the provocative slogan *All power to the Palestinian resistance* during the 1970 war in Jordan, in an obvious imitation of the Bolshevik slogan *All power to the Soviets*.

The ideology of Palestinianism as it was espoused and practiced by PLO organizations subordinated the concerns of Arab opposition groups in the host countries to the interests of the PLO agenda in these countries. A narrow Palestinian outlook alienated the population in Jordan and distanced the Jordanian opposition movement, which was originally sympathetic to the Palestinian cause. More importantly, the PLO did not even associate itself closely with the Palestinian middle class in Jordan, which later became a champion of Hashemite Jordanian nationalism, introduced as an attractive alternative to the PLO in Jordan.

The aim of independent Palestinian decisionmaking, however, clashed with the PLO's need for Arab financial aid. Only for a brief period of time ending with the 1970s showdown in Jordan was the PLO able to achieve a relative state of political independence. The rise of the bureaucracy within the organizations of the various PLO groups required a continuous flow of Arab money, whether from the "conservative" Arab states to Fath or from the "radical" states to the PFLP and its allies in the Rejection Front of the 1970s.

Nowhere was the ideology of Palestinianism more evident than in the Lebanese phase of the PLO sojourn, lasting until 1982. The ability of the PLO to establish a solid infrastructure across the border from Israel rendered paramount the preservation of the post-1975 status quo in Lebanon. The fixation with maintaining the Lebanese base, which in turn meant increasing the dependence on Arab money and, consequently, policies, estranged the PLO from their allies in the Lebanese national movement. It could even be argued that the PLO was narrowly pursuing its own agenda prior to the eruption of the civil war in 1975.[9]

Nevertheless, it would be inaccurate to assume that the ideology of Palestinianism failed entirely. While it did not eliminate official Arab intervention in Palestinian decisionmaking and while it created an image of chauvinist Palestinian nationalism especially in Jordan and Lebanon, the PLO was successful in appealing to all Palestinians from all walks of life: those living under Israeli rule and those living in the diaspora. That this ideology permeated all Palestinian organizations is an indication of the diminution in the fundamental differences between the various PLO organizations.

While the "ideology of Palestinianism" prevails as the major doctrine for all PLO groups, there are differences among PLO groups concerning the nature of the would-be Palestinian state. These differences tend to determine the political variations between the elements of the PLO.

In the Fath movement, the leadership adopted a practical line. Deep ideological discussions about the nature of the regime in the future Palestinian state were avoided and dismissed as a distraction from the primary objective of *at-Tahrir* (liberation). This was highly appealing to Arab and Palestinian masses, who resented the intensity of ideological squabbles and the acute state of factionalism within the Palestinian Left. Fath promoted some vague formulations about the necessity of unification and "national independence." But Fath's major advantage vis-à-vis other Palestinian organizations resides in its heterogeneous structure. Its organizational bodies contain all ideological elements: Marxist, Muslim fundamentalist, Ba'thist, and right-wing leaders and elements. In the Lebanese popular political lexicon, Fath has all kinds of ideological *dakakin* (shops), to please everybody. This loose ideological formation has caused certain organizational weaknesses within Fath, like disunity, divisiveness, schismatic tensions within the leadership, and lack of discipline within the movement as a whole.

But the peculiar ideological characteristics of Fath broadened its popular base and its circle of regional and international alliances. Furthermore, Fath enjoyed a larger degree of maneuverability and flexibility in its decisionmaking than other PLO groups. Fath was very responsive to the changing public moods of the Palestinian community within and without the occupied territories. It has, for example, adapted to the rising tide of Islamic consciousness among the Arab masses. This has led to confusion among the leftist groups in the PLO. They are no longer able to promote dogmatic Marxist arguments among youths turning increasingly to religiosity.

The PFLP has been characterized by a distinct ideological line. It has stood as a representative of the leftist and "rejectionist" component of the PLO. But it should be remembered that Habash and most of the current leaders of the PFLP only grudgingly advocated Marxism-Leninism. They were, after all, leaders of "the rightist faction" in the Movement of Arab Nationalists (see AbuKhalil, 1987: 362–363). The PFLP's attachment to Marxist-Leninist ideology was less out of conviction than out of necessity. Their audience at the time wanted to adhere to an alternative ideology. The 1967 defeat brought about the intellectual and political bankruptcy of Arab nationalism, especially in its Nasserite version, as a course for the liberation of Palestine.

The PFLP's ideological transformation should be explained in terms of power politics within the Palestinian radical movement. While the PFLP declared its dedication to "scientific socialism" (the Arab communists' favorite euphemism for Marxism-Leninism, given the Arab popular detestation for the doctrine), it had to distinguish its ideology from that of its bitter rival, the DFLP. The PFLP found it expedient to follow the Maoist version of communism in order to underline its independence from Soviet policies in the Middle East and to remind Palestinian masses of Nayif Hawatmah's blind allegiance to Soviet policies. Moreover (and in more practical terms), the Soviet Union considered the PFLP too adventurist in the late 1960s and early 1970s and consequently denied them military and financial aid. On the other hand, China found in the PFLP a useful tool for furthering its aims in the Middle East and for countering the Soviet leverage among Arab communists. Over the last decade the PFLP has become a loyal follower of Soviet policies and, as will be explained, developed few ideological differences with the DFLP. However, both organizations exaggerate their differences to justify their raison d'être.

The DFLP has been consistent in its allegiance to Soviet views on the Palestinian question, including the inappropriateness of the objective of the liberation of all of Palestine. The DFLP (1975: 49–60) was an early advocate of the two-state solution to the Palestinian problem. They also distinguished their version of communism from that of the PFLP. They considered their version to be the "real 'revolutionary' leftist" one, while they considered the PFLP's version to be "nihilist, negativist," and infantile (see Hawatmah, 1977: 13–17). The DFLP, hoping to become the sole official Communist party in the would-be Palestinian state, also emphasizes Marxist-Leninist indoctrination in training its members. Furthermore, the proliferation of Palestinian Marxist-Leninist organizations, like the PFLP, the DFLP, and the three factions of the Palestinian Communist party (the Palestinian Popular Struggle Front, the PFLP–General Command, and the Palestinian Communist Workers' party) increases the pressure on the DFLP to prove and demonstrate its unbending loyalty to the Soviet line. It is possible that Soviet policy encourages a multiplicity of Palestinian communist organizations in order to play them off against each other.

There are, of course, other, less significant Palestinian organizations with their own ideological characteristics. The PFLP–General Command (PFLP–GC), for example, broke off from the PFLP in late 1968 to protest what they considered the heavy ideologization of the organization. The PFLP–GC emphasizes military activity as its primary concern. This is why it was able to attract a significant number of the PFLP's military cadres who were uninterested in the PFLP's ideological deliberations. It was only in August 1973 that the Fourth Congress of the organization approved a comprehensive political program that included the adoption of "scientific socialism."[10] But because of its obsession with military activity, the PFLP–GC failed to leave an ideological impact on Palestinian politics. Its only contribution to Palestinian thought and practice was its military doctrine. While all PLO organizations believed in guerrilla warfare and "popular liberation war," the PFLP–GC believed in conventional methods of warfare, probably influenced by Ahmad Jibril's training in the Syrian Army.

There are no noted ideological traits in other PLO organizations. The Arab Liberation Front, for example, is a mere tool of Iraqi policy, while As-Sa'iqah, is a tool of Syrian policy. Fath–Revolutionary Council (Fath–RC) of Abu Nidal changes its ideological orientation as it changes its patrons. Originally a Ba'thist organization, Fath–Revolutionary Council now seems to identify simultaneously with Iran (especially when it uses the name Organization of Socialist Muslims) and with Libya (especially when it uses the name Arab Revolutionary Brigades).

The Fath–Uprising, which split off from Fath in 1983, mirrors the confusion and ideological vagueness that have characterized the parent organization. Like the leaders of Fath, the leaders of Fath–Uprising do not share one ideological outlook. Abu Musa, for example, is a staunch anticommunist who sees no value in ideological indoctrination and theorization. Abu Khalid al-'Amlah, another influential leader of the movement, is a Marxist who believes in formulating a specific ideological program for the movement.

Finally, it should be emphasized that the existence of small splinter groups within the PLO should be attributed to personal rivalries rather than to ideological distinctions. Thus, these factions are often associated with the idol (secretary general) and not with a particular ideology. For example, the PFLP is associated with Habash, the DFLP with Hawatmah, the PFLP–GC with Jibril, the Fath–RC with Abu Nidal.

THE AIM OF LIBERATION

The political objectives of PLO organizations have undergone significant changes over the years in spite of the rigidity that tends to dominate Western characterization.[11] The search for a solution to the Palestinian problem has been the raison d'être for the emergence of the PLO. While disagreeing over methods, liberation was the simple and ultimate objective of all Palestinian groups. Initially, all of historic Palestine was considered occupied land, but a search for a more pragmatic and moderate solution (to use the terminology of Walid Khalidi [1978: 703]) led to the emergence of the two-state formula in the Palestinian body politic.

The Fath movement adopted—albeit secretively—the two-state solution as early as late 1967, when the central committee of the movement agreed to a phased program entailing the establishment of a Palestinian entity in the West Bank and Gaza (see Abu Nidal, 1984: 45). This same program was discussed in the Second Congress of the movement in 1968 in az-Zabadani in Syria. The idea did not gain Palestinian official or popular endorsement until the 1970s, when the DFLP "theorized" in favor of a state in the West Bank and Gaza.

The DFLP's efforts to win popular approval for the two-state solution preceded the twelfth session of the Palestinian National Council (PNC) in 1974, which adopted the "ten points program," which stipulated that the PLO would establish its "national authority" on a part of historic Palestine (see Abu Nidal and an-Nashshash, 1984: 100). The adoption of this program led to the withdrawal of the PFLP from the Executive Committee of the PLO and to the formation of the Rejection Front "against liquidationist settlements."[12]

The DFLP's enthusiastic support for the two-state solution was much more open and public than that of Fath, at least in the initial stage. In the summer of 1973, the organs of the DFLP devoted much time to the propagation of the efficacy of the two-state solution (see al-Hurriyyah, 1973a, 1973b). In one interview, Nayif Hawatmah described the insistence on the aim of liberating all Palestinian lands as "a nihilistic course" (see an-Nahar, 1973). The role of the DFLP in this respect should, however, not be viewed as a result of an independent soul-searching. Rather, it should be viewed as a decision reflective of Soviet policy by the most loyal client of the USSR at that time in Palestinian politics.[13]

The evolution of Palestinian political thinking in the direction of the two-state solution was the outcome of the series of defeats and setbacks encountered by the PLO. It was not able to achieve the liberation of any part of Palestine through military means. The promises of a "secular state in Palestine" were not matched by the military and political capabilities of the organization. Furthermore, the international diplomatic arena, as well as continued Israeli intransigence, diminished the likelihood of the fullfilment of Palestinian aspirations for full return and state building.

It would be fair to say that international and Arab indifference toward the Palestinian questions eventually lowered the level of political expectations and objectives; but the PLO also raised slogans that far exceeded the actual capabilities and resources of the organization. However, the strategy of the PLO is also a function of the general Arab situation, which has been characterized by weakness and disintegration. The 1973 war demonstrated the limitations of conventional Arab military power and led to the rise of Sadat's school of diplomacy, which was not rejected by Arafat's faction of the PLO before Sadat's trip to Jerusalem.

The aim of liberation, which constituted the cornerstone of the platforms of all PLO organizations, did not entail a concrete proposal for the form of government in the would-be liberated lands. Consistent with the ideology of Palestinianism, the aim of liberation was phrased in general and vague terminology (as the usage of the term *national* to describe the form of government in the future Palestinian state indicates) in order to appeal to the broadest sectors of Palestinian society. There was no attempt, as was said earlier, on the part of any of the Palestinian organizations to address problems intrinsic in Palestinian society.

In 1977 a consensus developed within the PLO around the two-state solution leading to the dissolution of the Rejection Front. The shift in strategy was also accompanied by a diminution in political autonomy. As the emphasis on the military option decreased, the dependence on the various Arab regimes to achieve a diplomatic solution to the Palestinian problem increased. It is important to note the role of the Arab regimes in exposing the shortcomings of the military path of liberation, as "one Arab border after another was closed to guerrilla action" (Sayigh, 1987: 50). The Arab regimes were not and are not prepared or willing to engage in a military confrontation with Israel, due to the superiority of the Israeli military capacity. Furthermore, a protracted military confrontation with Israel is a risk for Arab repressive regimes. A prolonged war with Israel could loosen the grip of these regimes over the army and society.

This is not to imply that the PLO itself had in the first place a comprehensive military plan for the liberation of Palestine. The past record of sporadic military attacks by the various PLO organizations against Israeli targets does not reflect "effective politico-military alternatives" (Sayigh, 1987: 50). Rather, these operations tended to serve the individual interests of the various organizations, which usually launch attacks to mark party anniversaries or to settle intra-Palestinian differences. The lack of coordination in military activities attests to the weakness of the military option as hitherto pursued by the PLO.

The original aim of the liberation of all of Palestine and the establishment of a secular state had been compromised. The PLO had been influenced by international and Arab pressures, as well as by its own impotence. All major PLO organizations now agree to confine Palestinian national aspirations to a ministate in the West Bank and Gaza. Nowhere is this Palestinian consensus more evident than in the PNC meeting in Algiers in 1987, where all groups adhered formally, once again, to the two-state solution and to the convocation of an international peace conference—tantamount to treason only several years ago according to the PFLP (1977). It is also noteworthy that the thirty-six communiqués issued by the Unified National Leadership of the Palestinian uprising between December 1987 and April 1989 contain nothing that contradicts official PLO objectives regarding the two-state solution and the convocation of an international conference.

The nineteenth extraordinary session of the PNC in Algiers in November 1988 attracted international attention, especially after Arafat fulfilled U.S. preconditions for the opening of dialogue between the United States and the PLO. Significant in the PNC meeting was the "declaration of independence," which proclaimed the West Bank and Gaza as an independent state under PLO rule. The PLO was undoubtedly influenced by the ideas of Jerome Segal (1989), who called for such a unilateral act. The PNC session was certainly a direct response to the momentum created by the Palestinian uprising. The resolutions of the PNC, as well as the PFLP's enthusiastic participation, demonstrate that the residents of the occupied territories seem to favor an untimid reconsideration of original PLO objectives and an official confinement of Palestinian national aspiration to the West Bank and Gaza. The results of the PNC were also a realistic reading of the passivity of Arabs living in Israel. The response of Palestinians in Israel to the uprising was clearly mute.

Despite the press focus on the changes in PLO policies and objectives in the PNC resolutions, these changes are not new. But the Western world has been unchanging in its attitude toward the PLO, associating the organization only with the 1968 charter. The series of PNC resolutions since that time, which transcended and often contradicted the charter,[14] have been ignored. The PLO, including the PFLP, has long advocated a two-state solution. What was new, however, was the articulation of PLO objectives in a political language more palatable to the West. Moreover, the PLO was far more explicit than ever in its resolutions. In one respect, this new political expression is indicative of the malaise in PLO ranks.

There are also some other significant changes in the PLO policies in the nineteenth session of the PNC. Not once did the term *armed struggle* appear in either the declaration of independence or the political statement. This contradicts the past fixation with armed struggle as the major (for Fath) or sole (for the PFLP) path toward the liberation of Palestine. Instead, the PLO affirmed its dedication to a peaceful resolution of the conflict.[15] The PFLP did not object to that principle. The decision to accept the 1947 partition plan of Palestine was also historic, not only because it implied a recognition of Israel but also because it conflicted with articles embodied in every charter of every Palestinian organization, including the PLO charter.

LEADERSHIP CHARACTERISTICS

Unlike the realm of ideology and strategy, the leadership of the PLO has undergone few changes over the years. It has become one of the fixed features of Palestinian political life. The continuity in the political leadership of the various PLO organizations has led to much factionalism and dissent in the Palestinian body politic. Given the tremendous impact of personality politics in Palestinian society, as well as in Arab society in general, each of the political organizations of the PLO has been associated with one supreme charismatic Palestinian leader. The charisma and popularity of the "sole" leaders serves as a major source of party recruitment and legitimacy. It can also be a source of disintegration when factions split in protest against the omnipotence of one person in the body of the organization. Nayif Hawatmah, Ahmad Jibril, Hashim 'Ali Muhsin, Wadi' Haddad, and many others split off from the PFLP as a result of strong personal rivalries with George Habash.

This is not to say that other political and ideological factors did not account for tensions and schisms in the organizational structure of the PLO. But ideological inclinations both within the PLO as a whole and within the individual organizations have been associated with certain leaders. George Habash has been associated with a radical maximalist line, Nayef Hawatmah with the Soviet line, and Wadi' Haddad with "international operations."

Forces of conservatism and traditionalism prevail in all PLO organizations when it comes to leadership changes and elite circulation. There appears to be a strong resistance to accountability and responsibility in the ranks of the elite. Major defeats and setbacks, like the humiliating 1982 evacuation of PLO forces from Lebanon, do not lead to resignations and organizational reshuffling. Instead, Arafat chose to promote those who were directly responsible for the shortcomings of the PLO in the 1982 war, triggering the dissident movement of Abu Musa and Abu Salih in 1983. In the words of a knowledgeable Palestinian writer, "Palestinian documents after 1982, especially those issued by the PNC in February 1983, use the same old terms and concepts, as if Beirut did not take place" ('Ayid, 1984: 200).

PLO leaders were particularly sensitive about criticism and self-criticism in their respective organizations, though the Palestinian community has been more pluralistic and less intolerant than other societies in the Arab world. Iron discipline was the norm, and collective leadership the exception. The

PLO did not encourage spontaneous political activism among the Palestinian masses in fear of losing control at the helm of the Palestinian community. Even within the respective organizations, democratization has been restricted; and decisionmaking has been managed by a small group of leaders. The leadership has been careful not to open up the political structure while it has been engaged in secretive diplomatic deals whose exposure could have caused serious political crises and embarrassment.

While the current leadership of the PLO includes a large number of representatives from the middle class, PLO organizations were careful never to address the question of class as embodied in Palestinian society. The ability of the PLO to ignore class differences and tensions enhanced its popularity and helped to unify its appeal across socioeconomic lines. In fact, the current leadership of the PLO struck an alliance with Palestinian traditional and bourgeois families in order to prevent the rise of more radical leaders from lower-income groups, especially in the occupied territories. In return, the Palestinian upper classes provided the PLO with generous financial support and unconditional political loyalty to curtail the growth of the radical Left.

The characteristics of the leadership within the Fath movement, the largest Palestinian group, are somewhat unique. Given the large size of the movement, there are several layers of leadership within the organization. At the top sits Yasir Arafat, who is described by none other than George Habash as being "incorruptible" (Hart, 1984: 38). Arafat's supreme control is largely due to his skillful manipulations of factions and leaders within Fath and within the PLO as a whole. He plays off factions and leaders one against the other in a manner that furthers his own political interests.

The leadership of Arafat is crucial in the discussion of PLO politics not only because he has been at the helm for over two decades but also because he was able to leave his imprint on the Palestinian body politic. Arafat's ability to survive the tremendous events in the Palestinian situation is due to his patience, astute political skills, antiideologism, correct reading of the political mood of the Palestinian community, flexibility, and the miscalculations of his many enemies.

Arafat was politically shrewd within his own movement and within the PLO as a whole. He established a wide network of alliances—and informants—in Fath as well as in all PLO groups. He knew when to delegate authority and when to keep things in his own hands (like dealing personally with his supporters in the leadership of non-Fath PLO groups). He also knew how to take credit for successes and how to let the blame fall on his subordinates for failures and defeats (like the swift defeat of PLO forces in South Lebanon in the course of the Israeli invasion in 1982).

His ability to remain at the helm of such a diverse movement should also be attributed to his personal—especially financial—integrity. He was able to maintain an image of the incorruptible leader in a movement rampant with corruption. It could also be argued that he used the existence of corruption to serve his own purposes. By compiling information on the corruption and misconduct of key PLO leaders both within and without Fath, he succeeded in curtailing the political ambitions of his rivals. He also was able to blackmail potential organizational troublemakers.

Arafat could not have maintained his supremacy without effective alliances in all PLO organizations. He would use his control over PLO finances to reward supporters and to punish adversaries. He could rely on the support of Bassam Abu Sharif within the PFLP (before his recent expulsion) and on Yasir 'Abd Rabbuh within the DFLP. Both were often his travel companions, a reward in itself. ("Traveling with the chairman" is a great honor in PLO circles.)

One should also underline his political flexibility as a source for his unusual longevity. His political obituary was very frequently prematurely announced, only to be followed by his reemergence stronger than ever. But his extreme flexibility could be equated with an unprincipled foundation for his leadership since he would switch alliances (from Syria to Iraq and vice versa, for example) with such ease and expediency.

Arafat's performance during the last PNC proceedings exhibited his political skills. It requires a master politician to please both the West (including the United States) and George Habash. It was unexpected that Arafat would go as far as he has gone recently in satisfying U.S. conditions for dialogue while maintaining national unity within the ranks of the PLO, notwithstanding the opposition by the hitherto less significant groups like the PFLP–GC and Fath–Uprising.

Arafat's leadership is consolidated from below by other layers of leadership. Each of the second-tier leaders heads his own faction, which explains the diverse organizational structure of Fath and broadens its political appeal, as each faction stands for a separate set of orientations. Munir Shafiq, for example, who heads the planning office, represents a faction of educated intellectuals with leftist leanings (he has recently been flirting with Islamic fundamentalism); Abu Salih headed a pro-Soviet faction before his defection from the movement in 1983; and Abu az-Za'im—who today heads an insignificant pro-Jordanian dissident Fath faction—stood for cooperation with Jordan and Egypt.

Corruption is another feature of the politics of the PLO. Although Arafat is personally uncorrupt, he is tolerant of corruption among his subordinates. Arafat often uses the power of money to manipulate the other leaders of the PLO, to keep them under his watch, and to check their political ambitions when necessary. Money is also used by Arafat to maintain a system of political patronage, both within the PLO body and also in the occupied territories. Money as well as the supply of weaponry were used by Arafat to buy off leaders, factions, and political organizations. It should be noted that Arab Gulf countries like Saudi Arabia and Kuwait, as well as the

Palestinian bourgeoisie in the Gulf, donated large sums of money to Fath to prevent the ascendancy of the Palestinian Left. On the other hand, other wealthy Arab countries, like Libya and Iraq—the latter at least until 1977— supplied large sums of money and arms to leftist Palestinian groups.

THE CIRCLE OF ALLIANCES AND FRIENDS

Nowhere does Arafat demonstrate his political acumen better than in the realm of regional and international alliances. He has been able to expand the circle of alliances and friends, while remaining a key player in the confusing maze of inter-Arab politics.

Whether the PLO is an independent political actor is a matter of debate. It is clear, however, that the PLO is not a client of the USSR, for example, as is sometimes maintained in the West. There are deep ideological differences between the Palestinian political culture and the Marxist-Leninist ideology (even or particularly in its Gorbachevian form) that frees the PLO from strict Soviet patronage.

But the vast PLO bureaucracy and the need for a constant flow of funds to maintain it requires stable relations with key states that have been major financial backers of the PLO. (It should be mentioned in this respect that there is no reliable information on PLO finances.)[16]

Arafat has been a constant player in inter-Arab politics for over two decades. He has never restricted himself to one regime or even to a sole axis in inter-Arab politics. Moreover, he never restricted his relationships to the governments in power; rather, he maintained good relations with open and underground opposition groups in most Arab states and in some Western states. The Arab Gulf countries have played a major role in the support of Arafat's leadership. It is partly due to Arafat's, as well as his collegues', past work experience in Kuwait and partly due to self-interest on the part of the Arab Gulf countries.

While the rise of Arafat's leadership posed a challenge to Arab governmental control over Palestinian affairs (especially since his predecessor was in effect a client of the Arab League), he quickly allayed the fears of certain Arab governments by demonstrating his willingness to cooperate with them.

Again, his track record in inter-Arab politics attests to his unusual flexibility. After the bloody showdown between the PLO and the Hashemite regime in Jordan in 1970, he accepted Nasser-sponsored reconciliation with King Husayn, against the advice of key leaders and the rank-and-file of all PLO organizations.

Arafat's relations with the Syrian regime of Hafidh al-Asad also reflect a willingness to overcome strong personal animosities and political differences for the sake of a larger strategy. In the aftermath of the 1976 military showdown between Syrian troops and PLO forces in Lebanon, Arafat again ignored the advice of some of his advisors and went ahead in a reconciliation with the Syrian regime.

But Saudi support of the Arafat leadership of the PLO needs special attention, not only because of the large sums of money the Saudi government donates to the PLO but also because Arafat's relations with the Saudi government never really worsened. Saudi Arabia saw in Arafat a moderating influence that could curtail Palestinian radicalism which was in ascendancy in the early 1970s. In a way, they saw a common enemy in Palestinian leftism. Arafat's wide network of contacts in the underground of the Arab world provided him with an intimidating power. He is also in a position to render secret intelligence services for some regimes when need be and for the right price.[17]

Although Arafat maintained good relations with the countries of the socialist bloc, he has paid special attention to Western countries, particularly the United States, notwithstanding the standard PLO rhetoric. In Arafat's calculations, very much like Sadat's calculations, U.S. influence is crucial in any possible future peace settlement.

CONCLUSION: MEASURING SUCCESS

In assessing the contemporary history of the PLO, it is difficult to present clear-cut judgments. It would be inaccurate to attribute the lack of a solution of the Palestinian problem to the failure of the PLO. The Palestinian problem emerged as a direct result of the creation of Israel, long before the PLO was created. The continuation of Palestinian statelessness and displacement should be viewed in the regional context of the Arab-Israeli conflict, where Israel refuses to acknowledge fundamental Palestinian rights and where the Arab regimes are unwilling to pay more than lip service to the Palestinian issue.

Furthermore, when one addresses the failures and weaknesses of the PLO, one is indirectly referring to Israeli military successes. Israel has been particularly successful in keeping its major Palestinian enemy in a continuous state of confusion and fragmentation. Military attacks against PLO bases in various parts of the Arab world, raids against Palestinian camps in Lebanon, and assassination campaigns against the most effective PLO leaders (the assassination of Abu Jihad in 1988 is one recent example) left the movement with no breathing space. It gave the PLO no luxury time for reassessment and reconsideration of its strategies and platforms. More often than not, it was Israel, through its military activity, that set the PLO agenda, thus rendering its action and policies to the realms of reaction and response.

But the PLO should be judged to the degree to which it was—or was not—able to achieve some of the objectives contained in its charter. On one basic level, the PLO has been highly successful in raising the consciousness of the Palestinian people and in solidifying Palestinian national identity. The PLO has also been successful in building at least the infrastructure of an independent society as a blueprint for the would-be Palestinian state. The construction of Palestinian institutions and services have made the promise of a state more realistic in the eyes of the Palestinian masses. It has also made the PLO more credible as the leader of the struggle for Palestinian national aspirations.

On an emotional and sentimental level, the PLO asserted Palestinian separateness at a time when the very national existence of the Palestinian people was threatened by Israel and Jordan, who sought to eliminate an independent Palestinian voice. The PLO affirmed a sense of belonging that tied together all Palestinians. It also created the political institutions that encompassed the wide range of the political spectrum and thus served as the representative body of the Palestinian people.

On another level, the PLO failed in liberating the land, or any part of the land. The initial objective of a secular democratic state is more remote than before, so much so that the PLO had to retract its position and adopt the two-state formula. Notwithstanding the regularization of Palestinian military forces and the spread of conventional military policies in contrast to earlier references to "people's war" and "guerrilla warfare," the PLO failed to pose a serious military threat to Israel. The practice of sporadic spectacular operations in balloons and dinghies is an indication of desperation. It is, of course, also an indication of how far some Palestinians will go in asserting their attachment to their land.

The continuing Palestinian uprising may shed some light on the status of the PLO among Palestinians. The very eruption of the uprising is reflective of the state of despair shared by Palestinians living under Israeli rule. It is reflective of the hopelessness felt by people who have relied on Arab regimes and later on the PLO to achieve independence and statehood. Contrary to Israeli wishful thinking, however, the popular uprising does not constitute a rupture in the relations of the PLO with the Palestinians in the West Bank and Gaza. It simply means a growing role for those Palestinians in PLO decisionmaking. The contents of all the communiqués issued by the Unified Leadership of the uprising (which comprises some PLO organizations and Islamic fundamentalists who themselves are represented within the PLO) in the PNC and in the National Central Council, the body that links the PNC to the executive committee, never deviated from the official line of the PLO.

The major reason behind the continuity of the popularity of the PLO has resided in its loose organizational structure and the vague formulation of ideological objectives. These two features have enabled the PLO to adjust to the changing public moods of the Palestinian people. It is evident now that

Palestinians under Israeli occupation are now setting the agenda for Palestinian political and military action. More attention by the PLO will be paid in the future to the attitudes and sensibilities of the Palestinians in the West Bank and Gaza. This will make PLO leaders more accountable to their constituents than in the past. That Palestinians under occupation refrained by and large from using firearms indicates a break with PLO military policies. Not surprisingly, the PLO now approves of the methods of civil disobedience, which originated indigenously in the occupied territories.

It is still too early to tell how the creation of an underground organizational structure of the PLO in the Occupied Territories will affect diaspora PLO organizations. It is still unclear whether a dramatic shift in the political weight of the PLO will occur in the direction of the Occupied Territories. The last PNC session indicated a larger role and voice for the Palestinians in the Occupied Territories.

The nature of the uprising and the intensity of popular participation in it underline a crucial aspect of the Palestinian revolution. Unlike conspiratorial movements or organizations (e.g., the Armenian Secret Army for the Liberation of Armenia [ASALA]) the PLO is an expression of the Palestinian national will, a vehicle for Palestinian political activism. It is highly unlikely that the PLO will soon disappear from Palestinian political life. It is likely, however, that the uprising will leave a strong impact on PLO policies and structure.

NOTES

1. See the statement of Golda Meir (1969).
2. A major Fath leader and close associate of Yasir Arafat, Khalid al-Hasan considers himself a "right-winger." Al-Hasan was an assistant to Mustafa al-Siba'i (a former leader of the Muslim Brethren in Syria) in the 1940s. See the revealing interview with al-Hasan (1988). Al-Hasan was reelected to the new Fath's central committee in August 1989 with the third largest number of votes (after Abu al-Lutf and Abu Iyad).
3. For Munir Shafiq the Marxist-Leninist-Stalinist-Maoist, see Shafiq (1974); for Munir Shafiq the Muslim fundamentalist, see Shafiq (1989: 32–33). Shafiq is one of the most sophisticated and influential ideologues within the Fath movement.
4. See al-'Adhm (1973: 115–117). Al-'Adhm maintains that Palestinian leaders treated the Palestinian question as if "it is entirely excluded from the class struggle."
5. See 'Ayid (1988). 'Ayid's study is probably the first scholarly analysis of the uprising.
6. The fundamental flaws of the terrorism paradigm stem from the very ideological thrust of the concept. The concept has become a mere propaganda tool, used by the United States and the USSR. The USSR has its own paradigm of, and books on, terrorism. (For a Soviet sample of the "communist terrorist

paradigm" see USSR (1983a, 1983b). Furthermore, the proponents of the paradigm of terrorism seem to have a fixation with Palestinians as major perpetrators of terrorism. A study of the coverage in the *New York Times* and the *Times of London* of what those papers defined as "international terrorist incidents" between 1968 and 1974 found that "while the Palestinian groups were responsible for one quarter of the terrorist incidents reported, they were the subject of over half the articles published" (*Jerusalem Post* 1988). In fact, in the public and official minds, the name *Palestinian*—and now *Shi'ite* also— is almost synonymous with *terrorism*.

Another characteristic of the paradigm of terrorism resides in the ideological bias of its proponents. Walter Laqueur (1976: 374–375), one of the major experts on terrorism, considers "indiscriminate bomb throwing in Arab markets and at bus stations" by Jewish underground groups before 1948 as acts of armed struggle. Palestinian organizations are often portrayed as mere instruments of the KGB. A sample of the works by these experts include Cline and Alexander (1984), Goren (1984), Dobson and Payne (1982), and Becker (1984). Furthermore, many experts of terrorism seem to underestimate the popular appeal of the PLO and exaggerate the Soviet commitment to a resolution of the Palestinian problem.

The rise of Islamic fundamentalism did not affect the obsessive fixation with the "international terrorism conspiracy" theory. Rather, most terrorism experts promoted an argument that ignored the fundamental ideological contradictions between Islam and communism. The conspiracy argument almost suggests that international terrorism is run simultaneously by a mullah and a KGB officer (see Netanyahu 1986). It is the inability to grasp the historical depth of the Palestinian-Israeli conflict that explains why the terrorism experts of the world render the Palestinian national movement as an outgrowth of international terrorism. The question of whether the PLO—or any other organization or state for that matter—is terrorist or not seems an issue to be determined on a purely subjective (i.e., political) basis. The study of terrorism—a field not generally recognized by social scientists—and the resulting application of a terrorist paradigm to the PLO, is not a legitimate academic activity. In other words, the paradigm of terrorism is inappropriate regardless of whether the PLO is terrorist and offers no insight into the question of legitimacy.

7. Israel and its proponents abroad have attributed "fixity" to the agenda of the Palestinian national movement. To recognize political changes within the PLO would undermine Israel's justification for its consistent refusal to deal with the genuine representatives of the Palestinian people. For a typical Israeli view, see the interview with Yitzhaq Rabin (Rabin 1989).

8. See the Fath anniversary speech by Arafat printed in a booklet by Fath (1986: 27).

9. For an analysis of the PLO in prewar Lebanon, see Franjieh (1972: 53–60).

10. See *Al-Mawsu 'ah al-Filastiniyyah* [The Palestinian Encyclopedia] (1984).

11. It is still popular, for example, to refer to the Rejection Front, although such a Front no longer exists. The Rejection Front (founded in 1974)

was dissolved in 1977 when all PLO organizations formally accepted the two-state solution to the Palestinian problem.

12. For the withdrawal of the PFLP from the executive committee of the PLO, see PFLP (1974).

13. The English translation of the minutes of meetings between Soviet and Syrian Party officials that took place in 1972 and in which the Soviet attitude toward the Palestine question was frankly presented is in *Journal of Palestine Studies* (1972: 50).

14. In the words of Walid Khalidi (1989: 6), "The contradiction between the Declaration for Independence in the 1988 PNC and these provisions [of the Charter] is not one of nuance. It is diametric and total."

15. It should be noted that this omission was not the result of a new nonviolent approach but was rather based on a willingness to appease the West and Israel.

16. Rashid Khalidi in a major book on PLO decisionmaking, states that "there are no reliable figures on PLO finances: all published estimates on its budget are based on speculation. This is an area where a large measure of secrecy has been maintained" (1986: 194).

17. In 1979, Saudi communist leader Nasir al-Sa'id was kidnapped from Beirut, never to be seen again. It was rumored at the time that followers of Abu al-Za'im kidnapped him and surrendered him to Saudi authorities in return for an unknown sum of money. See *Tariq al-Kadihin* (1987).

REFERENCES

AbuKhalil, As'ad (1987). "Internal Contradictions in the PFLP: Decision Making and Policy Orientation." *Middle East Journal* 41, no. 3 (Summer): 361–378.

Abu Nidal, Nazih (1984). *The History of Fath: From the Establishment to the Uprising.*

Abu Nidal, Nazih, and 'Abdul-Hadi an-Nashshash (1984). *The Palestinian Program Between the Course of Settlement and Liberation.*

al-'Adhm, Sadiq Jalal (1973). *A Critical Study of the Thought of the Palestinian Resistance.* Beirut: Dal al-'Awdah.

Al-Hurriyyah (1973a). July.

——— (1973b). August.

An-Nahar (1973). 17 August.

'Ayid, Khalid (1984). *The Train of Death: The Battle of Beirut in the Context of Zionist Terrorism and Expansion.* Beirut: Dar al-Sharaq al-Awsat.

——— (1988). *The Revolutionary Uprising in Palestine: The Internal Dimensions.* Amman: Dar al-Shuruq.

Becker, Jillian (1984). *The PLO.* New York: St Martin's.

Cline, Ray S., and Yonah Alexander (1984). *Terrorism: The Soviet Connection.* New York: Crane Russak.

Democratic Front for the Liberation of Palestine (1971). *The September Campaign and the Palestinian Resistance: Lessons and Results.* Beirut: Dar al-Tali'ah.

———— (1975). *The Political Program.*

Dobson, Christopher, and Ronald Payne (1982). *The Terrorist: Their Weapons, Leaders, and Tactics.* New York: Facts on File.

Fath (1970). *The Ten Basic Pillars in the Organization.* Amman: Fath Central Information.

———— (1986). Anniversary Speech by Yasir Arafat. Kuwait: Fath Information Office.

Franjieh, Samir (1972). "How Revolutionary Is the Palestinian Resistance? A Marxist Interpretation." *Journal of Palestine Studies* 1, no. 2 (Winter): 53–60.

Goren, Roberta (1984). *The Soviet Union and Terrorism.* London: Allen and Unwin.

Hart, Alan (1984). *Arafat: Terrorist or Peacemaker?* London: Sidgwick and Jackson.

al-Hasan (1988). Interview by al-Watan al'Arabi, 16 September.

Hawatmah, Nayif (1977). *The Revolution, Self-Determination, and the Independent State.* Beirut: DFLP.

Al-Hut, Shafiq (1986). *Twenty Years in the PLO: The Talks of Memories (1964–1984).* Beirut: Dar al-Istipal).

Jerusalem Post (1988). International edition, 2 April.

Khalidi, Walid (1978). "Thinking the Unthinkable: A Sovereign Palestinian State." *Foreign Affairs* (July): 695–713.

———— (1989). *At a Critical Juncture: The United States and the Palestinian People.* Washington, DC: Georgetown University.

Khalidi, Rashid (1986). *Under Siege: PLO Decisionmaking During the 1982 War.* New York: Columbia University Press.

Laqueur, Walter (1976). *A History of Zionism.* New York: Schocken.

al-Maswu'ah al-Filastiniyyah [The Palestinian Encylopedia] vol. 2 (1984). Damascus.

Meir, Golda (1969). Statement in *Sunday Times of London*, 15 June.

Netanyahu, Benjamin, ed. (1986). *Terrorism: How the West Can Win.* New York: Farrar, Straus, Giroux.

Popular Front for the Liberation of Palestine (1974). *The PFLP Announces Its Withdrawal from the Executive Committee of the PLO.* Beirut: Central Information Committee.

———— (1977). *Comrade George Hobash Talks About the Pressing Current Issues.* Beirut: Central Information Committee.

Rabin, Yitzhak (1989). Interview by Ha'aretz 21 April. Also in Foreign Broadcast Information Service (1989). Near East and South Asia, 25 April, pp. 31–33.

Sayigh, Yezid (1987). "The Politics of Palestinian Exile." *Third World Quarterly* 9, no. 1 (January): 28–66.

Segal, Jerome (1989). *Creating the Palestinian State: A Strategy for Peace.* Chicago: Lawrence Hill.

Shafiq, Munir (1974). *Marxism-Leninism and the Theory of the Communist Party.* Beirut: Dar al-Tali'ah.

———— (1989). Interview by *al-Majallah*, 25 April, pp. 32–33.

Tariq al-Kadihin (1987). "The Path of the Toilers." No. 34 (February).

USSR (1983a). *International Terrorism and the CIA: Documents, Eyewitness Reports, Facts.* Moscow: Progress.

——— (1983b). *Terrorism: An Indictment of Imperialism.* Moscow: Progress.

CHAPTER NINE

Anti-Marxist Insurgencies: Angola's UNITA

MARINA OTTAWAY

Whereas each of the previous chapters has focused on revolutionary movements or regimes for which there is little question of revolutionary legitimacy, this chapter examines a case whose claims to legitimacy are dubious at best. The elements that in our analysis have been associated with the legitimacy of revolutionary movements are, for the most part, absent in the case of UNITA. Nevertheless, UNITA continues to exist as the primary opposition to the currently revolutionary regime in Angola.

UNITA's claim for legitimacy reposes in two elements: the support of the Ovimbundu ethnic group of southeastern Angola and the significant appeal of its leader, Jonas Savimbi. But the primary source of support for UNITA derives (much as does that for Mozambique RENAMO) from the external support of key states. Indeed, Marina Ottaway makes the case that unlike any other revolutionary movement examined in this volume, UNITA would not survive without such external support. It is also true, however, that Angola's persistent internal discord suggests that the ruling MPLA government is also critically dependent on external support for its own survival. Therefore, we can begin to infer that revolutionary legitimacy within Angola has been, and continues to be, a challenged and scarce commodity.

*RENAMO's dependence on external support is even more decisive. While UNITA does possess a "pedigree" of revolutionary authenticity, it has shared with RENAMO critical dependence on a South African regime that lacks legitimacy among virtually all Africans. Thus, it is not so much the anti-Marxist orientation of these insurgencies that denies them legitimacy as their perceived link to the white minority regime in Pretoria.—*THE EDITORS

The National Union for the Total Independence of Angola (UNITA) is a very ambiguous movement, as its history shows. It started as a liberation movement with a leftist ideology, courting the support of communist China and North Korea. It tried to present itself as the party of reconciliation in 1975 during the crisis of independence. It ended as a movement pitted in a struggle against the Marxist regime in Luanda and receiving support from both South Africa and the United States.

UNITA's ideology, too, has undergone repeated metamorphoses. Jonas Savimbi, the movement's founder and to this day its leader, cultivated a Maoist image in the 1960s and the image of a champion of freedom and democracy (*freedom fighter* in Reagan doctrine terminology) in the 1980s. But documents published in Portugal and statements made by UNITA dissidents in the late 1980s suggested that the goal of the UNITA leadership might still be the setting up of a radical state (see *Africa*, 1988; *Espresso*, 1988). Just to confuse the issue, the same sources also indicated that UNITA was even willing to allow the continuation of a traditional sociopolitical system, complete with the burning of witches.

It should be clear at this point that UNITA defies an easy definition, in part because of its complex history, in part because Jonas Savimbi has a genius for public relations, telling everybody what they want to hear. In order to gain a better understanding of this protean movement, it is necessary to look beyond the statements of its leaders to the circumstances that have shaped it. It is my contention that UNITA's identity has been determined by the external support it has received and the circumstances under which it has fought to a greater extent than it is the case with most other movements. In particular, the relationship with South Africa since 1980 has affected the structure of UNITA very deeply.While Savimbi's goals have never been identical to South Africa's, the UNITA of the 1980s was in all fundamental aspects the product of that relation. The tripartite agreement between Angola, South Africa, and Cuba, brokered by the United States in December 1988, was very threatening to Savimbi because it forced South Africa to withdraw troops from Angola. The long-term effects of the decreased South African role could once again change the character of UNITA.

A THUMBNAIL HISTORY OF UNITA TO 1974

The history of the Angolan liberation movements is byzantine, and no attempt will be made to relate it here in all its complications. What follows is simply a brief sketch, explaining both why UNITA was formed and why it had such difficulty getting acceptance and support.

At the root of the conflicts that have wracked the Angolan movements since their inception is the fact that nationalist agitation started at the same time in different centers. Originally, the most important ones were the Bakongo exile community in what is now Zaire and the small, urban-educated class in Luanda, as well as the Angolan students in Lisbon. From the former would eventually rise the National Front for the Liberation of Angola (FNLA), from the latter the Popular Movement for the Liberation of Angola (MPLA).[1] Neither movement was well integrated ethnically. The FNLA was overwhelmingly Bakongo, the MPLA Mbundu (the dominant group in Luanda) as well as *mestico* and *assimilado*. The Ovimbundus of the central plateau, particularly what are now Huombo and Rio provinces, and the related groups in the scantily populated south and southeast portions of the country did not have significant representation in either movement, although they were at least a third of the population.

The first Ovimbundu to surface in a leadership position in the nationalist ranks was Jonas Savimbi; his rapid rise to prominence in the FNLA was greatly facilitated by Holden Roberto's desire to broaden the composition, and thus the appeal, of the movement. Savimbi left Angola in 1958 to study first in Portugal and later in Switzerland. Within three years, he was deeply involved in political activity, joining Roberto in late 1961 and immediately becoming the movement's general secretary. In April 1962 Roberto formed a government in exile, the Revolutionary Government of Angola in Exile (GRAE); and Savimbi became foreign minister. In this period Savimbi carefully cultivated his image as a young, radical African revolutionary. An admirer of Franz Fanon, he visited him on his deathbed in the United States (Marcum, 1969: 222).

Cooperation between Roberto and Savimbi did not last long. In March 1964 Savimbi resigned from the GRAE, accusing Roberto of leading the FNLA and GRAE in an authoritarian fashion, seeking U.S. support, and running an inefficient organization, ineffective as a guerrilla movement. It is an open question whether these problems were the real cause of Savimbi's resignation or whether he was simply too ambitious to be overshadowed by Roberto (see Henderson, 1979: 194).

Having resigned his post, Savimbi did not renounce political activity but encountered serious difficulties in obtaining support. He sought to strengthen his radical credentials by going on an extensive tour of North Korea, North Vietnam, and China; but he failed to convince their leaders, particularly the Chinese, that he deserved backing. He entered into negotiations with the MPLA about the possibility of joining that movement but was unsuccessful there also. He convinced President Kenneth Kaunda of Zambia to invite leaders of the FNLA and the MPLA to Lusaka to discuss unification, but with no result. This pattern of following very different and contradictory strategies at the same time would be repeated by Savimbi later, particularly at the time of independence.

In March 1966 Savimbi launched his own movement, UNITA. At the time he explained that the MPLA represented only the Mbundu and was influenced by communist ideas, that the GRAE represented only the Bakongo and sought U.S. aid and that both organizations, thus, invited superpower confrontation in Angola. Finally, there was need for a new organization promoting unity (Henderson, 1979: 207).

From 1966 until 1974, when the coup d'état carried out by the Armed Forces movement in Portugal drastically altered the situation in Angola, Savimbi faced an almost insurmountable problem obtaining enough external support to get UNITA off the ground. The problem was that as a latecomer,

UNITA found the field occupied and possible sponsors already committed. The Organization of African Unity had originally recognized the FNLA–GRAE as the movement to be supported and later extended recognition to the MPLA as well but was not interested in a third organization (Henderson, 1979: 230). Cuba and the Soviet Union had been backing the MPLA since the mid-1960s, although at times with qualms because of that movement's endless internal conflicts. The United States, while keeping a very low profile in order to avoid antagonizing Portugal, had established contacts with Holden Roberto. China, which Savimbi had openly courted, had picked as its man Viriato da Cruz, an MPLA leader who later defected to the FNLA, with the paradoxical result that China and the United States found themselves on the same side.

The strongest backer of Savimbi was originally Kaunda; but the relationship did not last, because Savimbi violated an understanding that he would not attack the Benguela railroad, through which much copper from Zambia and Zaire was exported (Henderson, 1979: 207–208). However, attacks on the Benguela railroad were the only actions that would call attention to the UNITA's existence: the underpopulated southeastern part of the country offered no other highly visible targets. One of UNITA's first guerrilla actions, in late 1966, was an attack on the Benguela railroad. A second attack was launched in March 1967, while Savimbi was travelling. When he returned to Lusaka in June, he was promptly arrested and expelled. Exiled to Cairo, he managed to slip back into Angola in July 1968.

The difficulty of obtaining external support and Savimbi's break with Kaunda determined the character of UNITA for the next seven years. UNITA became a real guerrilla movement, operating exclusively inside the country, highly dependent on the support of the local population, and carrying out small-scale operations. The rival movements, on the other hand, were divided between outside representatives carrying out diplomatic and political activity from Zaire (the FNLA–GRAE) and the Congo (the MPLA) and the guerrilla commanders inside the country. The outside leadership tended to dominate.

The stereotyped image of UNITA as the guerrilla movement living among peasants like a fish in water and organizing from the bottom up is marred by the evidence that it was also busy making deals with the Portuguese authorities. This was not known at the time but became clear after 1974, when former colonial officials and officers in the Portuguese army in Angola started talking and when some documents from the period of the independence war became public. Savimbi, who apparently feared the expansion of MPLA activity in "his" area more than he feared the Portuguese, sought and obtained a deal with the colonial authorities, offering to fight the MPLA in exchange for safe passage for UNITA. It is not clear exactly when the contacts between Savimbi and the Portuguese authorities started. Published correspondence dates back to 1971. Other sources, more difficult to confirm, claim that Savimbi already had contacts with the International Police for the Defense of the State (PIDE), the Portuguese secret police, before 1969. There is no doubt, in any case, that deals with the Portuguese authorities were part of Savimbi's survival strategy.[2]

Another aspect of UNITA that emerged in this period is good organization. The FNLA and the MPLA were very poor in this respect. The FNLA had great difficulty in putting a fighting force in Angola despite easy access from Zaire. The MPLA fared somewhat better, but it was sapped by the endless infighting of the leadership and the equally endless splitting of the organization into factions. But Savimbi, with a small organization and personally in command and present inside the country all the time, kept the organization united and functioning. Through a combination of good public relations and an effective capacity to organize, Savimbi always managed to impress visitors—and to provide a distorted picture of his accomplishments. Thus Richard Gibson (1972: 238), a U.S. freelance journalist writing in 1972, described UNITA as a movement operating on five fronts over a very wide area. Furthermore, he reported that UNITA operated not only at the military level but also at the sociopolitical one, bringing about "important changes in the organization of Angolan rural life without destroying the existing communal society." The Portuguese estimated UNITA to have about three hundred men at the time. It is interesting also to note that Gibson represented Savimbi as a radical, hard-line Marxist, who had refused to join the MPLA because he was opposed to its revisionism. Savimbi would try hard two years later to dispel the image he had cultivated.

By 1974, in conclusion, UNITA had been shaped by circumstances into an internal guerrilla movement; it had been forged by Savimbi into a cohesive group; it had a radical image but was making deals with the Portuguese colonial authorities; and it remained a very small movement (Portuguese estimates put UNITA's strength at between three hundred and six hundred men in early 1974). It remained rather obscure and had little outside support. As John Stockwell (1978: 138), the head of the CIA Angola task force during the civil war put it, UNITA was "the Angolan long shot."

THE CIVIL WAR

Between the April 1974 Armed Forces movement coup d'état in Lisbon and the disappearance of Savimbi in the bush of southeastern Angola in March 1976 after the South African withdrawal, UNITA succeeded in obtaining recognition as a major player in Angola. This period confirmed the overwhelming importance of outside support for UNITA, as well as Savimbi's political ability. Above all, by establishing the link between South Africa and UNITA, it opened the way to what would become after 1980 the most important factor determining the character of UNITA.

Shortly after the coup d'état Savimbi quickly discarded the image of an uncompromising revolutionary leader, trying instead to cast himself as the most moderate of the Angolan nationalist leaders and the champion of national reconciliation. Savimbi's decision to play the moderate made him the man on whom Portuguese settlers in Angola, moderate elements in the new Portuguese leadership, and the South African government counted to keep the MPLA in check. By June 1974 Savimbi had signed a cease-fire and was hinting that he was willing to accept the plan set forth by General Spinola, the new Portuguese head of state, for slow decolonization within the federal framework of a "Lusitanian Commonwealth" (Heimer, 1979: 45n.). He had also stepped up the effort to create a political organization, particularly in the central highlands. But military recruiting also increased. By August 1975, the CIA estimated that Savimbi had four thousand trained guerrillas and six thousand trainees.[3] The growing political strength of UNITA was shown by the fact that by mid-1974 it was the dominant political movement in three provincial capitals (the MPLA controlled eleven and the FNLA two) (Hanlon, 1986: 156).

However, all movements were growing rapidly at this point because of the bandwagon effect created by the imminence of independence. The MPLA, which after an internal split had been down to perhaps three thousand men prior to the April coup, had some twenty thousand by summer 1975. The FNLA was supposed to have fifteen thousand in the same period.[4] UNITA thus remained the smallest movement and was still considered the least important by all analysts. However, UNITA soon proved much more effective than the FNLA, which remained as ineffective as ever on the battlefield and collapsed politically immediately after the installation of an MPLA government in Luanda. Behind UNITA's success were good organization and South African support.

In January 1975 the three Angolan liberation movements signed the Alvor Agreement with Portugal. It provided for the formation of a joint transitional government, which would organize elections for a constituent assembly within nine months, in preparation for independence in November. The Alvor Agreement proved unworkable; and soon the situation degenerated into civil war, with the three movements seeking outside support against each other.

Exactly at what point in the civil war Savimbi decided to accept South African aid is not clear. By September 1975, however, South Africa was training UNITA guerrillas; and by October it had troops in Angola. Contacts had undoubtedly started much earlier; but Savimbi was still exploring alternate options as late as August, when UNITA for a brief time entered into an agreement with the MPLA (see Heimer, 1979: 66–76). Later that month, however, the situation, which had been fluid since the signing of the Alvor Agreement, crystallized, with the FNLA and UNITA siding against the MPLA. With that decision, South African aid became crucial for Savimbi, particularly since the United States was still channeling most of its aid to the FNLA (Stockwell, 1978: 155).

South African troops allowed UNITA to advance through the central highlands almost to Luanda, something it could not have done on its own. It was a short-lived victory. A few days after Angola became officially independent on 11 November, in the midst of a raging civil war, the Western press discovered that South African troops were fighting in Angola on the side of UNITA.[5] This caused the movement to lose its newfound legitimacy. African countries, hitherto supporting the concept of a coalition government in Angola, hastened to recognize the MPLA regime, a move soon followed by the entire international community with the exception of the United States. UNITA found itself once again politically isolated.

From then on, the situation deteriorated very rapidly for UNITA. Cuban intervention in support of the MPLA and the collapse of the FNLA increased the cost of the war for South Africa. By January Pretoria decided to pull out rather than increase its commitment to match that of Cuba and the Soviet Union. By late March 1976 the South African withdrawal was complete.

UNITA was left without outside support and little hope of getting any. The United States, which by late 1975 had started channeling more aid to UNITA, judging it to be a more effective movement than the FNLA, discontinued all support for the Angolan opposition after the passage of the Clark Amendment in February 1976. UNITA was thus forced to withdraw, abandoning the towns and territory it had controlled. UNITA's troops withdrew further and further, eventually disappearing once again in southeastern Angola. By March 1976 UNITA had again become a small, internal guerrilla movement with no bases outside the country and little external support. The saga to which the UNITA leadership, with Maoist nostalgia, refers as "the long march" had started (Bridgland, 1987: 194–218).

Three years later, UNITA seemed to be a waning movement. People's Armed Forces for the Liberation of Angola (FAPLA) was establishing control over the central highlands with Cuban support, and most of the peasants who had taken to the bush following UNITA's retreat had come back to their farms.

UNITA SINCE 1980

A change in South African policy—and later in that of the United States, revived UNITA. The movement that had been condemned to a marginal position in the liberation struggle by the lack of outside support was built up into a major threat to the Angolan government by external circumstances. Briefly stated, by 1980 South Africa emerged from a period of political uncertainty and established a new, more activist and aggressive policy toward all its neighbors. Mozambique National Resistance (RENAMO) was the other major beneficiary of the new policy. In the new South African design, UNITA was to play a major role in keeping the Angolan army from the Namibian border, depriving SWAPO of safe areas in southern Angola. Guerrilla activity in other parts of the country, particularly the diamond-producing region of the northeast and the agricultural highlands, would keep the Angolan economy weak. The issue of whether South Africa saw UNITA as a potential governing party in Angola or just a factor of destabilization is much less clear.

South Africa maintained a military presence in southern Angola almost constantly between 1981 and 1989 despite the signing of the Lusaka accord in February 1984, which provided for South African withdrawal from southern Angola as along as SWAPO bases were kept out of the area. South Africa has also repeatedly provided support for UNITA in major battles, in particular at Mavinga and at Guito Guanavale. This support has been crucial for UNITA.[6] In late 1988 South Africa had an estimated eight thousand troops in Angola.

My focus, however, is on the changes UNITA has experienced since South African aid caused it to grow into a major movement. I will discuss change in four areas: (1) the goals of the movement, (2) the structure of the organization, (3) the emergence of conflicts within UNITA, and (4) the relationship with the United States.

The Goals of UNITA

The goals of UNITA have never been clear, but they have become even murkier since 1980. What makes it so difficult to define these goals is the fact that Savimbi always played a complex game. In the early period Savimbi ostensibly fought the Portuguese while secretly making deals with them. After 1980 Savimbi became South Africa's ally in destabilizing Angola, but UNITA representatives tried to convey the impression that the movement was at the forefront of the struggle against apartheid and that its relationship to South Africa has been misunderstood and misrepresented. Furthermore, while UNITA has been fighting against the MPLA since before independence, the official goal of UNITA in 1989 was national reconciliation.

There is little doubt that Savimbi nurtured goals of his own and that these have never been identical to South Africa's. This created friction at times: for example, during the battle for Mavinga in October 1987, the South Africans found it necessary to publicize their role there as a reminder to Savimbi of his dependency on their help, lest he develop illusions of autonomy. The problem is not to find evidence that Savimbi had goals of his own but to define precisely what they were beyond the satisfaction of personal ambition and the survival of UNITA.

More importantly, Savimbi's own vision of UNITA's role was much less important in shaping the character of the movement than the circumstances under which it operated. UNITA was extremely dependent on South Africa for maintaining the level and character of operations it undertook during the 1980s, and this determined the nature of the movement and its short-term goals. This is not to say that UNITA would disappear without South African aid. Savimbi has shown before that he could, and was willing to, go back to the bush and to small-scale guerrilla warfare. But the UNITA of 1989, with the sixty-five thousand men under arms it claimed, was a creature of South Africa.

The Structure of UNITA

The structure of UNITA changed a great deal after 1980. Inevitably, the growth of the movement made it more diversified and complicated, thus increasing the possibility of conflict. UNITA was in fact beginning to display some of the typical liberation movement problems that it had avoided earlier.

The most important and most significant is the division between the inside and the outside, a problem UNITA had not experienced earlier because it did not have outside bases. Technically, this was still true; but in practice, the southeastern corner of Angola where Savimbi had his "capital," Jamba, was so safe from MPLA attacks that UNITA could function as if outside Angola. Jamba was linked to South Africa by road and air. Visitors came and went without difficulty: a trip to Jamba was not a particularly dangerous or taxing undertaking in the late 1980s (see Honey, 1988). They found not guerrilla headquarters under siege but a thriving installation far away from the fighting—an "outside" base.

Parallel to this division between the inside and the outside was that between the regulars and the guerrillas. This was not only a difference in armament and training but also in the relation to the organization and the leadership. The regulars were the ones closest to the central leadership of UNITA, more in contact with headquarters. They were the ones supplied by the storerooms at Jamba, receiving regular rations, wearing the uniforms made in the Jamba workshops. They were also the ones fighting the major, most visible battles in close coordination with South Africa.

The guerrillas operated under very different conditions. Whether in the central highlands or, increasingly, in the eastern and northeastern provinces, they were on their own, with much looser contacts with headquarters. There were no clear signs of conflict between the two at the time of this writing, although there were rumors of dissatisfaction. Nevertheless, the potential for trouble existed.

After March 1988 the distinction between the inside and outside was accentuated by the formation of a formal UNITA government in Jamba (Honey, 1988). Savimbi became president, and his deputy, Jeremias

Chitunda, prime minister, presiding over an eleven-man cabinet. UNITA representatives claimed that the formation of a formal government was a purely internal development, necessitated by the complexity of administering the liberated areas. UNITA was not seeking international recognition for its government, they argued, nor was it seeking to partition the country. In fact, the formation of the government was seen by many as a diplomatic maneuver to enhance UNITA's status in the eventuality of negotiations with the MPLA. Nevertheless, the existence of a formal government apparatus, no matter how rudimentary, had internal repercussions and accentuated the diversity of the movement and thus the possibility of tensions.

The withdrawal of South African troops and the independence of Namibia may, paradoxically, partially reduce the potential conflict between inside and outside forces by forcing UNITA to fall back exclusively on guerrilla operations. It is too early to say, however, whether permanent frictions have been created within the organization.

The size of the UNITA forces and of the population it controlled have always been a matter of debate. In April 1988 Savimbi claimed sixty-five thousand men under arms—thirty-seven thousand guerrillas and twenty-eight thousand regulars (Honey, 1988). Somewhat earlier estimates put the size of UNITA at between fifty thousand and sixty thousand (Carpenter, 1986). The amount of territory controlled by UNITA was also under dispute. UNITA maps showed the entire southeast quarter of Angola up to the Benguela railroad and almost as far west as Bie to be a liberated zone. The maps have not been changed since at least 1985. Yet Savimbi claimed to control half a million people in 1986 and two million in 1988. An independent estimate in late 1986 put the number of people under UNITA administration at no more than 250 thousand based on the population of Cuando Cubango, the vast but underpopulated area that is undoubtedly in Savimbi's hands (Hodges, 1987).

The Emergence of Conflicts

One result of UNITA's growth has been the increased potential for internal conflict. I have already mentioned the possibility of friction between inside and outside, but there appeared to be other tensions as well. Tracking down the problems precisely is difficult—there were many rumors and little solid evidence. But it is still worth mentioning the most important and credible. One potential problem had to do with the duration of the war and the lack of clear results. Savimbi founded UNITA at a time when all nationalists in the Portuguese colonies were convinced the struggle would last a very long time. This core of UNITA was committed to a war of long duration. To this core was added in 1974–1975 a second layer convinced that the end of the fight was imminent. Most of the followers from this period left UNITA after

1976—we know that by 1979 UNITA was again a small organization. After 1980 UNITA added a third, and very large, layer of recruits. There were occasionally reports that this new, enlarged membership was less committed to a lifetime of struggle and that Savimbi was under pressure to show some concrete progress toward a settlement.

Another problem beginning to affect UNITA was that of conflict within the leadership. Savimbi has not faced major challenges in the past. His leadership was facilitated by his personality, his deftness at handling public relations, and his organizational ability. It was also facilitated by the small size of the organization. But in the late 1980s there have been reports of challenges. One worth mentioning is the criticism of Savimbi and the movement first voiced by several UNITA dissidents in Portugal (see *Africa*, 1988; *Espresso*, 1988). The allegations were published extensively in the Portuguese magazine *Africa*, which is strongly pro-MPLA and anti-UNITA. The picture of UNITA that emerged from the accusations was full of contradictions, but this may simply confirm the fact that UNITA had become so large and diverse that Savimbi, trying to accommodate all constituencies, followed contradictory policies. The accusations centered on three issues: (1) the burning of witches, following traditional customs; (2) a *Practical Handbook for Cadres*, which used ideas and terminology in the best Marxist-Leninist tradition; and (3) the arrest or disappearance of UNITA officials critical of Savimbi's dictatorial attitude, including Wilson Dos Santos, the man responsible for preparing Savimbi's visit to Washington in 1986 (*Africa*, 1988; *Guardian*, 1988). Interestingly, UNITA's representatives in Washington did not deny either that traditional customs were still practiced in UNITA-controlled areas or that the handbook cited by the dissidents was an authentic document. But they dismissed the first point with the argument that traditions cannot be changed overnight and that a lot of time and education is necessary before UNITA can be expected to eradicate reprehensible customs such as the burning of witches. As for the handbook, they argued that UNITA accepted some Marxist-Leninist concepts of party work and organization, but certainly not the entire doctrine. Instead, UNITA was seeking to develop an ideology based on the Angolan identity, not on ideas imported form the Eastern bloc or the West.[7]

Tensions in UNITA were likely to increase if negotiations between UNITA and the MPLA got underway seriously. It was known that the MPLA would be more willing to make a deal with UNITA if Savimbi was removed from the scene. African heads of state meeting with both Savimbi and Angolan president Eduardo Dos Santos at Gbadolite, Zaire, in June 1989 even claimed that Savimbi had agreed to step aside at least temporarily in order to facilitate a compromise. While Savimbi himself vehemently denied that such an agreement had been reached, it was clear that there was considerable pressure on him to do so. Such a situation could only encourage conflict within UNITA.

The Relationship with the United States

The relationship with the United States has also undergone considerable change since South Africa resumed its aid to Savimbi. In the first place, it is South African aid that made UNITA into an organization the United States could consider backing in 1985, after the repeal of the Clark Amendment. If UNITA had been a languishing movement, rather than one already bolstered by South African aid, the Reagan doctrine would have been much more difficult to implement in Angola.

Beginning in late 1985, when the Reagan administration announced that the United States would start covert aid to UNITA, efforts were made to portray Savimbi as a champion of democracy in Angola. Savimbi, the public relations firm he hired, and the Reagan administration glossed over the relation with South Africa, concentrating instead on the fact that Savimbi was fighting the Soviet- and Cuban-backed MPLA.

U.S. aid, amounting to about fifteen million dollars a year, has been delivered through Zaire rather than South Africa, both for political reasons and in order to help UNITA escalate activity in the northern part of Angola, which is most easily reached from Zaire. This created considerable tensions between Zaire and Angola. But the two countries also made periodic attempts to smooth their relations again, since they were mutually vulnerable. With its long common border with Angola, Zaire can provide UNITA major support just by letting it operate on its territory; but Angola can always retaliate by allowing the Zairean opposition to invade the economically crucial Shaba province again.

UNITA attacks in northern Angola increased steadily after 1985, though U.S. aid was not the only reason. UNITA has to move out of the "land at the end of the world" (as the Portuguese called southeastern Angola) and into the heart of the country. The economically important areas are the crucial ones. UNITA has disrupted agricultural production in the central highlands, the country's breadbasket, since the civil war; but that was not enough. Since 1985 it has moved increasingly into the diamond-producing areas and has attempted to carry out attacks on the oil installations of the Cabinda enclave. The opening of the northern front was thus crucial.

In mid-1988 the Angolan government accused the United States of causing the escalation of fighting in the north. It alleged that the United States was arming and training UNITA guerrillas at six bases in Zaire, including one ominously close to Cabinda. The MPLA saw a grand U.S. design in this northern strategy, namely, an attempt to give UNITA a new image as independent of South Africa (Brooke, 1988). In fact, some observers expanded on the concept, talking of a U.S. effort to wean UNITA away from South Africa (see, e.g., *Africa Confidential*, 1988).

The signing of the tripartite agreement in 1988, which reduced the importance of South Africa for Savimbi, has put the relationship of UNITA and the United States to a test. A year later, evidence remained contradictory.

President George Bush declared from the very beginning his intention to continue supporting Savimbi; and indeed, aid continued to be provided. Nevertheless, the new administration was not very active in trying to find a solution to the problems of Angola, letting African heads of state take the initiative. There was also some evidence that in the new atmosphere of improved Soviet-U.S. relations "freedom fighters" like Savimbi were beginning to lose their luster. In an atmosphere of superpower confrontation Savimbi could be seen as a U.S. ally in the East-West struggle. In an atmosphere of détente, Savimbi was in danger of being downgraded to a participant in a distant regional conflict of little interest to the United States.

CONCLUSIONS

All liberation movements are influenced by the foreign support they get, but UNITA appears to be more so than most. The reason for this is that UNITA was never able to rely for support on countries sharing its purported objectives. UNITA developed late, found the field already occupied, and settled for whatever support it could get. Savimbi's supporters have been Portugal, South Africa, and more recently the United States—unlikely allies for an African nationalist leader who originally tried to establish radical credentials. It is this aid that allowed UNITA to survive and achieve concrete results. The MPLA, too, was dependent on outside support, but the character of the movement was not determined by that support. It did not turn to Marxism-Leninism because it received Cuban and Soviet aid but received that aid because of the ideological position it had embraced in the first place.

The history of UNITA has also been influenced by its internal characteristics, namely, strong leadership and good organization. External assistance, as the case of the FNLA shows, does not help much without an organization and leadership ready to take advantage of it. UNITA had both. This allowed it to survive in the periods when it had little outside support and to grow rapidly when it did. The example of the FNLA, which collapsed because of its organizational weaknesses during a period when external aid was forthcoming, is a good reminder of the importance of these internal factors.

Strong leadership and organization have allowed UNITA to survive for over twenty years. The vagaries of external support have given the movement the protean character that keeps it from being easily classified. During the 1980s UNITA has depended mostly on South Africa, thus becoming, despite Savimbi's denials, an instrument of South African policy. However, this phase in the history of the movement may be drawing to a close. The signing of the tripartite agreement and the overall improvement of Soviet-U.S. relations have decreased the UNITA's usefulness to South Africa and the United States. Even with much decreased external support UNITA could survive as a guerrilla organization and could possibly force the MPLA to reach a political settlement. But as external support for UNITA and the circumstances under which it operates change once again, the movement can be expected to undergo another metamorphosis.

NOTES

1. In order to avoid unnecessary confusion, we will refer here to the movement led by Holden Robert at the FNLA. Technically, the FNLA was only formed in March 1962 when previously existing movements joined. See Marcum (1969), pp. 243ff.

2. The most important source on this issue is a series of letters originally published in the Portuguese magazine *Espresso* on 17 and 24 November 1979. Some more appeared later in *Afrique-Asie*. These and other documents have been collected and translated in Minter (1988). Former Portuguese colonial officials have confirmed in interviews the existence of a deal with Savimbi, although not the details. See Holness (1986).

3. See Stockwell (1978: 155). Apparently, these are Savimbi's own figures.

4. See Stockwell (1978: 91). The author admits that these CIA estimates were to some extent "arbitrary."

5. A first article, written from Lusaka, appeared on 22 November in the *Washington Post*, and the story was immediately picked up by all major newspapers.

6. For a brief account of the major military events, see Hanlon (1986: 162ff).

7. The surfacing of Marxist-Leninist concepts in UNITA documents could be interpreted in other ways as well. It could be a sign that Savimbi remains the radical he genuinely was in the 1960s. Or it could indicate that Savimbi, after instrumentalizing radical ideas early on in order to get support from radical countries, ended by internalizing some of them. See Laidi's essay in Chapter 3.

REFERENCES

Africa (Lisbon) (1988). 11 May.
Africa Confidential (1988). 27 May.
Bridgland, Fred (1987). *Jonas Savimbi: A Key to Africa*. New York: Paragon House Publishers.
Brooke, James (1988). "Angola Says US Uses Zaire Bases To Train Rebels." *New York Times*, 26 May.
Carpenter, Ted Galen (1986). "US Aid to Anti-Communist Rebels: The Reagan Doctrine and Its Pitfalls." Policy Analysis no. 74. CATO Institute.
Espresso (Lisbon) (1988). 7 May.
Gibson, Richard (1972). *African Liberation Movements: Contemporary*

Struggles Against White Minority Rule. New York: Oxford University Press.

Guardian (1988). 2 May.

Hanlon, Joseph (1986). *Beggar Your Neighbors*. Bloomington: Indiana University Press.

Heimer, F. W. (1979). *The Decolonization Conflict in Angola, 1974–76*. Geneva: Institute Universitaire de Hautes Etudes Internationales.

Henderson, Lawrence (1979). *Angola*. Ithaca: Cornell University Press.

Hodges, Tony (1987). *Angola in the 1990s: The Potential for Recovery*. London: Economist Intelligence Unit.

Holness, Marga (1986). "Angola: The Struggle Continues." In David Martin and Phyllis Johnson, eds., *Destructive Engagement*. Harare: Zimbabwe.

Honey, Peter (1988). "Angola: The Bush War." Three-part series. *Baltimore Sun*, 24–26 April.

Marcum, John (1969). *The Angolan Revolution*. Vol. 1. Cambridge: MIT Press.

Minter, William (1988). *Operation Timber: Pages from the Savimbi Dossier*. Trenton: Africa World.

Stockwell, John (1978). *In Search of Enemies*. New York: W. W. Norton.

PART THREE

CONCLUDING PERSPECTIVES

CHAPTER TEN

Patterns of Legitimacy and Future Revolutions in the Third World

BARRY M. SCHUTZ
ROBERT O. SLATER

Practitioners and analysts of international affairs are frequently astonished by the substance and context of revolutionary change in the Third World. In this book we have observed the attachment of such change to Marxism-Leninism, variants of revolutionary socialism, militant nationalism, and resurgent traditional religion. In the final analysis, what seems critical is the ability of the state to maintain or enhance its own legitimate authority, particularly when confronted by popular disaffection or deprivation.

In our theoretical discussion in Chapter 1 we introduced the concept of legitimacy as the primary factor in defining and distinguishing revolutionary movements and challenges to established regimes. Perhaps it is not so much legitimacy but popular *perceptions* of the illegitimacy or eroding legitimacy of such regimes that provides the context for Third World revolutionary movements. With the increasing acknowledgement of regime illegitimacy, these movements begin to acquire the elements of legitimacy necessary for their eventual success in achieving power and maintaining authority. More often than not, revolutionary movements face difficulty in transforming their legitimacy as a movement into legitimacy as a government.

What stands out in the cases presented in this volume is the rich ideological diversity that characterizes revolutionary movements. This diversity includes elements of nationalism, anticolonialism, anti-Westernism, eclecticism, and the instrumentalization of external revolutionary models. These diverse, inherently *external* ideological prescriptions are borrowed and reinterpreted to accommodate the concrete social and cultural contexts faced by the movements. Also in evidence, in contemporary international politics, is an apparent erosion in the popular belief and confidence in the movement's ability to deliver its ideologically premised revolutionary message.

It can, however, be problematic and misleading to overgeneralize these patterns. For example, the case of Islamic resurgence is not easily accommodated by these general inferences about Third World revolutions. More than anything, the case studies demonstrate the distinctive character of each revolutionary context and movement. Nevertheless, in all of the cases there is evidence of commonality in political and ideological dynamics.

Certainly, the prominence of anti-Western or anticolonial attitudes cuts across all Third World revolutionary movements.

As discussed in Chapter 1, prior conceptualizations offer an analytical map for comparing Third World revolution and political change. Samuel Huntington's distinction of Western and Eastern types of revolution provides an effective starting point for such comparisons. While Huntington's distinction comprehends most Third World revolutionary types, it fails to include certain major movements that were occurring during the period of his analysis nor, obviously, does it include cases that have occurred since the 1960s. Revolutionary movements, since then, have evolved into what we might describe as "hybrid" in terms of Huntington's Western and Eastern dichotomy.

All Third World revolutionary movements are manifestations of nationalism. In many cases this nationalism is directed against a perceived colonial dominance. The colonial presence may indeed be residential, that is, characterized by a government representing, and legitimized by, a resident population that can be traced to a past immigration from a Western source. In the knotty cases of South Africa and Israel, the nationalism evident in the ANC and PLO is clearly directed against regimes that are regarded by these movements as Western, oppressive, and illegitimate. The government of South Africa is an international pariah because of its explicit application of racial criteria as a legal means to restrict the political rights—indeed, the very citizenship—of the majority of the South African population. The ANC derives its revolutionary legitimacy from the perceived illegitimacy of the South African government. Israel, on the other hand, from its inception, achieved and maintains legitimacy from the international community. Despite this legitimacy, the PLO bases its own legitimacy on a Palestinian perception that rights have been denied by the policies of the state of Israel. The comparison of the ANC and the PLO in this volume has not been made with the intent to compare the international legitimacy of South Africa and Israel. Rather, it has been useful in pointing out the similarity in direction and perception within two movements making claims for revolutionary legitimacy.

The form of external dependency of a Third World state may very well determine the character of a revolutionary movement. We identify three forms of such dependency: residential colonial, formal colonial, and external hegemonial.[1] Residential colonialism engenders revolutionary movements like that in Algeria, the ANC, and the PLO.

Formal colonialism occurs when the presence of the colonial power does not develop into an extensive—and eventually distinct—residential presence. As Chaliand has noted in Chapter 2, the British colonial presence in Malaya provides a classic case of formal colonialism. The case of the Philippines (see Chapter 7), with its extended U.S. colonial presence, furnishes an illuminating example of the impact of formal colonialism within a Third

World revolutionary context. On the one hand, the New Peoples' Army (NPA) builds and instrumentalizes much of its revolutionary legitimacy on the perceived Filipino colonial and neocolonial dependency on the United States. On the other hand, the historical absence of a significant U.S. residential population apart from the U.S. military presence reduces the capacity of the NPA to optimize that legitimacy. The U.S. colonial presence firmly embedded in the Philippines both a political-institutional inclination toward an elective process and the core for a sufficiently viable middle class. The product of this process, coupled with the persistent socioeconomic stagnation, is a stalemate between a partially legitimized revolutionary movement and a potentially legitimate elected government.

The third form of external dependency is the manifest dominance of an external power on an economically weak and politically vulnerable state. In this case, landowners and upper classes of the dependent state tend to monopolize and aggrandize wealth and power. While occasional state violence is in evidence, the predominant character is the softness of state control, in the sense of the state's lack of capacity to maximize popular support and to legitimize its own rule. Regime illegitimacy is a salient characteristic of the soft state, often leading toward ultimate revolutionary mobilization. Such is the case in much of Central America, where a combination of politically bankrupt regimes and the decreasing impact of the external hegemon has yielded revolutionary situations. The more the external hegemon, by tradition and perceived strategic necessity, attempts to intervene and impose its influence on the dependent state, the more it provides an opportunity for revolutionary legitimacy.

In contrast, the more established the Third World state, the more instrumentalized the external power. Ethiopia's revolution demonstrates remarkable similarities to the great revolutions. Yet military dependence stimulated an appeal for extensive Soviet military aid by the Ethiopian revolutionary regime. By tradition and strategic practice, Ethiopia has instrumentalized the ideologies of more technologically developed actors. Soviet Marxism-Leninism may be as pervasive in Ethiopia in the twentieth century as Portuguese Roman Catholicism was in the sixteenth century.

Furthermore, the organized Ethiopian revolutionary movement never came to power. The existence of an entrenched bureaucracy and military created the conditions for the cooptation of the revolution and its movement by a military junta under Mengistu. This pervasive and continuing military control of the revolutionary process and government deprives this regime of actual or potential legitimacy.

Peru offers yet another example of an established state's engendering an unorthodox revolutionary process. The traditional propensity for military or government intervention; the pervasive impact of relative economic deprivation; and the immense social, economic, and cultural chasm between the largely Hispanic-mestizo upper and middle classes and the predominantly

Indian peasants in the countryside combine to spawn revolutionary responses by disaffected elements of the population. The persistent and unseemly success of the eclectic and dogmatic Sendero Luminoso manifests the deepening revolutionary situation in Peru.

The cases of UNITA (as well as RENAMO) reflect our attempt to inquire into the legitimacy of these ostensibly anti-Marxist movements. UNITA, we conclude, is a movement that has no revolutionary legitimacy nor ideology. RENAMO is a "movement" that lacks not only ideology but even goals and a program. External interests dominate—and may even define—one or both of these organizations.

Third World instability will persist. Shifting demographic patterns such as intensifying urbanization, further decreases in the already imperiled quality of social and economic life, the political emergence and activism of ethnic minorities (in some cases majorities), and continuing endemic violence ensure the likelihood of more revolutionary activity directed against Third World regimes. Outside interests, already a factor in the emergence of revolutionary movements, will likely become even more intensive as global interdependence intensifies. The diminution of superpower rivalry in the Third World may in the long run exacerbate, rather than inhibit, revolutionary challenges to Third World regimes. We ignore these trends at our peril.

NOTES

1. These distinctions have been set forth in a different form by Arghiri Emmanuel (1972). "White Settler Colonialism and the Myth of Investment Imperialism," *New Left Review* 73, pp. 35–57.

About the Contributors

As'AD ABUKHALIL is a specialist on the politics of the Middle East and North Africa. He has studied extensively politics and society in Lebanon, Palestinian politics and society, and the politics of the Arab-Israeli conflict. Dr. AbuKhalil has been a consultant to the media on Middle East affairs and has taught at both Georgetown University and Tufts University. He has published in major journals including *The Nation, Third World Affairs*, and the *Middle East Journal.*

GERARD CHALIAND is a French political scientist and a student of revolutionary change in the Third World. He has spent twelve years in Africa, Latin America, the Middle East, and Southeast Asia. Altogether, he has lived more for than eight months among guerrilla groups in Guinea-Bissau, Vietnam, Colombia, Jordan and Lebanon, Eritrea, Iranian Kurdistan, Afghanistan, Central America, Angola, Peru, and the Philippines. Dr. Chaliand is the author of twenty books, of which thirteen have been translated into English. He currently teaches at the French Ecole Nationale d'Administration and is an adviser to the Center for Analysis and Planning for French Foreign Relations.

HENRY DIETZ is associate professor in the Department of Government at the University of Texas at Austin. Dr. Dietz has done considerable field work in Peru over the last twenty-five years, concentrating basically on urban poverty and its political ramifications. He has also done work on civil-military relations in Latin America. His most recent publications include *The Military as a Vehicle for Social Integration.*

WILLIAM FOLTZ is professor of Political Science at Yale University, associate director of the Southern Africa Research Program, and director of the Yale Center for International and Area Studies. He is a specialist in Africa's politics and international relations, and in the foreign policies of the United States and other great powers as they affect Africa and other parts of the Third World. Professor Foltz has been a member of the Yale faculty since 1963, and has been a visiting professor at Makerere University, the

University of Cape Town and the University of Chad, and helped found Yale's Southern Africa Research Program.

EDMOND J. KELLER is professor in the Department of Political Science at the University of California, Los Angeles. Dr. Keller is an internationally recognized scholar of African politics and has studied extensively the nature and ideology of revolutionary regimes. He has concentrated much of his work on the study of Ethiopian politics and has published *Revolutionary Ethiopia* as well as numerous articles on the subject in major journals. He is also coeditor of *Afro-Marxist Regimes: Ideology and Policy.*

ZAKI LAIDI is a senior fellow at the Centre National de la Recherche in Paris and teaches at the Centre d'études et de recherces internationales of the Fondation nationale des sciences politiques. Dr. Laidi is a scholar of Third World politics and is editor of *USSR and Third World* (1988) and *Superpowers and Africa* (1986). He has published more than thirty articles in scholarly reviews.

WILLIAM LEOGRANDE is professor of political science in the Government Department of the School of Public Affairs at The American University. He has been at The American University since 1978 and served as director of the Political Science Program from 1980 to 1982. Dr. LeoGrande has been an International Affairs Fellow at the Council on Foreign Relations and worked with the Democratic Policy Committee of the Democratic Caucus Task Force on Central America. He has written widely in the field of Latin American politics and U.S. foreign policy, with a particular emphasis on Central America and Cuba. He is author of *Cuba's Policy in Africa* (1980) and *Confronting Revolution: Security Through Diplomacy in Central America* (1986).

T. DAVID MASON is associate professor of political science at Mississippi State University, where he also holds partial appointments with the University's Social Science Research Center at its Center for International Security and Strategic Studies. His research on civil violence has appeared in the *American Political Science Review*, *Comparative Political Studies*, *International Studies Quarterly*, *Western Political Quarterly*, and *Asian Studies*. He is coeditor of *US-Japan Trade Friction: Its Impact on Security Cooperation in the Pacific Basin.*

MARINA OTTAWAY is associate professor at the School of International Service, The American University, and also serves as adjunct professor at the School of Advanced International Studies at the Johns Hopkins University. Dr. Ottaway has researched and published extensively on Africa, focusing on issues involving Southern Africa and the Horn of Africa. She is author of

"The Crisis of the Socialist State" in *The African State in Transition: Flucuat Mergitur* and coauthor of "State Power Consolidation in Mozambique" in *Afro-Marxist Regimes: Ideology and Public Policy*.

DAVID ROSENBERG is professor of political science at Middlebury College, Vermont. He was a Fulbright Research Professor at the University of the Philippines' Asian Center in 1988. Dr. Rosenberg is contributor to the *Encyclopedia of Asian History*, the *Yearbook on International Communist Affairs*, and an editor of *Pilipinas: The International Journal of Philippine Studies*. His most recent publication is "Social and Cultural Factors of Development and Democracy in the Philippines" in Thomas Robinson, ed., *Development and Democracy in East Asia*.

BARRY M. SCHUTZ is professor of Third World and African Studies at the Defense Intelligence College and adjunct professor in the National Security Studies Program at Georgetown University. He is a specialist in Third World political dynamics with extensive academic and government analytical experience in African, Soviet, and other Third World regional affairs. Dr. Schutz has published on Southern Africa with emphasis on Zimbabwe; political culture; and the Soviet impact on Africa. His most recent piece is "Political Change and the Management of Ethnic Conflict in Zimbabwe" in Joseph V. Montville, ed., *Conflict and Peacemaking in Multi-Ethnic Societies*.

ROBERT SLATER is director of research at the Defense Intelligence College in Washington DC. In his capacity at the college, Dr. Slater also directs the Defense Academic Research Support Program (DARSP), a program designed to promote scholarly exchanges between academic scholars and U.S. government analysts on Third World issues. Dr. Slater is a scholar of international politics and has published in major journals, including the *American Political Science Review*. He is also coeditor of *Current Perspectives of International Terrorism*.

JOHN VOLL is professor of history at the University of New Hampshire. Dr. Voll specializes on the Middle East and has written most widely on religion—and particularly Islam—and politics. He has studied under fellowships provided by the Ford Foundation Foreign Area Training, Danforth Graduate Fellowship, Fulbright-Hays Research Abroad, Social Science Research Council, and Hebrew University Institute for Advanced Studies. Dr. Voll has published widely on religion, including *Islam: Continuity and Change in the Modern World* (1982), *The Sudan: Unity and Diversity in a Multicultural State* (with Sarah Voll, 1985) and "Renewal and Reform in Islamic History," in *Voices of Resurgent Islam* , ed. by John Esposito (1983).

FRED R. VON DER MEHDEN is the Albert Thomas Professor of political science at Rice University. He formerly taught at the University of Wisconsin-Madison, where he was director of East Asian Studies, and has written widely on issues of religion and politics and religion's relationship to development. He has recently concentrated on the Islamic revival in Southeast Asia, and is author of *Religion and Modernization and Southeast Asia*.

Glossary

ACP	Armed City Partisans (*see* Philippines)
AFCC	Armed Forces Coordinating Committee (*see* Ethiopia/the Derg)
ANC	African National Congress
ANP	Alliance for New Politics (*see* Philippines)
APRA	Popular American Revolutionary Movement (*see* Peru)
ASALA	Armenian Secret Army for the Liberation of Armenia
BCM	Black Consciousness Movement (*see* South Africa)
CHDF	Civil Home Defense Force (*see* Philippines)
CNC	Christians for National Liberation (*see* Philippines)
COPWE	Commission to Organize the Party of the Working People of Ethiopia
COSATU	Congress of South African Trade Unions
CPP	Communist Party of the Philippines
DFLP	Democratic Front for the Liberation of Palestine
ECHAAT	Revolutionary Struggle of the Oppressed Ethiopian Masses
EGP	Guerilla Army of the Poor (*see* Guatemala)
EPLF	Eritrean People's Liberation Front (*see* Ethiopia)
ERP	People's Revolutionary Army (*see* El Salvador)
FAPLA	Armed Forces for the Liberation of Angola
FAR	Rebel Armed Forces (*see* Guatemala)
FARN	Armed Forces of National Resistance (*see* El Salvador)
FDR	Revolutionary Democratic Front (*see* El Salvador)
FMLN	Farabundo Marti Front for National Liberation (see El Salvador)
FNLA	National Front for the Liberation of Angola
FPL	Popular Liberation Forces (*see* El Salvador)
FRELIMO	Front for the Liberation of Mozambique
FSLN	Sandinista National Liberation Front (*see* Nicaragua)
GAD	Grand Alliance for Democracy (*see* Philippines)
GPP	Prolonged Popular War Tendency (*see* Nicaragua)
GRAE	Revolutionary Government of Angola in Exile
IU	United Left (*see* Peru)
KMU	May First Movement (*see* Philippines)

This list serves as a selected glossary to the acronyms in this book; it is not inclusive.

255

MAN	Movement of Arab Nationalists (*see* PLO)
MIR	Revolutionary Leftist Movement (*see* Peru)
MNLF	Moro National Liberation Front (*see* Philippines)
MNR	Social Democratic Party (*see* El Salvador)
MPLA	Popular Movement for the Liberation of Angola
MRTA	Tupac Amaro Revolutionary Movement (*see* Peru)
NDF	National Democratic Front (*see* Philippines)
NEC	National Executive Committee (*see* ANC)
NPA	New People's Army (*see* Philippines)
OAU	Organization of African Unity
OLF	Oromo Liberation Front (*see* Ethiopia)
ORPA	Organization of the People in Arms (*see* Guatemala)
PAC	Pan-African Congress (*see* South Africa)
PAIGC	Guinea-Bissau African Independence Party of Guinea and Cape Verde
PCGG	Presidential Commission on Good Government (*see* Philippines)
PDC	Christian Democratic Party (*see* El Salvador)
PDRE	People's Democratic Republic of Ethiopia
PFLP	Popular Front for the Liberation of Palestine
PGT	Guatemalan Labor Party
PLO	Palestine Liberation Organization
PNC	Palestinian National Congress
RAM	Reform the Armed Forces Movement (*see* Philippines)
RENAMO	Mozambique National Resistance
RIM	Revolutionary Internationalist Movement (*see* Peru)
SACP	South African Communist Party
SPLA	Sudanese People's Liberation Army
SWAPO	Southwest African People's Organization
TP	Proletarian Tendency (*see* Nicaragua)
TPLF	Tigre People's Liberation Front (*see* Ethiopia)
UDF	United Democratic Front (*see* ANC)
UNITA	National Union for the Total Independence of Angola
URNG	Guatemalan National Revolutionary Unity
WPE	Workers' Party of Ethiopia

Index

About the Book

Revolutions and insurgencies at both national and regional levels increasingly are dominating contemporary international politics. This book provides a comparative and theoretically based exploration of the dynamics of revolution and political change in the Third World. The framework presented in the first chapter outlines the elements used consistently throughout the book to identify what kinds of political changes are taking place in the developing countries and under what conditions. These elements provide the foundation for comparing cases and drawing conclusions about the thrust of political change.